Dilution Anxiety and the Black Phallus

Margo Natalie Crawford

THE OHIO STATE UNIVERSITY PRESS / Columbus

Library of Congress Cataloging-in-Publication Data
Crawford, Margo Natalie.
Dilution anxiety and the black phallus / Margo Natalie Crawford.
p. cm.
Includes bibliographical references and index.
ISBN 978–0–8142–5168–3 (pbk. : alk. paper)—ISBN 978–0–8142–1091–8 (cloth : alk. paper) 1. American literature—20th century—History and criticism. 2. Human skin color in literature. 3. Politics and literature—United States—History—20th century. 4. Human skin color—United States—Psychological aspects. 5. Human skin color—Social aspects—United States. 6. Race awareness in literature. 7. Race in literature. 8. Race relations in literature. 9. Miscegenation in literature. 10. Body, Human, in literature. 11. Difference (Psychology) in literature. I. Title.
PS228.S57C73 2008
810.9'3552—dc22
2008015056

This book is available in the following editions:
Cloth (ISBN 978–0–8142–1091–8)
Paper (ISBN 978–0–8142–5168–3)
CD-ROM (ISBN 978–0–8142–9171–9)

Cover design by Janna Thompson-Chordas.
Text design by Jennifer Shoffey Forsythe.
Type set in Adobe Minion Pro.
Printed by Thomson Shore, Inc.

∞ The paper used in this publication meets the minimum requirements of the American National Standard for Information Sciences—Permanence of Paper for Printed Library Materials. ANSI Z39.48–1992.

9 8 7 6 5 4 3 2 1

contents

illustrations

acknowledgments

THE book gained wings during my graduate studies at Yale University with the invaluable guidance of Margaret Homans and Robert Stepto. I thank them for the type of dialogue and feedback that greatly enriched every layer of this project. At Yale, Laura Wexler taught a seminar, "Photography and the Body," that propelled my initial work with Black Arts movement photography. Her excitement about Bob Crawford's photographs greatly encouraged me. Richard Brodhead provided superb insight on the contradictions that Faulkner crystallizes. At Yale, seminars taught by Margaret Homans, Vera Kutzinski, Hazel Carby, Sara Suleri, Michael Denning, Michael Holquist, Bryan Wolf, and James Szwed provided a wealth of new ways of seeing and new ways of thinking. I thank Wai Chee Dimock for a reading of the dissertation that foregrounded the metaquestions and helped immensely as I moved to the Black Arts movement and Black Power movement as a pivot point in this story about images of black bodies.

During the middle life of the writing of this book, Lisa Gail Collins and I coedited *New Thoughts on the Black Arts Movement* (Rutgers 2006). As we worked on that project, many parts of this book were nurtured. I thank Lisa Collins for being such a kindred spirit. The annual James A. Porter Colloquium on African American Art, held in the art history department at Howard University and organized by Floyd Coleman, has offered lively and engaging feedback. The 2006 Porter Colloquium provided a rare focus on both the literature and the visual culture of the Black Arts movement.

Houston A. Baker, Jr. has been a consummate mentor. I have deep gratitude for his sense of the "Sade tones."

I thank Sonia Sanchez for telling me at the 2004 MLA conference to "continue doing exactly what you're doing." I first met Kimberly Benston at a 2006 conference on Larry Neal at Brooklyn College. His encouragement has been precious. Hortense Spillers' groundbreaking work has been a bridge over troubled waters. I thank Jacqueline Goldsby for hearing what I was saying at the exact moment when I needed to be sure that it was being heard and for being an exemplary model of the black feminist scholar.

At Indiana University, George Hutchinson has offered the type of genuine support and camaraderie that often made all the difference. Many conversations with Trica Keaton have simply sustained me. I am very grateful to Purnima Bose for her insight and rare generosity.

Many others have provided that necessary dialogue and vital inspiration: Haki Madhubuti, Cheryl Clarke, Olaf Berwald, Lewis Gordon, William Van Deburg, James Mumford, Quincy Troupe, Cathy Bowman, Cheryl Wall, Eleanor Traylor, John Bowles, Bennie Johnson, Mae Henderson, James Smethurst, Radhika Parameswaran, Amor Kohli, Dwight McBride, Jennifer De Vere Brody, Mike Sell, Uma Narayan, Wendy Graham, Pat Brantlinger, Salah Hassan, John McCluskey, Audrey McCluskey, Michelle Wright, Evie Shockley, Howard Rambsy, Valerie Grim, Joyce Joyce, Vivian Halloran, Badia Sahar Ahad, Esiaba Irobi, Komozi Woodard, Carter Mathes, Wakisha Malone, Tiffany Mann, Tommy Lott, Aldon Nielsen, and Ross Gay. Many of my graduate students have shared my passion for black body politics. Some of the most fruitful exchanges have occurred with Ursula McTaggart, Jackson Brown, Vanessa Reece, Clark Barwick, Kristen Gentry, Aisha Sharif, and Asha French.

During the final stages of this book, Marta Caminero-Santangelo was incredibly generous with her time and close reading. Her deep insight and encouragement have greatly nurtured this book. Working with the anonymous readers truly enhanced this book. Their engagement with the material was a crucial part of the writing process. Sandy Crooms made this book possible. I have been fortunate to have such an encouraging and committed editor. Working with her was a sheer pleasure.

I give my deepest expressions of gratitude to my mother. Julio Finn, Bob Crawford, Renee Arnold, Dagny Bloland, Anupama Rao, Tijuana Murray, Karama Neal, Nikki Taylor, Darren Hutchinson, Vicki Bond, Joe Razza, Paula Bryant, and my siblings remain ideal readers.

introduction

WHEN one of my students proposed that, in contemporary films and Hip Hop culture, dark-skinned black men are now "in style," another student queried, "Is it because light-skinned men are rendered effeminate?" This student then proposed that we should also think about the relatively new use of "very" dark-skinned black female supermodels who sometimes look androgynous. The conversation then moved to images of dark-skinned black female supermodels as one big black phallic symbol. In a 2008 article in the *Wall Street Journal,* interviewees connect Barack Obama's brown-skinned wife and his ability to gain the support of both middle-class and lower-class African American voters. One interviewee states, "Many of our male celebrities, sports figures, they marry white women or light-skinned wives. [. . .] We all see that on television. But you turn on the TV and you see Michelle Obama and she looks black. I can identify with her. [. . .] I can tell you this: He would have a lot less votes if his wife were light-skinned or white."[1] Another interviewee claims that Barack Obama "married up." This language rewrites the longstanding post-slavery script in which people "marry up" when a light-skinned spouse becomes a type of racial uplift. In the Harlem Renaissance play *Color Struck* (1925), Zora Neale Hurston depicts a dark-skinned female character's inability to believe that any suitor would really prefer her over a "high-yaller," a light-skinned black woman. Her internalization of this light-skinned preference ends her relationship with John, the character who, contrary to Emma's assumptions, never displays any signs of being "color struck." When John returns to Emma after twenty years in order to profess his never-ending love, he is surprised to find that the dark-skinned Emma, who constantly accused him of secretly desiring "yellow" women, is now the mother of a light-skinned "mulatta" child who is ill. The father of this child is not present. Theatergoers (or readers) are led to wonder if Emma, in her great frustration over light-skinned privilege, decided that giving birth to a light-skinned child, even outside of wedlock, would increase her social status. This child, however, does not finally redeem Emma's dark-skinned blues. The child dies, in the final scene, when Emma does not immediately contact the doctor because she fears leaving John alone with her child and begins to see her child as yet another light-skinned female threat to any possibility of a dark-skinned black woman's happiness.

These fictional and nonfictional accounts dramatize the need to ask what is really at stake in the ongoing fetishism of shades of blackness (light-skinned blackness and dark-skinned blackness). The fetishism of *glowing* dark-skinned blackness often competes, within contemporary American visual culture, with the longstanding fetishism of the light skin color of the *tragic* mulatta. Freud's "narcissism of minor differences" is an apt description of the fetishism of shades of blackness.[2] Frantz Fanon, in *Black Skin, White Masks,* contrasts the "dramatic" encounter between the white person and the "Negro" who has no "ontological resistance" to the white gaze and the nondramatic "little gulf that exists among the almost-white, the mulatto, and the nigger" (110). Fanon explains, "I was satisfied with an intellectual understanding of these differences. It was not really dramatic" (110). Twentieth-century American literature often makes this "little gulf" "dramatic." The term "colorism" is often used as a way of distinguishing between the black and white color line and the intraracial dynamics of lighter- and darker-skinned blackness. In American literary studies, colorism (the full spectrum of color fetishism, not only the fetishism of lighter-skinned blackness) is just beginning to receive the attention that it has gained in sociology and psychology.[3] Gaining real momentum in the 1980s, there has been widespread interest, among sociologists and psychologists, in the different experiences of black people with lighter and darker skin.[4] In this study, I turn to twentieth-century American literary depictions of colorism.

After the "Black is Beautiful" movement of the 1960s, colorism is overdetermined by both the familiar fetishism of light skin as well as the counter-fetishism of dark skin. These stories about colorism are often the authors' attempts to capture a collective post-slavery trauma that shapes ways of seeing African American bodies.[5] Images of the post-slavery body, carrying the sign of slavery, the brand, need to be connected to the ongoing marking of black bodies on the spectrum of lighter and darker skin. In "Mama's Baby, Papa's Maybe: An American Grammar Book" (1987), Hortense Spillers persuasively argues for more acknowledgment of the complicated ways in which the branding of black bodies has been passed through the post-slavery generations. She writes, "We might well ask if this phenomenon of marking and branding actually 'transfers' from one generation to another, finding its various symbolic substitutions in an efficacy of meanings that repeat the initiating moments" (207). Some of the most complicated aspects of this generational transference revolve around the gender and sexual politics of lighter- and darker-skinned blackness.

How has the fixation on the lightness or darkness of blackness become an unspoken story about contradictory images of white male power (the white phallus), black male power (the black phallus), the feminizing of light-skinned blackness, and the masculinizing of dark-skinned blackness? How do obsessions with the black phallus and the white phallus haunt images of light- and dark-skinned blackness? The very story that was used as the prime biblical justification for American slavery was the story of Ham looking at Noah's nakedness. The descendants of Ham, within these justifications for slavery, were cursed because their progenitor dared to look at the naked father figure. The sight of the father figure's nakedness is rendered the cause of black people's enslavement. The descendants of Ham are blackened, and Noah becomes the white father figure. In some interpretations of this biblical story, Ham laughs when he sees Noah's nakedness. In *Sex and Race* (1952), J. A. Rogers describes the accounts of the amused Ham. He writes, "Noah, according to this bit of folk-lore, had been drunk and exposing his person, and Ham had laughed at him, while the other sons had covered his nakedness; accordingly, the eldest son of Ham, mark you, not Ham, himself, was doomed to eternal servitude" (22). The use of this story about the son's sight of the father's penis as a means of justifying slavery reveals the fixation on the phallus in American slavery's particular version of antiblack racism. Within the post-slavery American imagination, images of the black and white phallus continue to be tied to the sensationalizing of the visual differences between light- and dark-skinned blackness.

The words "black phallus" and "white phallus" have very different meanings. Lacan insists that "the phallus is a signifier," whereas Fanon decides that the "Negro is the genital" (180). Fanon's assertion that the "Negro is the genital" is deeply connected to his image of the "amputation" that "spatters" the "whole body with black blood" (180, 112). The

"Negro" is castrated when he is reduced to the genital. To reclaim the "black phallus" as "black power," the very idea of the "black phallus" must be separated from the ongoing objectifications that make the "Negro" the "genital." When the word "black" is added to the term "phallus," Lacan's use of the word "phallus" gains a fundamentally different shape. In *Desiring Whiteness: A Lacanian Analysis of Race* (2000), Kalpana Seshadri-Crooks presents whiteness as a "master signifier (without a signified)."[6] This formulation is very compatible with the idea that the phallus is a signifier, not a body part. The question of the black phallus, given both antiblack racism and patriarchy, is the tension between the disempowerment tied to blackness and the power tied to maleness.[7] In *Bad Faith and Antiblack Racism* (1995), Lewis Gordon theorizes the black phallus in the following manner: "Blackness is regarded as a hole in being. Black men are hence penises that are holes; and black women are vaginas that are holes—holes that are holes. If blackness is a hole, and women are holes, what are white women, and what are black men in an antiblack world?" (124). This key question must be connected to colorism. How does the fetishism of darker- and lighter-skinned blackness reveal the "holes" tied to black men, black women, and white women? How does biracialness and the light-skinned blackness associated with interracialness often become another type of phallic hole? The American one-drop rule aimed to make biracialness unintelligible: one "drop" of blackness makes you black, not biracial. Questions about the black phallus need to be connected to the one-drop rule. Was the one-drop rule always the *one drop of sperm* rule? The American one-drop rule (the idea that one drop of "black blood" makes someone black) assumes that blackness has reproductive power. Blackness penetrates white purity and creates pure blackness. The fear and fantasy of black reproductive and erotic power undergirds the one-drop rule.

In *Who is Black? One Nation's Definition* (1991), the sociologist F. James Davis studies the peculiar survival of the one-drop rule through slavery and reconstruction, the Negro Renaissance of the 1920s, and the 1960s Black Power movement. Building on Joel Williamson's work in *New People: Miscegenation and Mulattoes in the United States* (1980), Davis argues that the one-drop rule, "this American cultural definition of blacks[,] is taken for granted as readily by judges, affirmative action officers, and black protesters as it is by Ku Klux Klansmen" (5). As Davis explains in *Who is Black?* by 1785 Virginia legally defined a black person as anyone with one black parent. This definition was the legal norm in the Upper South until there was pressure to make the legal definition match the social definition of blackness in the Upper South, the one-drop rule.[8] In addition to the need to analyze the one-drop rule as one of the prime roots of the fetishism of shades of blackness, the distinctions between light- and dark-skinned blackness during American slavery have also become a common means of explaining the contemporary investment in these different shades. It is worth noting, however, that historians have different opinions about the role of colorism in determining the roles of field versus house slaves on Southern plantations. Eugene Genovese, for example, in *Roll, Jordan, Roll,* argues, "However much the quadroon and mulatto servants, stiffly parading in full dress, dominated the Big House of the legend, they did not dominate the Big House of reality [. . .] As often, as not, southern slaveholders, in sharp contradistinction to the slaveholders of the British Caribbean, enjoyed being served by blacks—the blacker the better—as well as by light-skinned Negroes" (327–28). The slippage between what Genovese labels the "legend" as opposed to what he deems the historical facts reveals that the difference between light-skinned house slaves and dark-skinned field slaves is a type of post-slavery trauma that has been naturalized, not due to a strictly historical truth, but rather due to the need to explain the longevity of colorism, the continued reality of colorism. This slippage between the historical facts and the cultural imagination that shapes our ways of seeing bodies demonstrates that the analysis of the ongoing fetishism of shades of blackness is not simply an historical or sociological space for analysis. Some aspects of this fetishism cannot be historically placed in a rigid manner. The topic demands a more speculative query that makes post-slavery trauma a necessary question, not the all-encompassing answer.

In "The Paper Bag Principle: Of the Myth and Motion of Colorism" (2005), Audrey Elisa Kerr examines the ways in which many people's understanding of the history of colorism in African American communities pivots on the circulation of myths about the paper bag tests that created social settings and group affiliations that only included people with complexions lighter than a brown paper bag. Through a range of interviews, Kerr discovers that the paper bag is sometimes remembered as the absent object that defines who can enter a social gathering or who can join a group. As Kerr searches for the actual history of the paper bag test, she discovers that the folklore surrounding the paper bag test continues to create people's sense of the historical underpinnings of colorism. As the interviewees retell the stories they were told about the paper bag tests, "paper bag parties, paper bag churches, brown bag clubs, or brown bag social circles," Kerr shows that any analysis of the meaning of lighter- and darker-skinned blackness in African American imaginations must include an analysis of the historical circulation of myths and representations.[9] The literature examined in this study demonstrates the historical circulation of images of lighter- and darker-skinned blackness. Toni Morrison, in a 2003 interview, describes the symbolic meaning of the paper bag test in African American imaginations. She states, "There was something called 'the paper bag test'—darker than the paper bag put you in one category, similar to the bag put you in another, and lighter was yet another and the most privileged category." In her novels *The Bluest Eye, Tar Baby,* and *Paradise,* Morrison shapes this historical speculation ("there was something called") into a deep analysis of the reasons why African Americans sometimes fetishize shades of blackness.

As F. James Davis in *Who is Black?* combines history and speculative analysis, he views the 1960s Black Power movement as a fundamental shift in the status of light-skinned blackness within black communities. Drawing on Joel Williamson's work in *New People: Miscegenation and Mulattoes in the United States,* Davis writes, "In the 1960s, lighter persons in general often felt they had to prove their loyalty to the black community and some complained of discrimination from other blacks (Williamson 1980, 190). What a change from the historical advantages of lightness!" (74). The Black Power movement's reaction to the one-drop rule demands even more analysis. During the artistic counterpart of the Black Power movement, the Black Arts movement, there was a great focus on an all-encompassing blackness ("black" as the unifying term that heals the violence of the white gaze's fascination with shades of blackness), as well as a great policing of blackness, that which A. B. Spellman addresses in his manifesto, "Big Bushy Afros" (1998), when he writes, "I only regret the culture cops." This policing of "authentic" blackness often stemmed from the fear of dilution, the fear of loss of what was imagined as pure and authentic blackness. The dilution anxiety of the Black Arts movement is encapsulated in the poems "The Self-Hatred of Don L. Lee" (1963), written by Haki Madhubuti, and "The Life of Lincoln West," written by Gwendolyn Brooks in 1963 and published in 1970. "The Self-Hatred of Don L. Lee" celebrates the "all black" interior as it explains the fetishism of dark-skinned blackness during the Black Arts movement. In this poem, a contrast is presented between Madhubuti's love of his "all black soul" and his hatred of his "light brown outer."

i
began
to love

only a
part of
me—
my inner
self which
is all
black—
&
developed a
vehement
hatred of
my
light
brown
outer.[10]

In the psychoanalytic understanding of fetishism, the fetishized subject is reduced to a body part, or the entire body becomes a fetishized part (in the objectification of the female body). The fetishism of that which is "all black," the blackening of his "inner self" as a huge overcompensation for the "dilution" of his skin, the "light brown outer," is a striking example of the insidious move from a racialized surface to a racialized essence.

The "light brown outer" is akin to the castrated body in the Freudian script. As the poem progresses, the speaker revels over the "pitchblack paragraphs," the black aesthetic that shapes his writing and redeems the dilution anxiety, his hatred of his "light brown outer." Gwendolyn Brooks's "The Life of Lincoln West" can be read as the "mother" text that explains "The Self-Hatred of Don L. Lee."[11] In "The Life of Lincoln West," the dark-skinned child, Lincoln West, is assaulted by both the white gaze and the light-skinned African American gaze. Lincoln West hears a stranger, a white man, refer to him as "the real thing" as opposed to "those diluted Negroes."[12] Brooks describes this white stranger as the "author of his new idea," Lincoln's newfound sense that his "undiluted" blackness is a source of comfort (488). The last words in the poem are "It comforted him" (489). This "new idea," the "real thing" syndrome that counters the supposedly "diluted Negro," is at the core of the Black Arts movement, the first Black cultural movement that fully indulged in black fetishism of blackness and the reclamation of the black phallus.

To move beyond the longstanding focus on the tragic mulatta and make room for the study of the fetishism of both light-skinned and dark-skinned blackness, I analyze the modernist, Black Arts, and post–Black Arts gazes in the work of Gertrude Stein, Wallace Thurman, William Faulkner, Black Arts poets, James Baldwin, Toni Morrison, and John Edgar Wideman. I argue that dilution anxieties and dilution fantasies surrounding black bodies need to be added to the current "race and psychoanalysis" work that foregrounds the role of castration in our cultural imagination. This emergent inquiry, often too flexible to be codified, that which Hortense Spillers calls "race and psychoanalytics," has gained wings by virtue of groundbreaking scholars building on the work of Frantz Fanon in *Black Skin, White Masks* (1967) and the French original (1952). These trailblazers include Hortense Spillers ("All You Could Be Now if Sigmund Freud's Wife Was Your Mother: Race and Psychoanalysis" and "Mama's Baby, Papa's Maybe"), David Eng (*Racial Castration*), Anne Cheng (*The Melancholy of Race*), Jean Walton (*Fair Sex, Savage Dreams: Race, Psychoanalysis, Sexual Difference*), Kalpana Seshadri-Crooks (*Desiring Whiteness*), Jean Wyatt, and Kobena Mercer ("Reading Racial Fetishism: The Photographs of Robert Mapplethorpe"). This amorphous field of "race and psychoanalysis" is the ideal zone for an analysis of African American body politics that seeks to explore the questions about racialized gender and sexuality that sociology cannot answer. Within this open field, Kobena Mercer, in his study of Mapplethorpe's images, has shown how the fetishism of "glossy black skin" becomes a racialized fetishism that cannot be separated from sexual fetishism. Mercer complicates Homi Bhabha's contrast of race as the "most visible of fetishes" versus the hidden sexual fetish, the "secret."[13] Mercer shows that racialized skin color emerges as the literal cover and mask when viewed through the lens of the Freudian story of the sexual fetish revolving around lack and the masking or covering of lack. Hortense Spillers has laid the foundation for a focus on the centrality of the trauma of the middle passage in any psychoanalysis of African American gender politics. As she wonders about the lack of gender differentiation in the oceanic state of the middle passage, she does not imagine a total erasure of gender difference in the lives of African Americans. She does, however, wonder if many African Americans, as a result of post-slavery trauma, live a certain disavowal of gender difference.

The visual images of the restroom signs during the era of legal segregation in the South underscore this disavowal of gender difference for the "colored" (figure 1). This study explores the connections between this gender confusion and the fetishism of light-skinned blackness as well as the fetishism of dark-skinned blackness. The fetish, in psychoanalysis, is the disavowal of difference that overcompensates for the recognition of dif-

Figure 1. *Segregated public restrooms (© D'Azi Productions)*

ference. The coexistence of the one-drop rule and the imagined difference between shades of blackness shapes African American skin-color fetishism into a prime example of the peculiar simultaneous recognition of difference and the disavowal of difference.

Why is it helpful to use the psychoanalytic understanding of the fetish to theorize about the racial signifying power of skin color? As the field of "race and psychoanalysis" continues to emerge, we need to think about the relation between the psychoanalytic idea of "having" the phallus (the male body) versus "being" the phallus (the female body) and the tension, cemented by the American idea of the "one-drop rule," between "having" visual signs of whiteness and "being" black. In the psychoanalytic fiction, the woman "is" the phallus in the sense that, once she is objectified, her body is a substitute phallus. In the Freudian story about castration anxiety, the male child sees the mother as both lacking and possessing the male sexual organ. When the male child fetishizes the mother's femininity, supposedly, her body becomes the peculiar site of both presence and absence. The psychoanalytic language of the male, who "has" the phallus, and the woman, who "is" the phallus, can be applied to the light skin/dark skin "narcissism of minor differences" that structures colorism.[14] If the phallus is the signifier of cultural power and cannot be reduced to the male sexual organ, it includes white skin. The idea of lack being covered might apply in a literal way to the fetishism of gradations of nonwhite skin color. Du Bois' explanation of double consciousness as "two warring ideals in one dark body" might be a concrete example of a bodily surface becoming a fetishized resolution of a contradiction, the bodily absence and destruction created by the white gaze and the simultaneous singularity of the bodily presence "whose dogged strength alone keeps it from being torn asunder."[15] To think about the usefulness and limitations of applying psychoanalytic understandings of the fetish to race, it is necessary to think specifically about the relation between the sexual fetish and the racial fetish. Since psychoanalysis has traditionally centered on the sexual fetish, we must acknowledge that the sexual fetish, of course, has clear parallels to the racial fetish, but racial fetishism sometimes becomes a very specific type of sexual fetishism.

In psychoanalytic theories of the sexual fetish, "having" the phallus is the position of power, whereas "being" the phallus, the reflection of the phallus, is the site of disempowerment. The one-drop rule makes "being" white the privileged term and refuses to make "having" whiteness a reflection of the phallus. Antiblack racism is constantly being both internalized and subverted by African Americans, so that an imagined phallus of blackness sometimes emerges in addition to a certain dilution anxiety, the sense that dark-skinned blackness is the visual signifier of "roots" and cultural authenticity and that light-skinned blackness is a visual signifier of assimilation and cultural hybridity. To understand black fetishism of blackness, the emergent field of race and psychoanalysis needs to focus more on the peculiar coexistence, in the African American imagination, of desire for "whiteness" and dilution anxiety (fear of loss of "blackness"). This "dilution anxiety" is present in Jean Toomer's explanation of the impetus for writing *Cane* (1923): "The folk-spirit was walking in to die on the modern desert."[16] In a letter to Waldo Frank, Toomer writes, "There is one thing about the Negro in America . . . As an entity, the race is loosing [*sic*] its body . . . One is even led to believe that the thing we call Negro beauty will always be attributable to a clearly defined physical source. But the fact is, if anything comes up now, pure Negro, it will be a swansong."[17] This idea of an authentically black body and culture, the "pure Negro," is, of course, a glaring example of racial essentialism at its worst, but it is also an example of an imagined black phallus, a state in which blackness signifies cultural power and the state before castration, the mythologized "original body" in Aristophanes' speech in Plato's *Symposium*.

When Toomer thinks about the disappearing black body, he anticipates the dilution anxiety that is given concrete form in Eldridge Cleaver's Black Power treatise *Soul on Ice* (1968). As Cleaver critiques racial self-hatred that desires dilution, he puts his fear of the lightening of blackness on full display. He writes:

> Quite simply, many Negroes believe, as the principle of assimilation into white America implies, that the race problem in America cannot be settled until all traces of the black race are eliminated. Toward this end, many Negroes loathe the very idea of two very dark Negroes mating. The children, they say, will come out ugly. What they mean is that the children are sure to be black, and this is not desirable. From the widespread use of cosmetics to bleach the black out of one's skin and other concoctions to take Africa out of one's hair, to the extreme, resorted to by more Negroes than one might wish to believe, of undergoing nose-thinning and lip-clipping operations, the racial death-wish of American Negroes—Yacub's goal—takes its terrible toll. What has been happening for the past four hundred years is that the white man, through his access to black women, has been pumping his blood and genes into the blacks, has been diluting the blood and genes of the blacks—i.e. has been fulfilling Yacub's plan and accelerating the Negroes' racial death-wish. (127)

Cleaver makes this dilution a sexual act, the act of penetration. He rages against the white phallus's creation of light-skinned blackness. The "pumping" of "blood and genes into *the blacks*" (italics mine) captures the post-slavery American trauma that continues to make blackness a collective body. As Cleaver laments the racial self-hatred that leads to the desire for lighter skin, he imagines that dark-skinned blackness is the original state of the collective black body. This investment in the notion of a collective black body is the key issue that overdetermines the fetishism of shades of blackness. This belief in the collective black body often makes skin itself into the boundary that seemingly connects black subjects. In the 1960s African Americans first began using the term "skins" as an affectionate way of addressing each other. The hand greeting "Give me some skin" was also a popular greeting in 1960s black expressive culture. A. B. Spellman remembers the 1960s Black Arts movement itself as "the sensuality of a collective consciousness that declared itself on sight." This lush description of the black aesthetic of this movement is an apt image of the Black Arts attempt to literally *feel* the collective skin of a collective body. In *In Our Terribleness* (1970), Baraka describes this collective black body in the following manner: "So we are parts of a body. [. . .] And what is the changing same for us, the reality beneath illusion that binds us, as the body is bound by its motion its intent. From the kids the simbas to the old folks, sweet sisters in between, what will hold us in motion, with the content of the black chemist the black magician, the changers of what is to what must be, what but our selves" (133). Investments in the authentic black body and the fetishism of the altered black body (the hybrid body) are the result of the ongoing naturalizing of the collective black body. To move beyond biological understandings of authenticity and hybridity, we must denaturalize the collective black body and the concomitant idea of dilution.

As I add images of skin color dilution as a type of castration to this field of race and psychoanalysis, I extend Toni Morrison's focus on white American writers' "playing in the dark" to the ways in which white and black writers "play in the light and the dark," the shades of lighter- and darker-skinned blackness. In *Playing in the Dark: Whiteness and Literary Imagination,* Morrison makes *Three Lives* and *Absalom, Absalom!* two of her core examples of the "underscored omissions, startling contradictions, [and] heavily nuanced conflicts" arising from the "black presence" in the white literary imagination (6). In reference to *Three Lives,* she insists, "It is hard to think of any aspect of Gertrude Stein's *Three Lives* that has not been covered, except the exploratory and explanatory uses to which she puts the black woman who holds center stage in that work" (14). She is as puzzled by signs of blackness in *Absalom, Absalom!* She writes, "We are reminded of other images at the end of literary journeys into the forbidden space of blackness. Does Faulkner's *Absalom, Absalom!* after its protracted search for the telling African blood, leave us with just such an image of snow and the eradication of race?" (58). Morrison moves from a survey of texts such as *Three Lives* and *Absalom, Absalom!* that make blackness a metaphor without brakes to a listing of the principal tensions emerging from this "playing in the dark" (a listing that hopes to hail critics who will do this work). The fetishism of shades of blackness is one of the tensions she highlights. Taking Morrison's lead, I begin with images of colorism in the white modernist gaze and compare these images to Harlem Renaissance images. In different but similar ways, Stein and Thurman capture the gender confusion often connected to the fetishism of shades of blackness. Faulkner, in *Absalom, Absalom!* as he reveals the fetishism of female interracialness and the feminization of black male interracialness, uncovers the post-slavery fear and fantasy of dark-skinned black virility. As I turn to more recent representations of these shades of blackness, I focus on the work of Toni Morrison and John Edgar Wideman. While analyzing their representations of the fetishism of shades of blackness, I introduce dilution anxiety and the reclamation of the black phallus as the fear of loss of authentic blackness. This dilution anxiety is often tied to the fetishism of dark-skinned blackness at the center of the black gaze of the 1960s and 70s Black Power and Black Arts movements.

In *Just Above My Head* (1979), as James Baldwin muses on the bizarre and unspoken entanglements of skin-color fetishism and the fetishism of the black penis, he writes, "It was more a matter of its color than its size, or perhaps, its color *was* its size" (105). In *Hung: A Meditation on the Measure of Black Men in America* (2005), Scott Poulson-Bryant, echoing Baldwin, writes, "The size is the color. The color is the size" (75). *Hung* is an example of the contemporary work on African American masculinity that brings to the forefront Fanon's realization that the "Negro is the genital."[18] The coloring of the phallus plays a huge role in the sexual and gender politics of light- and dark-skinned blackness in the literature analyzed in this study. An undercurrent of light-skinned blackness as a type of castration emerges within an ongoing story about the fear and fantasy of the dilution of the black phallus. This imaging of dilution begs to be connected to the celebration of the powers of unadulterated melanin in contemporary Afrocentrism. Some of the titles within this "underground" African American publishing include *Melanin: A Key to Freedom* (1994), *Melanin: The Chemical Key to Black Greatness* (1998), and *The Isis Papers: The Keys to the Colors* (1991). In "What Freud Was Really Talking About" (1975) in *The Isis Papers: The Keys to the Colors* (1991), Frances Cress Welsing argues that the truth underneath Freud's theory of penis envy is "white envy of the black phallus."[19] According to Welsing, white supremacy is a reaction against the abundance of the black body (an abundance of melanin and the size of the black male's penis, an imagined excess that Welsing accepts as a biological truth). As Welsing focuses on white envy of the black body, she fetishizes melanin and the black male's penis. She presents whiteness as "skin albinism" (96), the lack of melanin. She naturalizes "white lack" and "black abundance." Welsing treats the black phallus as both the black male sexual organ and the black cultural power that white supremacy destroys.

In spite of her essentialism, homophobia, and acceptance of gender roles, Welsing's text gains real force when she includes drawings that show how male genitalia has been abstracted into the cross and the swastika. In this part of the text, she demonstrates that the very notion of the phallus relies on the embodiment of abstraction. When she "abstracts" the drawings of the penis to arrive at the cross, she presents the phallus as the quintessential sham of transcendence. The phallus and the cross are both privileged signifiers, but the phallus is a signifier, like race, that cannot transcend its writing on the body. When Welsing includes the drawings, she discovers the fear of the black phallus that shapes the white phallus, the "white" cross. She writes:

> Whereas the testicles are those aspects of the male anatomy that contain the dominant genetic material, the penis is the aspect that transports the genetic material, which initiates the production of life and skin color. If one were to make a simple schematic diagram of the genital organs of the male anatomy, that diagram might look like Diagram I. [. . .]
>
> A further abstraction of the same drawing could be represented as Diagram II.
>
> Or, if further abstracted, it could be represented simply as two lines, one vertical, the other horizontal—one crossing near the top of the other. (See Diagram III.) [. . .] It is clear that Diagram III, a highly abstracted line drawing of the male genitalia, is a "cross." (62–64)

Welsing's use of "abstraction" as a method, a means of deconstructing the phallus, is fascinating, given the fact that race so often revolves around the embodiment of abstraction. When she refers to the penis as "initiat[ing] the production of life and skin color," her use of abstraction as a method raises questions about color itself being an abstraction that race makes into a "thing," a body part. After she presents whiteness as "skin albinism," her connection of the "production of [. . .] skin color" and the ejaculation of the penis demonstrates how the fetishism of black masculinity becomes tied to the fetishism of dark-skinned blackness. In the process of "abstracting" the visual sign of the phallus, Welsing reinforces the embodiment of "black masculinity," another abstraction. One of Welsing's principal points, throughout the entire text, is the "dominant genetic material" of blackness. Fear of the black phallus, in Welsing's account, is fear of the "dominant genetic material" (62).

When Welsing discusses reproduction, in a peculiar manner, she does not focus on the black woman's body. In her diagrams, the shape of the penis includes the shape of a receptacle. As opposed to the typical images of the woman's body as the receptacle, the black male penis is imagined as the repository of the "dominant genetic material." As she enters a masculinist discourse of black power, she attributes reproductive power to dark-skinned black masculinity. Welsing's focus on the power and significance of high levels of melanin places her work in a tradition of Afrocentric texts, such as *Melanin: The Chemical Key to Black Greatness* (1988). A story about fetishized melanin occupies a central place in the contemporary, some-

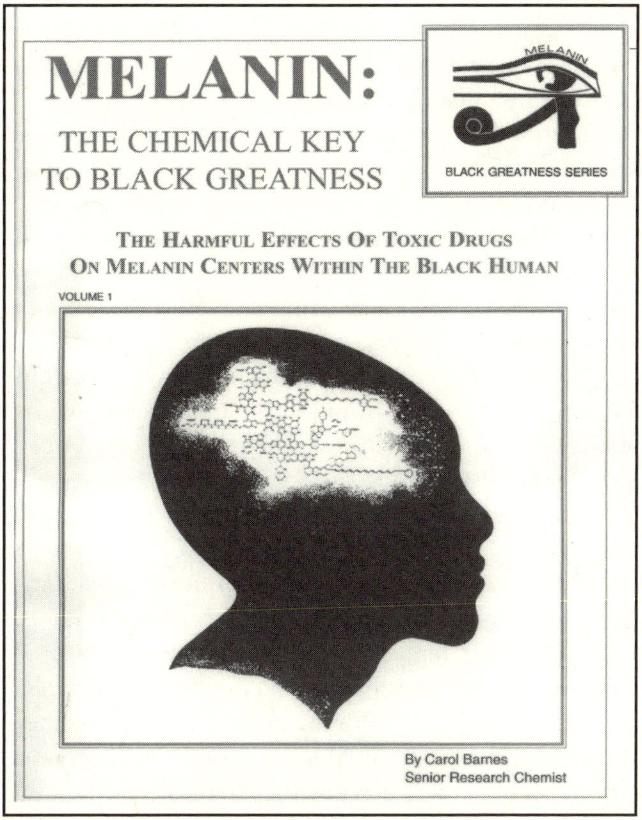

Figure 2. Melanin: The Chemical Key to Black Greatness *(Carol Barnes, 1988)*

times self-published texts that are often labeled "Afrocentric." In *Melanin: The Chemical Key to Black Greatness,* a form of "scientific" Afrocentrism emerges as a reaction against nineteenth-century "scientific" racism (figure 2). As blackness is essentialized in these texts, something meaningful remains—a psychoanalysis of black fetishism of blackness. Welsing and Barnes assume the indisputable truth of this "dominant genetic material." Their investment in this claim of superiority is less significant than the larger American fantasy and fear of black male erotic power. This fantasy stems from the breeding of black bodies that occurred during American slavery. In *Breeding the Black Body* (2006), Pamela Bridgewater argues that the breeding, during American slavery, continues to overdetermine legal and cultural understandings of black women's reproduction.

Questions about the continued effects of this breeding of the black body and the post-slavery trauma over the differentiation between shades of blackness are at the heart of this study. I argue that the post-slavery fear and fantasy surrounding the black phallus is inseparable from the ongoing fetishism of shades of blackness. The phallus, in psychoanalysis, is the prime abstraction that becomes embodied in the male sexual organ. As Susan Bordo argues, "The phallus, remember, is not a real body part. Having one or not requires the permission of culture and/or the exercise of attitude more than the possession of a particular kind of body. Having a penis (even one that is imagined to be extremely large) does not protect one from being divested of phallic authority, from being a 'man manqué' (as Richard Majors describes the historical situation of the black man)."[20] As I explore the role of the black phallus and the white phallus in literary representations of colorism, I begin, in the first chapter, with an analysis of the role of heterosexuality in the normative darkening of virility and lightening of femininity. Through a comparison of the queerness in Stein's *Three Lives* and Thurman's *The Blacker the Berry,* I expose the heterosexual underpinnings of the colorist racial uplift that was cemented in the early 1900s. The representations of colorism and queerness in *Three Lives* and *The Blacker the Berry* ultimately lead to questions about the power of the erotic to destabilize the repression and gender norms naturalized by the racial uplift discourse. As opposed to Stein's and Thurman's critique of racial uplift as they explore the fetishism of shades of blackness, Faulkner often endorsed the progressive lightening of black bodies as a natural path to racial uplift. In chapter 2, I argue that the fear *and* fantasy of diluted blackness in *Absalom, Absalom!* has not been fully connected to the feminizing of interracial maleness. I uncover the ways in which the representations of the white phallus and the black phallus stifle any possibility of the articulation of the interracial phallus. *Three Lives* and *Absalom, Absalom!* reveal that light-skinned blackness, within the spectrum of shades of blackness, has been constructed as the feminine or castrated position. Stein depicts the yellow woman's desire to escape this position of "being" the phallus as opposed to "having" the phallus. Faulkner depicts white Southerners' unsuccessful attempts to separate blackness from virility. I argue that the end of the novel signals the white fear of and seduction by the idea that black virility, the black phallus, will "conquer the western hemisphere" even as it is "bleach[ed]."[21]

Whereas Faulkner presents interracialness as the delicate, "silken" alternative to the roughness of "pure" blackness,[22] and Stein and Thurman unveil the dark father figure and the yellow daughter as symptomatic of the gendering of shades of blackness, the Black Arts movement fully explodes the often unspoken gendering of shades of blackness in the American post-slavery landscape. A new edition of *The Blacker the Berry* was published in 1970 (figure 3). On the back cover of this edition, the text reads, "Emma Lou is defenseless against the haunting chimera of intra-racial prejudice. She must face her darkest self in order to survive—for black is truth if not beauty—and it is her only hope."[23] With the words "black is truth if not beauty" and the reference, in this same book cover description, to the "contemporary sociological masterpiece, *Black Rage*," Thurman's Harlem Renaissance depiction of colorism and self-hatred is given a Black Arts movement frame. The reference to *Black Rage* (1968), in this packaging of the 1970 edition of *The Blacker the Berry*, gains significance when the analysis of black manhood and womanhood, in *Black Rage*, is compared to Thurman's representation of the association of black female attractiveness and a light-skinned complexion. In *Black Rage*, the psychiatrists William Grier and Price Cobbs foreground the race, gender, and sexuality issues that create the black body politics of the 1960s and 70s Black Arts movement. Grier and Cobbs insist that "femininity, as it is defined in these times, is something she [the black woman] cannot achieve" and that "[f]or the black man, attaining any portion of manhood is an active process," whereas "for a white man in this country, the rudiments of manhood are settled at birth by the possession of a penis and a white skin."[24] This reference to "a penis and a white skin" highlights the discussion of the phallus in this 1960s field of black psychology (psychologists connecting their analysis of black subjects to the psychologists' own lived experience of blackness). As Grier and Cobbs argue that the gender roles between black men and women must be understood as maneuvers within a "latter-day version" of the "slave family," they propose that, contrary to the myth of African American matriarchy, many black households are a type of "patriarchy without a patriarch" (83–84, 61).

In chapter 3, I analyze Black Arts male writers' relation to this "patriarchy without a patriarch" as they attempt to feminize and castrate whiteness and rescue the black male warrior from the castrated black men produced during slavery and its legacies. When the Harlem Renaissance is explicitly feminized by Harold Cruse in *The Crisis of the Negro Intellectual* (1967) as Cruse echoes Haki Madhubuti and Larry Neal's critique of the desire for integration and dependence on white patronage, it is clear that the assumption of the black phallus was the veritable pulse of the Black Arts movement.[25] In the poem "Tell It like It Is" (1973), as Dudley Randall thinks about the connections between Black Power performances of virility and the Black Power fetishism of dark-skinned blackness, he muses, "If you want to be virile / be virile, / but you ain't gonna get virile / By

Figure 3a.
The Blacker the Berry
front cover
(Wallace Thurman, 1970)

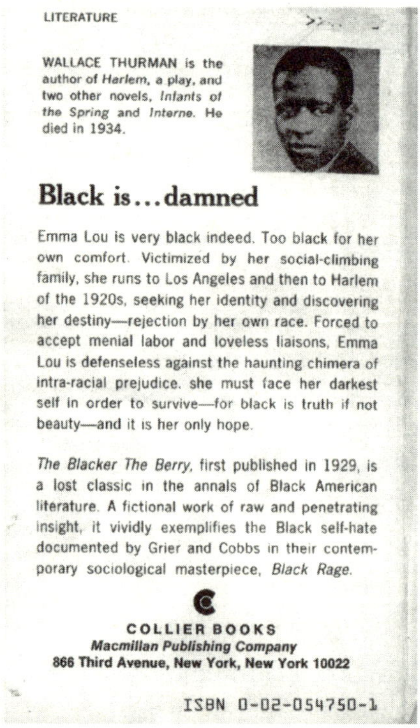

Figure 3b.
The Blacker the Berry
back cover
(Wallace Thurman, 1970)

saying somebody else ain't virile. / And if the white boys are all faggots, / like you say, / how come we got all these black poets / with yellow skin?"[26] During the Black Arts and Black Power movements, "yellow" blackness was denigrated as virile; dark-skinned blackness was proclaimed as authentic blackness. In chapter 4, I place Toni Morrison's novel *The Bluest Eye* in the context of this explosion of dilution anxiety and reclamation of the black phallus.

The Bluest Eye was published by Holt, Rinehart and Winston in 1970, while Morrison was an editor for Random House in New York City. While Morrison was working at Random House, the publishing company wanted to tap into the black readership that had been created by the rise of black nationalist literature. In the 1993 afterword, she explains that the "Black is Beautiful" ethos greatly influenced her first novel. She wrote the novel during the full span of the Black Arts movement, between 1962 and 1970. As the Black Arts movement and the "Black is Beautiful" consciousness raising was at its height, she contemplated, in this first novel, racial self-hatred (the internalization of antiblack racism). *The Bluest Eye* reveals that the "Black is Beautiful" sensibility was indeed aesthetic warfare aiming to transpose racial self-hatred into racial self-love. Both the racial self-hatred described in *The Bluest Eye* and the "Black is Beautiful" ethos of the Black Arts movement naturalize the notion of racial self-love. In post–Black Arts movement African American literature, there is an emergent critique of this very idea of racial self-love; race itself is shown to be the ugliness that cannot be beautified. The critique, in post–Black Arts movement African American literature, of the fetishism of both light-skinned and dark-skinned blackness gains a new space that adds new layers to the Black Arts critique of light-skin privilege, racial self-hatred, and desire for whiteness. In chapters 4, 5, and 6, I unveil the critique of dilution anxiety, the fear of loss of authentic blackness, that emerges in novels written by Toni Morrison and John Edgar Wideman. Novels such as *Tar Baby* (1981), *Sent for You Yesterday* (1983), *Paradise* (1997), and *Philadelphia Fire* (1990) are quintessential post–Black Arts movement texts in that "Black is Beautiful" is taken for granted to the extent that the novelists can critique belief in the embodiment of blackness even as they celebrate an elusive cultural and historical quality that is presented as specifically black, not withstanding its hybrid forms.

These novels written by Morrison and Wideman are emblematic of a larger, emergent post-dilution anxiety in contemporary African American literature. In *Temple of My Familiar* (1989), as Alice Walker, like Morrison and Wideman, envisions the loss of dilution anxiety, she blurs the boundaries between the primitive and the new as she presents a new version of Afrocentrism that is irrevocably tied to cultural syncretism. *Kindred* (1979), *Two Wings to Veil My Face* (1983), *Thereafter Johnnie* (1991), *One Dark Body* (1993), *South to a Very Old Place* (1991), and *Mama Day* (1993) are examples of other post–Black Arts movement novels that interrogate both the teleological understanding of blackness (the move from the "old," dark-skinned blackness to the "new," interracial or light-skinned black body) and the imagined relation between blackness and the primitive. Bakhtin's theory of the chronotope, the spatialization of time, illuminates the time-line aspect of the fetishism of shades of blackness, the way that skin color is imagined as a condensation of time. According to Bakhtin, "Time, as it were, thickens, takes on flesh."[27] The chronotope of dark-skinned blackness, the temporal meanings that "take on flesh" when dark skin blackness is fetishized, is represented vividly in *One Dark Body* when the wrinkles of the young girl Raisin are described. When Charlotte Sherman describes the relation between the dark-skinned young girl named Raisin and the light-skinned young boy named Sin-Sin, she thinks about the temporalities written on their bodies. Although she is a young girl, Raisin's dark skin is old and wrinkled, as opposed to the skin of Sin-Sin, which is "so bright it shines" like the bright sun of a new day (11). Raisin's darkness is rendered "old": "Whenever they start talking about how wrinkled up and black I am, I just close my eyes and think of a warm soft place like a tub of hot water I can lay my body down in, or a nice dark space like a womb" (8). At a crucial moment, Raisin tires of being the "old" storyteller while Sin-Sin listens. She insists that he begin to tell stories, and when he does, the oldness inscribed on her body is transferred to him: "He finally sit still and look at me with a face that older than mine" (16). When she refuses to make the light-skinned Sin-Sin remain a listener as opposed to assuming the heaviness of the storytelling, Sherman critiques the notion that the dark-skinned black body is endowed with a type of cultural authenticity and black cultural memory that the light-skinned black body lacks.

In one of the magical realism passages, when Sin-Sin sees "a great black face carved into the trunk of [an] elm" (180), Sherman captures the way that dark-skinned blackness, as opposed to Sin-Sin's light-skinned blackness, has been rendered, in the African American gaze, an icon of roots, origins, and untainted nature. When Sin-Sin thinks about Raisin's mother, he envisions "[o]ld blue-black" and the "black at the beginning of the world" (133). The blackness of Raisin and her mother is imagined as a spatialization of time (Bakhtin's chronotope), the embodiment of the "beginning of the world." In one version of the evolutionary "family tree" of nineteenth-century "scientific" racism, the lowest branch is labeled "Negritos," and the highest branch is labeled "Aryans."[28] To fully understand the significance of the light-skinned Sin-Sin viewing dark-skinned blackness as "a great black face carved into the trunk" of a tree, we must remember this morphological tree of the human race that placed "Negritos" on the lowest branch. Sin-Sin's desire for "unadulterated blackness" allows him to imagine dark-skinned blackness as the tree trunk and as the "beginning of the world." Underneath this desire for "unadulterated blackness," however, is the internalization of the antiblack racism that constructed blackness as the lowest branch in the evolutionary tree.

The antiblack literary tradition of depicting dark-skinned blackness as a living fossil and the lowest level in the evolutionary tree is fully displayed in *Absalom, Absalom!* (1936). The wife of the interracial Charles Etienne is described as a "coal black and ape-like woman" and "an authentic wife resembling something in a zoo" (166, 169). As Mr. Compson narrates the story of Charles Etienne, immobility and the grotesque are linked to the dark-skinned black body. Faulkner describes the "backwater" to which the dark-skinned wife of the interracial Charles Etienne is tied, but Leon Forrest, in *Two Wings to Veil My Face* (1983), rewrites this "backwater" time. In *Two Wings to Veil My Face*, "backwater" is the incredibly tangible presence of the past in the present and a bodily experience of the past (the bodily "site of memory").[29] Whereas the "two dimensional backwater" of the wife of Charles Etienne is comparable to that "aghast and automaton-like state in which she had arrived" (166), Leon Forrest makes "backwater time" signify the "unrecorded backbone of history and what really stirred at the bottom—never to rise unless [you] touched down upon it" (13). As opposed to the "two dimensional[ity]" of the character that Faulkner associates with the "backwater," Forrest's African American characters become most alive and complicated (three-dimensional) when they "stir" the backwater or when the backwater stirs their very bodies. During experiences of "backwater time," Forrest's characters realize that the "very feel of history [is] ingrained in the texture" of their bodies (13). Forrest uses the branding of slaves' bodies to signify the heaviness of these bodily sites of memory.

The continuation of colorism aids the continual branding of black bodies. This study confronts the web of beautified or eroticized brands and scars, created by colorism, crisscrossing race, gender, and sexuality. The depiction of the horror of these aestheticized brands and scars begins in the white- and black-authored modernist literature examined in the first chapters. A call for the end of the ongoing branding emerges with sheer force in the post–Black movement novels examined in the final chapters.

one

"She Should Have Been a Boy"

Shade of Blackness in *Three Lives* and *The Blacker the Berry*

IN *Playing in the Dark: Whiteness and the Literary Imagination,* Toni Morrison argues that when blackness becomes a metaphor without brakes in the white literary imagination, it has an "enabling" factor. She insists that critics have not unveiled the deeper significance of Gertrude Stein's use of blackness in "Melanctha," the central story in *Three Lives.* Part of the work that Morrison calls for is the comparison of the "playing in the dark" that happens in white and black literary imaginations. When studying colorism, the playing in the dark often becomes "playing in the light." We need to think more about the differences and commonalities between the ways in which black and white authors depict, critique, or fall prey to the seductions of colorism. Stein's engagement with gender, sexuality, and colorism can be usefully compared to Wallace Thurman's representation of the same issues in a novel, *The Blacker the Berry* (1929), published two decades after *Three Lives.* Both *Three Lives* and *The Blacker the Berry* foreground the role of colorism in the racial uplift efforts of African Americans. Stein and Thurman confront the phenotypical racial uplift that, in the early 1900s, often became darker-skinned people marrying lighter-skinned people or lighter-skinned people only marrying other light-skinned people to keep families "light." Furthermore, they are both drawn to the dynamic of lighter-skinned black women historically becoming the means for some darker-skinned men to gain more economic and class privileges. Both Stein and Thurman use this "survival of the lightest" marriage system to introduce and frame their depictions of gender, sexuality, and colorism. When these texts are compared, the intriguing connection is the nexus of skin-color fetishism and homoeroticism. In *The Blacker the Berry,* there is the final move to sexual relations between men, and sexual desire between women is represented in both *The Blacker the Berry* and *Three Lives.* Both texts depict the horror of colorism and then gesture toward "queering" colorism and the meanings attached to the black phallus and the white phallus.[1]

The most recent criticism on images of race in *Three Lives* wrestles with the reiteration *or* undoing of racial stereotypes in "Melanctha." Deborah Mix analyzes the productive tension that emerges when an African American poet, Harryette Mullen, experiments with Stein's experiments with representing blackness.[2] As opposed to Mix's focus on the exhilarating energy in the call and response between Stein and this contemporary African American poet, Daylanne English, in *Unnatural Selections: Eugenics in American Modernism and the Harlem Renaissance* (2004), argues that images of race in *Three Lives* are strangled by Stein's absorption of eugenics. The most provocative criticism on *The Blacker the Berry* analyzes the relation between this text and the more overt representation of homoeroticism in Thurman's later text, *Infants of the Spring* (1932).[3] In this chapter, as I bring *Three Lives* and *The Blacker the Berry* together, I argue that what Stein ultimately does and does *not* do with the racial stereotypes in *Three Lives* is very related to the subtle questioning of the heterosexuality of colorism in both *Three Lives* and *The Blacker the Berry.*

Stein uses images of shades of blackness, with a specific focus on black women's bodies, as she reshapes her first novel, *Q.E.D.*, an autobiographical lesbian love triangle. As she includes some of the same language in *Three Lives,* the colorism that shapes black women's lives leads her to the issues of the phallus at the core of *Q.E.D.* (how can a woman gain access to the phallus?). In contrast to the physicality of the tragic mulatta that dominates most modernist depictions of colorism, there is a lack of emphasis, in *Three Lives,* on the beauty standards that privilege light-skinned female blackness over dark-skinned female blackness. Stein, in fact, does not physically beautify Melanctha; Melanctha is "subtle," "mysterious," "wandering," and represents "a new kind of beauty," but this "beauty" is not rendered as the archetype of the beautiful woman (207). *The Blacker the Berry,* on the other hand, is overdetermined by the trauma caused by white beauty standards.

As a darker-skinned black person, Wallace Thurman personally experienced the trauma of the shunning by lighter-skinned blacks of that which is "too black." In *The Collected Writings of Wallace Thurman,* the editors Amritjit Singh and Daniel Scott explain that the "novel, whose protagonist is haunted by the darkness of her skin, has often been read in relation to Thurman's own dark skin—a reading inspired in part by Hughes's stress in *The Big Sea* on Thurman's dark skin as a source of his bitterness" (442). Stein's engagement with colorism is not tied to any personal experience of its effects. As she creates the story of the yellow Melanctha, she develops a narrative voice and white gaze that has a certain amount of distance from and intimacy with black people. Early in the text, this narrator wonders, "Why did the subtle, intelligent, half white girl Melanctha Herbert love and do for and demean herself in service to this coarse, decent, sullen, ordinary, black childish Rose, and why was this unmoral, promiscuous, shiftless Rose married, and that's not so common either, to a good man of the negroes, while Melanctha with her white blood and attraction and her desire for a right position had not yet been really married" (86). This question is Stein's starting point as she creates the story of "half white" Melanctha's insatiable desire and multiple love affairs.

Her relationship with Rose is difficult to identify as necessarily an erotic relationship, yet there are key passages that suggest a sexual dimension to this relationship. Melanctha's desire to serve darker-skinned Rose becomes a latent sadomasochistic relationship in which Stein recasts the dark-skinned black mammy stereotype as the person with the phallus and makes the light-skinned femme fatale the person who desires to be dominated and feels a sense of power while serving the dominatrix. In *The Blacker the Berry,* as Thurman develops the story of the "too black" Emma Lou, whose dark skin shuts her out from her family's social set of light-skin black privilege (the "blue vein" society), he begins with the question "Why had her mother married a black man? Surely there had been some eligible brown-skin men around. She didn't particularly desire to have had a high yaller father, but for her sake certainly some more happy medium could have been found" (3). As Stein and Thurman begin with questions about what does not make sense within the hegemonic world of colorism (Melanctha as the light-skinned "servant" for the dark-skinned Rose and Emma Lou's mother marrying a "black man"), they depict both the precarious nature and the stability of skin-color fetishism. They also depict normative sexuality, as well as homoeroticism. Their focus on both the normative structure of skin-color fetishism and the exceptions becomes a "queering" of racialized heterosexuality, a queering that reveals that sexual relations between men and sexual relations between women do not escape the skin-color traps but do complicate the positions of "dark-skinned men" as the epitome of virility and "light-skinned women" as the epitome of femininity.

Stein "queers" the archetype of the "high yellow" by creating a yellow character who is more "blue" than high and not strictly heterosexual. Thurman "queers" the normative story of dark-skinned black women's limited marriage possibilities (a story that continues to be heralded in contemporary black magazines such as *Essence* and *Ebony*) by adding homosexuality (a story that is now "queered" in "real life" by the recent great focus on the "down low" black men who secretly have sexual relations with men). The queering in both texts leads to images of non-normative femininity and maleness. In *Three Lives,* yellow Melanctha is ultimately more "manly" than feminine. In *The Blacker the Berry,* the dark-skinned Emma Lou ultimately has a life-changing experience that makes her want to both "strike" her lighter-skinned mate and comfort him in a maternal manner. By ending the novel with the image of Emma Lou as the maternal phallus, the phallic mother figure who can strike and comfort, Thurman "queers" the colorism that makes Emma Lou's family feel that "she should have been a boy," since her dark skin would not be as much of a liability for a boy.

From Q.E.D. to "Melanctha"

With *The Blacker the Berry,* Thurman gave public exposure to black racial self-hatred. A complicated type of latent Jewish self-hatred may underpin Stein's representation, in *Three Lives,* of colorism and black self-hatred. In *Jewish Self-Hatred* (1986), as Sander Gilman analyzes the complexity of Jewish self-hatred, he persuasively argues that Jewishness, for Freud, was the racial otherness that Freud displaced as he created his theories of gender. When we take Sander Gilman's lead in *Freud, Race, and Gender* and remember that when Stein wrote *Q.E.D.* and *Three Lives,* Jewish maleness was often feminized through the larger pathologizing of Jewish circumcision, we arrive at a necessary comparison of the "negro is the genital" (Fanon's recognition of the black person, whose body itself becomes the huge overcompensation for not "having" the phallus, but rather "being" the phallus) and the "Jew (Jud) as the clitoris" (language that Gilman reveals as a pivotal part of the racial discourse surrounding Jewishness at the beginning of the twentieth century).[4] Gilman argues that Freud's latent Jewish self-hatred led him to the fetishism of sexual difference, as if the racial discourse that he could not confront was transmuted into a naturalized sexual difference. In a similar sense, Stein does not include any images of Jewishness in the quasibiographical text *Q.E.D.* that includes a full focus on the ethnicities of the three women in the lesbian love triangle, but makes blackness, in *Three Lives,* a means of exploring a castration anxiety that is very similar to that attached to Jewish bodies in the early 1900s.[5]

In *Gertrude Stein and Richard Wright: The Poetics and Politics of Modernism,* Lynn Weiss argues that in *Three Lives* Stein puts on a "black mask" (82). When and how Stein herself peeks through this "black mask" is a question that illuminates the different meanings and functions attributed to "blackness" in the white modernist literary imagination. To understand the significance of Stein's "playing in the dark," we must compare images of race and sexuality in the earlier texts *Q.E.D.* and *Three Lives.* In both texts, white characters are described as yellow and brown, but the yellowness and brownness of white characters is represented as being fundamentally different from the yellowness and brownness of nonwhite people. In a key passage that insists on the difference between white brownness and the brownness of "colored" people, Stein uses an image that evokes photography and the layering of colors. The brownness of white people is "brown with the clear color laid flat on the light toned skin beneath" (240). White brownness allows light to pass through, whereas nonwhite brownness absorbs light. In this same passage, the narrator emphasizes that the brown of "blonde races" is different from the "yellow or the red or the chocolate brown of sun burned countries" (240). Stein does, however, describe white characters, in *Q.E.D.* and *Three Lives,* as yellow. In both texts, white yellowness is tied to repression and a sense of loss. In "Melanctha" the yellow black character Melanctha desires to escape the repression and loss tied to racial uplift, the supposed progress of the Negro race. Stein moves from white yellowness to the meaning of yellowness in ways of seeing black bodies.

The rewriting of *Q.E.D.* as "Melanctha" is ultimately the shift from the thwarted, repressed desire of white women to the thwarted but *insatiable* passion of the yellow black woman struggling against the repression of the racial uplift discourse. As Stein captures the fetishism of yellowness in our post-slavery landscape, she combines images typical of the "high yellow" paradigm (the privileging of yellowness over darker shades) and images of a mellow yellow woman searching for "knowledge and power" (97). Stein explicitly connects Melanctha's search for "knowledge and power" to her "big black virile" father. The narrator explains repeatedly that the "real power in Melanctha's nature came through her robust and unpleasant and very unendurable black father" (90). Stein plays with the stereotypes of dark-skinned raw masculinity and light-skinned raw femininity as the following questions emerge. Can the yellow woman gain access to the dark-skinned phallus? Can the yellow woman find access to a lesbian phallus?

To unpack Stein's engagement with skin-color fetishism (the fetishism of "shades" of blackness), the specific points of comparison between *Q.E.D.* and *Three Lives* must be unveiled. The following two passages reveal that the "negro" body, when rendered the "sexual primitive" in *Three Lives,* is set up as a contrast to the "drag of unidealised passion" of the white characters in *Q.E.D.*

> Mabel Neathe had the angular body of a spinster but the face told a different story. It was pale yellow brown in complexion and thin in the temples and forehead; heavy about the mouth, not with the weight of flesh but with the drag of unidealised passion, continually sated and continually craving. (*Q.E.D.* 55)

> Melanctha Herbert was a graceful, pale yellow, intelligent, attractive negress. She had not been raised like Rose by white folks but then she had been half made with real white blood . . . Rose laughed when she was happy but she had not the wild abandoned laughter that makes the warm broad glow of negro sunshine. Rose was never joyous with the earth-born, boundless joy of negroes. Hers was just ordinary, any sort of woman laughter. (*Three Lives* 86)

When the "pale yellow brown" is represented as the antithesis of the "angular body of the spinster," uninhibited emotion and sexuality are tied to that which is not white. The "drag of unidealised passion" is rewritten as "the earth-born, boundless joy of negroes," a quintessential description of the "negro primitive." The juxtaposition of these two passages reveals that the very idea of the "negro primitive" emerges from frustrated "white" desire.

Modernist primitivism was often an embrace of that which is imagined as racially "other" and sexually taboo.[6] When Stein recasts a lesbian romance as a "negro" romance overdetermined by primitivism, she makes the "racial other" a screen on which she projects the angst of *Q.E.D.*'s lesbian love triangle, which is, in many ways, autobiographical.[7] In 1926 Carl Van Vechten, one of the central figures in the Harlem Renaissance, includes a lengthy passage from *Three Lives* (1909) in his controversial novel, *Nigger Heaven.* In this novel that purposefully caricatures the prim and proper uptightness of the black middle class and the passion and freedom underneath this middle-class conformity, *Three Lives* represents both high culture and a critique of the inhibitions and blandness of the black middle class. Van Vechten imagines the character Mary remembering a passage from *Three Lives* as she muses on the superficiality of her black middle-class life. As Mary thinks about her biracialness, she wonders if her "white side" is tied to repression and restraint. She muses:

> She had an instinctive horror of promiscuity, of being handled, even touched by a man who did not mean a good deal to her. This might, she sometimes argued with herself, have something to do with her white inheritance, but Olive, who was far whiter, was lacking in this inherent sense of prudery. At any rate, whatever the cause, Mary realized that she was different in this respect from most of the other girls she knew. The Negro blood was there, warm and passionately earnest: all her preferences and prejudices were on the side of the race into which she had been born. She was as capable, she was convinced, of amorous emotion, as any of her friends, but the fact remained that she was more selective. Oh, the others were respectable enough; they did not involve themselves too deeply. On the other hand, they did not flee from a kiss in the dark. (54)

When Mary proceeds to recall an exact passage in *Three Lives,* it is clear that she has literally internalized the racialized primitivism in *Three Lives* that epitomizes the classic binary of white repression versus black naturalness and uninhibited sexuality and desire.

Primitivism in *Three Lives* becomes most heightened when it takes the form, in "Melanctha," of the celebration of uninhibited, raw desire. Rose, as the "black primitive," is "earthy" like "negro sunshine," whereas "yellow" Melanctha is imagined as "complex" and "mysterious" (87, 90, 93, 200, 210). Melanctha, however, is the character through which Stein explores uninhibited desire. Melanctha represents raw desire, unlike other characters whose desire and sexuality have been delimited by societal restraints. As Stein differentiates between the "real black[ness]" of Rose and the biracial subtlety of Melanctha, the skin color gradations of "blackness" become filters for the lack of emotional intensity and desire attributed to "whiteness." Descriptions such as "dark, frowning anger" (172), "black heat" (209), "hot southern negro sunshine" (209), and a "black oath" (183) reveal that "blackness" is imagined as intense emotion and desire, a primitive state of mind and body. When *Three Lives* is compared to *Q.E.D.,* it is clear that desire itself and earthiness are rendered "negro" and "biracial" in *Three Lives.*

In *Q.E.D.* Gertrude Stein describes Mabel as "yellow" (55). In *Three Lives,* yellowness is attributed to Melanctha, the light-skinned black woman who is "complex" and "mysterious." In "The Gentle Lena," the brownness of Lena is differentiated from the "brownness" of the "sun burned countries" (240). Comparing the references to yellowness and brownness in *Q.E.D.* and *Three Lives* unveils the way that "white" ethnicity is constructed as being different from racial otherness. In *Q.E.D.* and *Three Lives,* foreignness is separated from racial otherness only after Stein makes connections between constructions of foreignness and constructions of racial otherness. Shortly after completing *Three Lives* in 1906, Gertrude Stein wrote a letter of lament from Paris to her friend Mabel Weeks: "I am afraid that I can never write the great American novel. I don't know how to sell on a margin or do anything with shorts or longs, so I have to content myself with niggers and servant girls and the foreign population generally" (Peterson 140). In this statement, African Americans, the lower class, and foreigners become a collective "other."

In *Three Lives* when Stein separates the brownness of the German Lena from the brownness of African Americans, we see that "negroes" are attributed an otherness that is more opaque than that of foreigners. The passage reads:

> Lena was a brown and pleasant creature, brown as blonde races often have them brown, brown not with the yellow or the red or the chocolate brown of sun burned countries, but brown with the clear color laid flat on the light toned skin beneath, the plain, spare brown that makes it right to have been made with hazel eyes, and not too abundant straight, brown hair, hair that only later deepens itself into brown from the straw yellow of a german childhood. (240)

The language of photography embedded in this passage is significant considering the simultaneous photographic realism and experimental abstraction in *Three Lives.* The photographic realism takes the form of the "quick and easy" captions, such as "Rose Johnson was a real black, tall, well built, sullen, stupid, childlike, good looking negress" and "Melanctha Herbert was a graceful, pale yellow, intelligent, attractive negress" (85, 86). The abstraction of this realism occurs when these litanies of adjectives are repeated and rearranged, in a relentless fashion, until the bodies being described morph into blurred shapes and colors that somehow remain, even in the midst of the experimentation and "play," actual bodies on which race has been written. The realism is transformed, by the repetition and playfulness of the language, into abstract art. If the "corporeal enactment" of race is so often the embodiment of abstraction, Stein abstracts the racial embodiment of abstraction until it seems that the abstract nature of the experimental language in *Three Lives* undoes the signifying power of the abstractions (the ideas, the emotions) tied to race even as race is reiterated.[8] Stein deconstructs race as she reiterates it; as she experiments with repetition itself, her reiteration of race leads to a deconstruction that is neither didactic nor overt, but rather one possible way of interpreting the puzzling mix of racial stereotypes and subversive twists.

When Stein includes the language of photography as she describes Lena's brownness that does not make her "negro," she invokes the idea of "white light." The light underneath Lena's brownness differentiates her brownness from that of "negroes." Jacques Lacan illuminates the ways in which this description of "white light" becomes a disturbing description of personhood, subjectivity itself, as "white." In *The Four Fundamental Concepts of Psychoanalysis* (1973), Lacan presents subjectivity itself as the process of "light [being] embodied" (106). The text reads:

> What determines me, at the most profound level, in the visible, is the gaze that is outside. It is through the gaze that I enter light and it is from the gaze that I receive its effects. Hence it comes about that the gaze is the instrument through which light is embodied and through which—if you will allow me to use a word, as I often do, in a fragmented form—I am *photo-graphed.* (106)

Like Stein's image of the light beneath Lena's brownness, Lacan uses the photography metaphor of "enter[ing] light and "embod[ying] light" to explain the very process of becoming a subject. These usages of photography reveal the racial fetishism, the skin-color fetishism, embedded in black-and-white photography. Stein uses photography, the prime art form of realism, as she presents the disturbing realism of antiblack racism, the sensationalizing of the difference between the "white" brownness of Lena and the brownness that signals that one is a descendant of "sun burned countries."

As opposed to this rendering of the "black primitive" in *Three Lives,* in the opening pages of *Q.E.D.,* Adele (the character who can easily be read as Stein's depiction of herself) is tied to the primitive and the earthy in an explicit manner: "She nestled close to the bare boards as if accustomed to make the hard earth soft by loving it. She made just a few wriggling movements to adapt her large curves to the projecting boards of the deck, gave a sigh of satisfaction and murmured 'How good it is in the sun'" (56). Being "in the sun" in *Three Lives* is figured as being "negro." Before the sunshine is imagined as "Negro sunshine," it is tied to Stein's image of her own bodily repose (if we accept the very easy interpretation of Adele as a representation of Stein). In *Three Lives,* the "hard earth" is an image of white self-repression. When Stein adds "blackness" to the love triangle in *Q.E.D.,* she "make[s] the hard earth soft by loving it" (56). Stein's discussion of the "black primitive" in *The Autobiography of Alice B. Toklas* (1933) illuminates the nature of Stein's desire "to make the hard earth soft by loving it."

In *The Autobiography,* Stein wryly explains, as she differentiates between European primitivism and American primitivism, that "as an american she likes primitive things to be more savage":

> She had a definite impulse then and always toward elemental abstraction. She was not at any time interested in african sculpture. She always says that she liked it well enough but that it has nothing to do with europeans, that it lacks naïveté, that it is very ancient, very narrow, very sophisticated but lacks the elegance of the egyptian sculpture from which it is derived. She says that as an american she likes primitive things to be more savage. (64)

Later in *The Autobiography,* in the following passage, Stein insists that the African American is "nothing" as opposed to "primitive."

> Once a southern woman, a very charming southern woman was there, and she said to him [Paul Robeson], where were you born, and he answered, in New Jersey and she said, not in the south, what a pity and he said, not for me.
>
> Gertrude Stein concluded that negroes were not suffering from persecution, they were suffering from nothingness. She always contends that the african is not primitive, he has a very ancient but a very narrow culture and there it remains. Consequently nothing does or can happen. (238)

From these passages, can we uncover what the word "primitive" meant to Stein? Perhaps she insists that the "primitive" is not "african" or "negro" because she wants to claim a personal connection to the primitive. When she writes, "that it [african sculpture] has nothing to do with europeans, that it lacks naïveté," Stein directly implies that the type of primitivism that is connected to "europeans" is "naïveté." Making "the hard earth soft" can be interpreted as Stein's explanation of what it means for a person socialized as white and "sophisticated" to reclaim a connection with primitive naïveté. These passages reveal Stein's great awareness of the tendency, in the 1920s and 30s, to conflate the "primitive" and the "negro" or "african" and her interest in denaturalizing this imagined connection.

When Stein rewrites *Q.E.D.* as *Three Lives,* she makes the "negro" signify primitive raw desire and emotion, in spite of her later reluctance, in the 1930s, to link the "negro" and the "primitive." Melanctha's biracialness becomes Stein's means of reiterating the imagined connection between the "negro" and primitive raw desire even as she finds room to explore the primitive raw desire of "whiteness." Melanctha may, in many ways, be a persona of Stein. As Stein uses black characters in "Melanctha," she muses on the possibility of unrestrained desire and sexuality. This desire and sexuality is black on the surface and simply human underneath. The reiteration of racist stereotypes as the medium of this expression of fundamentally human desire and sexuality makes it possible to read "Melanctha" as potentially subversive blackface.

Throughout "Melanctha," as Stein experiments with shifting repetitions of phrases such as "real black," "simple beast," "wide, abandoned laughter," "glow of negro sunshine," "careless and [. . .] lazy," and "subtle, intelligent, attractive, half white," she demonstrates the seductiveness of these stereotypes as well as their emptiness. When *Q.E.D.* is transposed into *Three Lives,* is the addition of black, "enabling" characters problematic? One way to answer this question is to link the repeated images in "Melanctha" of "negro sunshine" and the contemporary white fascination with tanning. Richard Dyer has argued that tanning offers white people access to "brownness" without losing white privilege and power. The problem with the fetishism of light-skinned blackness while representing white love of the sun may be the "tanning" of white self-repression, the way in which Melanctha's yellowness, her inheritance from the "sun burned countries" (240), becomes the sheen of desire that contrasts with the "repressed Anna" and the "lifeless Lena."

From "Melanctha" to The Blacker the Berry

The place to begin, in the comparison of *Three Lives* and *The Blacker the Berry,* is the image of the dark-skinned father figure in both texts. In *The Blacker the Berry,* as Emma Lou laments her very dark skin and her mother's marriage to a very dark-skinned black man, she decides, "She didn't particularly desire to have had a high yaller father, but for her sake certainly some more happy medium could have been found" (3). Just as the 1920s politics of colorism dictate that darker skin is more of a liability for a young woman than a young man (the idea that Emma "should have been a boy"), the "high yaller father" is evoked as an oddity, an idea that Emma feels she could not "particularly desire" (3). As the "high yaller" within the post-slavery imagination is sometimes beautified, sometimes oversexualized, and sometimes stigmatized as the sign of shameful rape, it gains a feminine aura that makes it difficult for Emma to fetishize the idea of a "high yaller father." As Thurman develops Emma Lou's racial self-hatred and difficulties in the world of intraracial prejudice, he highlights the fact that light-skinned black women's bodies, in the body politics of racial uplift, became a type of currency for dark-skinned black men. Within this economy of color and desire, Thurman imagines that dark-skinned black women would have sometimes sought to increase their social capital by marrying light-skinned black men. The difference between the desire for the light-skinned women and the desire for light-skinned men is at the heart of the narrative assertion "[s]he should have been a boy, then color of skin wouldn't have mattered so much" (4). The "high yaller father" does not exclusively occupy the place of the black patriarch, whereas the "high yaller" woman, in the body politics of racial uplift, has occupied the position of social currency as light-skinned wives became economic trophies.

Thurman's real intervention within representations of this economy of color is his focus on the "very" dark-skinned black woman's search for a light-skinned male "trophy." Emma Lou's suffering as a dark-skinned black woman makes her seize the role scripted as the male suitor looking for a light-skinned wife. Thurman imagines a situation in which being dark-skinned is the one issue that forces an individual to lose her social status. Emma Lou is the daughter of a light-skinned mulatta woman who, along with other family members, has a social status denied to Emma by virtue of Emma's dark skin. When the family expresses their disgust over the skin color that Emma has inherited from the dark-skinned father, Emma learns that to be a part of the social world of her family, she must somehow redeem her dark skin, separate herself from her belittled dark-skinned father, and gain access to the privileges of light-skinned blackness. When Emma searches for a light-skinned husband, light-skinned blackness literally becomes the phallus she seeks. The images of the dark and light phallus are rendered explicitly in *Three Lives* when Melanctha encounters the different types of power tied to dark-skinned Rose, light-skinned Jane, and her dark-skinned father. Images of the dark-skinned and light-skinned phallus, in both *Three Lives* and *The Blacker the Berry,* illuminate the sexualized power relations tied to the shades of blackness.

The dark-skinned father figure haunts both texts. The presence of the absence of these dark father figures underscores that they represent both sexual power and social castration. In *The Blacker the Berry,* Emma Lou is tied to racial castration when she wishes her dark-skinned nose did not become so shiny on hot summer days. When she "powder[s] her shiny member" (84), Thurman creates a subtext in which the gaze that reduces Emma Lou to her dark skin color is comparable to the gaze, described by Fanon, that equates the "Negro" and the "genital." The fact that Thurman uses the word "member," which can refer to any body part in addition to the more specific reference to the penis, reveals that when dark-skinned blackness, for Emma Lou, becomes the curse of the father figure, Emma's entire body, in the words of Fanon, is "spattered [. . .] with black blood" (*Black Skin, White Masks* 112). When this subtextual image of Emma Lou as a woman with a phallic organ is brought to the surface and connected to other images in the novel of Emma as a transgressor of normative female traits, Thurman's depiction of the plight of this dark-skinned black woman, in the world of light-skinned privilege, insists that a dark-skinned black woman who transgresses the social script assigned to dark-skinned female bodies must also transgress normative roles of femininity and masculinity. Emma Lou becomes more of a sexual predator as opposed to the sexual prey that her mother and others assume a woman must be when they feel that as a very dark-skinned person she "should have been a boy." Thurman captures the ways in which she assumes the role of the male gaze: "He was too pudgy and dark, too obviously an ex-cotton picker from Georgia. He was unlettered and she couldn't stand for that, for she liked intelligent-looking, slender, light-brown-skinned men, like, well . . . Like the one who was just passing. She admired him boldly. He looked at her, then over her and passed on" (83). The image of the "ex-cotton picker from Georgia" who is "too pudgy and too dark" crystallizes the post-slavery trauma that shapes ways of seeing dark-skinned blackness. The "too dark" African American body, in this passage, is rendered the phenotype that recalls slavery and Eldridge Cleaver's "supermasculine menial."[9]

Emma's desire for light-skinned men is fueled by her determination to not be socially and economically limited because of her dark skin. Her mother feels that "no professional man is going to marry a woman dark as Emma Lou," but Emma is determined to marry a light-skinned professional man (51). In *Three Lives,* Stein does not attribute a color preference to Melanctha, but her two significant relationships with men are with mulatto suitors. The relationship that is explicitly homoerotic is with Jane, who is so light skinned she appears white. Jane is described as a "roughened woman" in contrast to the "graceful" Melanctha (107). Rose, the dark-skinned friend whose relationship with Melanctha has homoerotic undertones, is crude but proper. James Herbert, the dark-skinned father, represents "fierce," "angry," and "evil" power. Within the normative colorism scheme, very light-skinned female blackness is refined femininity, in contrast to rough dark-skinned female blackness and terrifying dark-skinned male blackness, and parallel to stereotypes of feminized light-skinned male blackness. Melanctha's yellowness is represented as a sign of a transgressive femininity that is in-between the roughness of Jane, the bland properness of Rose, and the "unendurable" masculinity of James Herbert. Thurman explores Emma Lou's attempt to "powder her shiny member" (84), to claim the white phallus and rid herself of the stain of the dark-skinned phallus. As Stein thinks about women's relation to the phallus, she reclaims "real power" as a passionate and free expression of sexuality that defies the mind/body split. This erotic intelligence is very similar to the theory of power that Audre Lorde presents many years later, in 1984, in her essay "The Uses of the Erotic."[10] Emma Lou, at the end of *The Blacker the Berry,* is forced to confront the shams of power tied to light skin, heterosexual masculinity, and racial uplift. When she decides that real power would be "acceptance of herself by herself" (208), Emma Lou approaches Melanctha's discovery of the "power" within herself: "When the excitement was all over, Melanctha began to know her power, the power she had so often felt stirring within her and which she now knew she could use to make her stronger" (95). Melanctha first discovers this power when her "big black virile" father rages against her sexual freedom, his fear that she is becoming erotically involved with "that yellow John" (90, 94). Melanctha begins to think about this power when her father assaults her; her fear and hatred of his dark-skinned virility lead her to first wonder about her own ability to find a ferocious sexuality. Her own power blossoms when she becomes intimate with the very light-skinned, "so white" Jane Harden, who "had power and [. . .] liked to use it" (103, 104). Situated between the hues of Jane and her father, Melanctha's yellowness is a sign of her need to negotiate the tension between the blackened virility and whitened femininity.

Melanctha's father is an explicit image of the black phallus. Melanctha has received her "real power" from the dark-skinned father as opposed to the light-skinned mother: "Melanctha was pale yellow and mysterious and a little pleasant like her mother, but the real power in Melanctha's nature came through her robust and unpleasant and very unendurable black father" (90). Virility is tied to dark-skinned black masculinity in "Melanctha," but dark-skinned black femininity is rendered as feminine lack, whereas light-skinned black femininity, the liminal space between dark-skinned black masculinity and dark-skinned black femininity, is imagined as partially virile. Whereas dark-skinned femininity, within post-slavery trauma and racism, has been masculinized in stereotypes of the asexual black "mammy" as femininity itself has been imagined as a quality of whiteness, Stein experiments with masculinizing light-skinned blackness even as she differentiates between the subtlety, the delicacy, of "yellowness" and the imagined "roughness" of dark-skinned blackness.

When Emma Lou "powders her shiny member," Thurman creates a vivid image of this relation between the black phallus and white femininity. When *Three Lives* and *The Blacker the Berry* are compared, it becomes clear that, just as Stein uses colorism as she explores women's relation to the phallus, Thurman is ultimately most interested in the colorism that shapes men's relation to the phallus. On the surface, it appears that *The Blacker the Berry* is about black women, but Thurman delves into the crisis of black masculinity as he develops the story of Emma Lou. He includes, for example, a pivotal scene in which three young black men express their lack of desire for very dark-skinned black women, and one of the "noisy lads" asserts, "Man, you know I don't haul no coal" (84). Thurman captures the everyday black vernacular that illuminates black men's attempt to separate themselves, through their shunning of very dark-skinned black women, from the degradation of that which Eldridge Cleaver identifies as the "supermasculine menial." The very dark-skinned black woman, the "coal," signifies that which is too coarse and menial as the men attempt to claim refinement and empowerment for themselves. By ending the novel with Emma Lou's shock when she sees Alva being intimate with "an effeminate boy," Thurman adds a new twist to the idea of "not hauling coal." Black male desire for a delicacy tied to male bodies is figured as that which ends any possibility of a harmonious relationship between Emma, the dark-skinned black woman, and Alva, the lighter-skinned man.

In this final scene revolving around Emma's shock, the earlier narrative statement, "She should have been a boy," takes on another meaning. Alva, having internalized the masculinizing of very dark-skinned blackness, may have unconsciously been attracted to the different type of femininity written on her dark skin. Alva's attraction to both Emma and the "effeminate boy" may be a similar attraction to gender ambiguity. Emma views Alva as a masculine "bulldog." As she remains fully conditioned by the gendering of shades of blackness, she contrasts Alva's "bulldog" traits and the "pallid" aura of other men. Thurman writes:

> Emma Lou couldn't get excited over any of them. They all seemed so young

> and so pallid. Their air of being all-wise amused her, their affected church purity and wholesomeness, largely a verbal matter, tired her. Their world was so small—church, school, home, mother, father, parties, future. She invariably compared them to Alva and made herself laugh by classifying them as a litter of sick puppies. Alva was a bulldog and a healthy one at that. (190)

Even though Emma wants to marry a light-skinned black man, she is repulsed by the "pallid[ness]" that she associates with weakness and effeminacy. In addition to the "lighter the better" beauty standards that she has internalized, she has also absorbed a more unconscious association of light-skinned blackness with weakness. Thurman reveals the peculiar simultaneity of her racial self-hatred and her belief in the castrated nature of "pallid" skin. Alva is presented as an exception to this light-skinned castration. The implied sexual stamina tied to Alva's "healthiness" is separated, in the continuation of this passage, from reproduction and racial uplift. In contrast to the eugenics that shapes Emma's family's and social set's attempt to become "lighter and lighter" as the generations pass, Alva, in Emma's viewpoint, seems to have no future: "Yet 'these sick puppies,' as she called them, were the next generation of respectable society folk. They had a future; Alva merely lived for no purpose whatsoever except for the pleasure he could squeeze out of each living moment" (190). Jeff Campbell, in *Three Lives,* views Melanctha, in a similar manner, as a pleasure seeker "having excitements all the time" and failing to think about the future and betterment of the race (116). By using Melanctha and Alva as a means of critiquing the repression that was often a part of African American attempts to prove the respectability and properness of the race, Stein and Thurman upset the normative sexuality of the racial uplift agenda. They demonstrate that the differentiation between darker- and lighter-skinned blackness occupies a key space in the racial uplift mission.[11]

As both authors explore colorism, they expose the fetishism of the very idea of racial mixture. Alva is often described as yellow, and in one passage, as "neither yellow nor brown" (89). His parentage is "an American mulatto" (his mother) and "a Filipino" (his father) (89). In *Three Lives,* Melanctha is sometimes described as biracial by parentage and sometimes as the light-skinned daughter of a light-skinned mother and a dark-skinned father. Melanctha is "half made with real white blood," but Rose is "raised [. . .] by white folks" (86). As Stein thinks about the visual hybridity tied to Melanctha's body in contrast to the cultural hybridity that Rose gained while being raised by "white folks," she questions the assumption that cultural hybridity is experienced only by light-skinned black bodies. In a similar sense, Thurman includes a key scene in which a character, Tony Crews, insists, "But you seem to forget [. . .] that because a man is dark it doesn't necessarily mean he is not of mixed blood" (134). Thurman shows that colorism is fueled by investments in visualizing hybridity and imagining that "mixed blood" is always visible. Emma Lou is seduced by the exotic, "different" color of Alva's skin (112). As she attempts to escape the stigma of her very dark-skinned blackness, she is attracted to his lighter color but also the "different" color (112). Thurman's description of the "oriental-like face" of Alva has a deeper resonance through the lens of racialized dilution anxieties and fantasies. As signaled by the very title, "Racial Castration," of David Eng's study of Asian American identity and culture, the "oriental" (male) face is the desexualized counterpart to the oversexualized black body.[12]

In African American body politics, yellowness, the color often evoked in images of castrated Asian male bodies, continues to often be a sign of female beauty (the "high yellow" beauty). When Stein describes Melanctha's father as a "big black virile negro" and her mother as "that pleasant, sweet-appearing, pale yellow woman" (90), the equation of dark skin and virility and light skin and femininity is shown to be the core binary that Melanctha defies.[13] At the end of *The Blacker the Berry,* Emma Lou decides that Alva is not the light-skinned prize but rather the "yellow nigger" that she will not serve and the "yellow nigger" who is attached to the "effeminate boys." Emma Lou vows that she will accept her blackness as "real and unchangeable" (208). She will no longer accept the idea that to be a refined woman, she must be attached to a light-skinned man. As Emma Lou vows that she will not be burdened by a "yellow nigger," she revises the colorist sentiment, "I don't haul no coal," echoed earlier in the novel by men who are repelled by dark-skinned black women. Thurman gives voice to the story of dark-skinned black women like Rose in *Three Lives.* At the end of "Melanctha," Rose is figured as the maternal anchor that makes Melanctha feel "solid" (231). Dark-skinned black femininity feels like "home" as Melanctha "wanders." But Melanctha loses this sense of home as Rose separates herself from Melanctha. Rose does not rescue Melanctha from the gender traps she has inherited, the dark-skinned virility and the soft, pleasing, yellow mother figure. Melanctha's mother is kind and gentle, but not "solid" and safe, as Rose is.

Dark-skinned black femininity, in the post-slavery landscape, evokes strong womanhood, not softness or delicateness. As Stein and Thurman explore the gender ambiguity of their respective protagonists, Melanctha and Emma Lou, they wonder about a new "shade" of woman that would be delicate and strong. They confront the ways in which gendered colorism makes dark skin both a sign of virility and a maternity that are tied to the lingering effects of slavery. Emma Lou, for example, is the dark-skinned "wench" who takes care of the yellow child (202); the word "wench" was one of the prime terms used in descriptions of slaves in auction advertisements and runaway postings. When the dark-skinned black woman, in "Melanctha," is described as a "simple beast" (85, 222), it is clear that she is the "raw primitive" that undergirds the "subtle" and "mysterious" primitive nature of Melanctha. This layering of primitiveness reveals that "dark-skinned blackness" remains the imagined original state of savagery and naturalness which the lighter-skinned black character can visit and tour before continuing to "wander." The opening sentence, "Rose Johnson made it very hard to bring her baby to its birth" (85), reveals that Rose gives birth to the "baby" that Melanctha gains: "the deepest of all Melanctha's emotions" (234). Rose is comparable to a surrogate mother. Emma Lou finally decides that she is simply a surrogate caretaker once Alva loses his yellow wife. Emma Lou remembers, "Hadn't she been warned that men didn't marry black girls? Hadn't she been told that they would only use her for their sexual convenience?" (52).

Both authors first depict and then aim to subvert the equation between dark skin and masculinity and light skin and femininity. Thurman writes, "There was no place in the world for a dark girl" (45), as the idea of a "dark girl" is shown to be a contradiction in the scheme of gendered colorism. Whereas "there was no place for her in the world [. . .] She was too black, black is a portent of evil, black is a sign of bad luck" (206), Melanctha has "no place in the world" because she has too much wanderlust. Melanctha's yellowness becomes a sign of bad luck, of the unruly woman. As they represent the sexual politics of colorism, both Thurman and Stein describe the different ways in which black womanhood is limited by the traps of the "black mammy" and the "yellow wife." In the mammy stereotype and the historical truth of American slavery, the black woman cares for white babies and their white mothers. Stein reverses this stereotype when Melanctha, the light-skinned black woman, serves the dark-skinned Rose.[14] Stein emphasizes the "peculiar" nature of this servitude when she writes, "Why did the subtle, intelligent, half white girl Melanctha Herbert love and do for and demean herself in service to this coarse, decent, sullen, ordinary, black childish Rose, and why was this unmoral, promiscuous, shiftless Rose married, and that's not so common either, to a good man of the negroes, while Melanctha with her white blood and attraction and her desire for a right position had not yet been really married" (86). As Stein repeatedly uses the word "wander" as she describes Melanctha's insatiable desire and quest for "knowledge and power" (97), Rose emerges as the more submissive and domestic woman, the dark-skinned black woman who is "stuck" at home as the "yellow" black woman "wanders." This is the very paradigm that traumatizes Emma Lou. The part of the story that Stein flattens is the layer that Thurman develops, and Thurman's uncomplicated images of yellow women are the layer that Stein develops.

Thurman makes the mammy trap a central part of the degradation of the dark-skinned black woman. By emphasizing that Emma Lou has all of the other traits of dominant beauty except the light skin, Thurman demands that readers confront the tendency, in the 1920s, for dark skin alone to make a black woman a "mammy" type as opposed to the refined, higher-class woman that Emma Lou desires to be. When Emma Lou becomes the caretaker of Alva's child, she is viewed by others as the "black mammy" who must care for the child that the light-skinned wife abandoned (203). After overhearing a neighbor gossiping about Emma and Alva, Emma decides, "That's what she was, Alva Junior's mammy and a typical black mammy at that" (203). At the end of the novel, when Emma finds Alva in the intimate pose with the "effeminate boy," she has conflicting feelings. She feels violated by Alva, and she also feels an urge to protect Alva, who seems, at that moment, vulnerable and childlike. Thurman captures the ways in which the "mammy trap" parallels the black macho trap. Alva, who is described earlier as the "bulldog" in Emma's lens, is rendered vulnerable in this final scene, when he is placed outside the heterosexual rubric. As Emma Lou packs her belongings, Thurman makes it clear that she will leave Alva, but the most intriguing part of this ending is Emma Lou's need to resist lapsing back into the caretaker mode and the fact that the witnessing of intimacy between men becomes her turning point. This ending must be connected to the gendered colorism that the novel confronts (the idea that "she should have been a boy"). Thurman ends the novel with the suggestion that compulsory heterosexuality has oppressed Alva, just as colorism has oppressed Emma Lou. As opposed to many images of the light color of his skin (relative to Emma's), Alva, in a key passage, is described as being "neither yellow nor brown but something in between" (89). The ambiguity of his sexual orientation parallels his in-between status on the color spectrum of light- and dark-skinned blackness.

What is the significance of the homoeroticism at the core of the images of colorism in *Three Lives* and *The Blacker the Berry?* Both texts demonstrate that colorism relies on a heteronormativity. When that heteronormativity is queered, the equation between light skin and femininity and dark skin and virility is upset. Through the images of shades of blackness in *Three Lives* and *The Blacker the Berry,* Stein and Thurman represent the racial unconscious that often lightens femininity and darkens masculinity. Shades of blackness become the medium through which Stein and Thurman explore the female protagonists' relation to power itself (to the phallus). Subtextually, it is significant that *The Blacker the Berry* ends with an image of Emma Lou "hardening inside" as she resolves to abandon Alva and empower herself: "Something snapped within her. The tears in her eyes receded, her features grew set and she felt herself hardening inside" (213). It is important to unearth this phallic subtext as we make visible the role of racialized castration in colorism. The often unspeakable nature of racialized castration anxieties makes the notion of dark virility and light femininity seem as familiar as the cliché "tall, dark, and handsome." The "tall, dark, and handsome" *white* man needs to be attached, even if symbolically, to this darkness in order to *have* the phallus, as opposed to the "tall, dark, and handsome" black man, who *is* the phallus. Having the phallus remains the privileged position. Emma Lou and Melanctha are black women who seek this privileged position of *having* the phallus. As Thurman and Stein capture the masculinizing of dark-skinned blackness, their respective light- and dark-skinned black female protagonists, as they try to find access to "knowledge and power" (Stein's very description of Melanctha's mission), assume roles assigned, within this color coding, to dark-skinned black maleness. Gender trouble is ultimately represented, in these texts, as that which emerges when one's gender status is determined not by "biological" sex but rather by the color of one's skin. As virility is tied to darkness and femininity is tied to lightness, the light-skinned Melanctha is haunted by the power that her dark-skinned father represents. Melanctha rejects the dark-skinned father figure when she reaches the point of feeling anchored only if she has the support of the dark-skinned black woman, Rose. In *The Blacker the Berry,* Emma Lou abandons, finally, her mission to marry a light-skinned black man as she resolves to find "knowledge and power" in an unabashed acceptance of her dark-skinned black womanhood.

two

The Fantasy and Fear of Dilution in *Absalom, Absalom!*

LIKE *Three Lives* and *The Blacker the Berry, Absalom, Absalom!* (1936) spectacularizes shades of blackness. When Faulkner ends the novel with an image of the "bleaching" of blackness and the fear of the black phallus, he brings to the surface the racialized castration anxiety that haunts *Three Lives* and *The Blacker the Berry.*[1]

At the end of *Absalom, Absalom!* Shreve and Quentin contemplate a final state of "Jim Bonds" who look white but "will still be Jim Bond" (302). As opposed to the idea of the "Negro race" vanishing to become white, the final image in this text is that of the "Negro race" "conquer(ing) the western hemisphere" (302), and becoming "bleach[ed] out" as it conquers, but always remaining "Jim Bond" (302). This bleaching and conquering of the "Negro race" is the ultimate contradiction presented at the end of *Absalom, Absalom!* One fresh way to understand this contradiction is to read it through the lens of Faulkner's views, twenty years later, on the most suitable approach to desegregation in the South. In interviews and public speeches, Faulkner endorsed the "Go Slow" approach to desegregation and connected this approach to what he viewed as the gradual lightening of the Negro. For instance, in an interview in 1956 with Russell Howe, he asserts, "In the long view, the Negro race will vanish in 300 years by intermarriage.

It has happened to every racial minority everywhere, and it will happen here."[2] When he claims that the "Negro race will vanish in 300 years," he insists on the inevitability of the assimilation of the "Negro race." This emphasis on assimilation is most direct, in 1955, during a presentation at the Tokyo American Cultural Center: "[I]n a few hundred years the Negro in my country will vanish away. He will be assimilated into the white race simply because there are more white people."[3] Unlike the image in *Absalom, Absalom!* of the final state of the bleached Negro always remaining Negro even as it is diluted, interracialness, in these interviews and speeches, is a transient state that gradually leads to the final state of whiteness.

"There is never time in the future in which we will work out our salvation," James Baldwin insists as he responds to William Faulkner's advocacy of the "Go Slow Now" approach to desegregating the South.[4] Baldwin counters Faulkner's "middle of the road" approach in "Letter to the North" (1956).[5] He counsels, in "Faulkner and Desegregation" (1954), the "time is always now" (126). For Baldwin, the most disturbing aspect of Faulkner's "Letter to the North" is the *mystification* of the immorality of antiblack Southern segregation. Baldwin writes, "He concedes the madness and moral wrongness of the South but at the same time he raises it to the level of a *mystique* which makes it somehow unjust to discuss Southern society in the same terms in which one would discuss any other society" (118; italics mine). The mystification of interracial characters in *Absalom, Absalom!* (1936) is inseparable from the mystification, at the end of this novel, of the eventual bleaching of Jim Bond. Just as Baldwin recognizes that, in "Letter to the North," there is a mystification of what is simply wrong and what simply needs to be done to correct the heinous immorality, the final image in *Absalom, Absalom!* of the diluted blackness that will "conquer the western hemisphere" seems to both terrify and excite Quentin and the narrator. This mystified ending, and the images of interracial characters throughout the entire novel, beg to be examined through the lens of Baldwin's critique of Faulkner's "Go Slow" approach. The representation of the fear and fetishism of interracialness in *Absalom, Absalom!* is deeply tied to issues of temporality. Images of lighter-skinned blackness reflect an in-between state, a state of becoming. The "Go Slow" approach, when connected to this novel's often beautified, and sometimes terrifying, images of interracial liminality, is not only Faulkner's stance on desegregation, but also the *slow* motion in his images of the cocoon-like state of suspension of some of the interracial characters. As he makes light-skinned blackness his "middle of the road" way of not confronting the fear and fantasy of the dark-skinned black phallus, interracial characters are tied to what is new as opposed to old, "pure" blackness, but they are also in a peculiar state of the slow motion of the process of *becoming*. The repeated images of the cocoons and the butterflies are the literary representations of the "middle of the road" discourse in "Letter to the North."

In "Letter to the North," Faulkner explains that he is against both compulsory segregation *and* compulsory integration. When this letter is applied to *Absalom, Absalom!*, the novel's final image of the bleached Jim Bond who "conquer(s) the western hemisphere" emerges as the fear of a compulsory integration that will lead to blackness overpowering whiteness. This fear surfaces when the emphasis is placed on "it will still be Jim Bond" (378). In *Absalom, Absalom!* Faulkner depicts both the fear and the fantasy of this compulsory integration, whereas in public talks and interviews, he depicts this compulsory integration through miscegenation as the fortunate inevitability of the literal fading of the Negro and the inevitability of less toxic race relations as this lightening occurs. This biological approach to integration is difficult to separate from the antiblack fantasy of black bodies being continually diluted as white Southerners escape the "threatful portent of the old" (126). At the end of the novel, Faulkner foregrounds the ongoing avoidance of the "big black phallus," the fear of the "hot equatorial groin of the world," at the heart of this dilution fantasy (92). Critics such as Eric Sundquist, Ben Railton, Philip Weinstein, Thadious Davis, and Hortense Spillers have greatly complicated readings of images of blackness in *Absalom, Absalom!* as prescriptive antiblack racism as well as impulses to assume that it is not productive to look at the ideological blind spots in his representations of race. The questions emerging from *Absalom, Absalom!* become even more complicated when we focus on the images of dilution anxiety and the black phallus. After a full indulgence, throughout the novel, in the aesthetics of interracial femininity (tied to male and female bodies), Faulkner ends with the invocation of a "bleached" black phallus that will "conquer the western hemisphere" (302). Since Faulkner becomes most drawn to the aesthetic experience (the very fantasy of beauty) when he is depicting interracialness, what he does with interracialness, fetishism, and the phallus becomes inseparable from what he does with the "more than" formulation in the aesthetic experience (the beauty that is always "more than" any actual object or actual body).

To appreciate the ways in which *Absalom, Absalom!* connects images of the phallus and images of the aesthetic, we must recognize Faulkner's use of the repeated meditations on "it" as a means of moving from explicit representations of race to representations of the abstract beauty and pain that is always "more than" race. The novel stages a tension between the racial fetish and the aesthetic. Ultimately, in *Absalom, Absalom!* the "more than" quality, the transcendent beauty, of the aesthetic experience is not different from the embodiment of abstraction that race becomes, that which is signaled when Faulkner refers to the very pigmentation of Clytie's skin as a sign of the Civil War: "Clytie, who in the very pigmentation of her flesh represented that debacle" (156). The fetishism of shades of blackness makes skin color the embodiment of abstractions; the "very pigmentation" represents these abstractions. As Faulkner is seduced by the "middle of the road," mystical nature of interracialness, he moves back and forth between a discourse of race that puts power in the center and a hyper-aestheticized discourse that masquerades as the realm of transcendence that can never be reduced to power relations. *Absalom, Absalom!* dramatizes how anxieties over white power *and* black power are evaded through pretty pictures of feminized interracialness. The novel underscores that, at the core of the fetishism of lighter- and darker-skinned blackness, there is the retreat to beauty as a means of rationalizing, and even mystifying, power. Faulkner is indeed an aestheticist; he does imagine that the aesthetic experience can transcend the ideological. But there is also an aestheticism often built into the post-slavery gazes that shape the fetishism of shades of blackness. The fetishism of the lighter skin tones of blackness is sometimes the lightening of the trauma of the heavy antiblack racist past *and* present.

The Racialized Phallus

The novel begins with a profound meditation on the heaviness of the past and the presence of absence. These images of the presence of absence become tied to the phallus when Faulkner moves from the opening descriptions of Rosa Coldfield's voice as the presence of absence ("Her voice would not cease, it would just vanish" [8]) to the first descriptions of Sutpen's violent intrusion ("Out of quiet thunderclap he would abrupt (man-horse-demon)" [8]). In "Desire and Dismemberment: Faulkner and the Ideology of Penetration" (1995), Anne Goodwyn Jones argues that the trope of penetration, what "men do with the phallus," not the "more familiar notion of the possession and/or loss of the phallus," is the central phallic issue in Faulkner's work. Jones focuses on images of dismembered bodies (in many novels written by Faulkner) that, in her reading, "wor[k] as a critique of the ideology of penetration" (130).[6] When we analyze images of the racialized phallus and racialized castration in *Absalom, Absalom!*, the crucial image is white men's "planting of the seed" that creates octoroon women. As Faulkner depicts the octoroon wife of Charles Bon, the prime image becomes the "mark of the unmarked." When he emphasizes that white men "plant the seed" that creates the "mark of the unmarked," the decentering of the black phallus is most evident. The mark of blackness, the one-drop rule, is rewritten as the unmarked whiteness. Why does Mr. Compson indulge in this rewriting? The story about the octoroon wife, told by Mr. Compson to Quentin, leads Faulkner to images of the white phallus as that which creates the "apotheosis of two doomed races" (91). The rewriting of the one drop of black blood as the one drop of white blood allows Faulkner to capture white Southern men's need to reclaim the virility of whiteness and efface black procreative power.

As opposed to the novel's final images of Jim Bond conquering through his acts of procreation, the white men who create the octoroon women are figured as the nonaggressive progenitors. Mr. Compson uses biblical allusions to the "sparrow" as he thinks about the "creation" of the octoroon women by white men. In the books of Matthew and Luke in the King James translation of the Bible, the "sparrow" is used as an example of how much God loves humankind. Jesus asks his listeners to imagine how much he loves humankind if he cares about "sparrows," one of which is "sold for a farthing" (Matthew 10:29) or "five . . . sold for two farthings" (Luke 12:6). Mr. Compson imagines Charles Bon purchasing his "octoroon" wife at a "ball" in New Orleans (93). The price of the sparrow in the biblical references is insignificant, and Mr. Compson believes the money exchanged for the octoroon women is insignificant and does not make them "whores" or "courtesans": "[f]or a price, of course, but a price offered and accepted or declined through a system more formal than any that white girls are sold under since they are more valuable as commodities than white girls" (93). In the biblical reference in the book of Matthew, the sparrow is "saved" by God: "one of them shall not fall on the ground without your Father" (10:29). In Mr. Compson's consideration of the "octoroon" woman as a "sparrow," God notices the sparrow's fall but does not "stop it" (92). Faulkner writes:

> Yes, a sparrow which God himself neglected to mark. Because though men, white men, created her, God did not stop it. He planted the seed which brought her to flower—the white blood to give the shape and pigment of what the white man calls female beauty, to a female principle which existed, queenly and complete, in the hot equatorial groin of the world long before that white one of ours came down from trees and lost its hair and bleached out—a principle apt docile and instinct with strange and ancient curious pleasures of the flesh (which is all: there is nothing else) which her white sisters of a mushroom yesterday flee from in moral and outraged horror. (92)

The actual body of the octoroon woman is signaled by words like "shape and pigment" and "pleasures of the flesh," but these concrete words aid the larger abstraction: the white man's idea of female beauty grafted upon an "essential" quality of black femininity. This essential quality is described as "apt docile and instinct with strange and ancient curious pleasures of the flesh" (92). The grafting of what the white man calls female beauty to this "essential" quality enables the octoroon woman to be consciousness-in-the-flesh, instead of pure corporeality. The octoroon woman transcends the thinglike, entirely pejorative images of "pure" blackness. Indeed, Mr. Compson proceeds to declare that the principle, which she represents, "reigns, wise supine and all-powerful" (93).

Mr. Compson tells Quentin that Henry must have viewed the octoroon wife of Charles Bon as the "apotheosis of two doomed races presided over by its own victim" (91), which is a pronounced example of the simultaneous abstracting and embodying of "race." According to Mr. Compson, Henry "looked" at the octoroon woman and saw the "apotheosis of two doomed races" and also saw the victimization of the woman "presid[ing] over" this deification (91). She is a victim, because her very body is the site where the "two doomed races" are deified. She herself represents the "apotheosis" of the "doomed" gender (the "Who-suffers") in addition to the "apotheosis of two doomed races" (91). She upsets the "erstwhile untroubled code in which females were ladies or whores or slaves" (91), because she transcends each of these categories, and this imagined power of the "victim" is yet another example of fetishism. When Mr. Compson explains, in a later passage, that the octoroon women were "culled and chosen and raised more carefully than any white girl, any nun, than any blooded mare even" (93), it is apparent that the octoroon woman cannot be fully assimilated to his concept of the "white girl," nor to that of the "blooded mare." She "divert[s]" Henry and Mr. Compson's attention from the meanings of whiteness and blackness, as constructed by antiblack racism (93). Indeed, he tells Quentin that her "sole end and purpose" is "to love, to be beautiful, to divert" (93).

The octoroon women, with their "strange and ancient curious pleasures of the flesh" (92), represent free and uninhibited sexuality, as opposed to the "moral and outraged horror" of their "white sister" (92). The word "horror" is used throughout the novel, along with "terror" and "outrage," when the trauma of the postbellum white Southerner is being described. At the end of the novel, in one of Rosa's streams of consciousness, she dreams that the "objects of outrage" were "no longer ghosts but . . . actual people to be actual recipients of the hatred and the pity" (302). Rosa wishes for an escape from the mystification of the Southern terror (the effects of the Civil War, the effects of slavery, and, most importantly for Rosa, the "living dead" aura of the South). When Mr. Compson describes the sheltered society of the octoroon women and the way in which they were protected by white men and perceived as the "only true chaste women, not to say virgins, in America" (93), it is clear that he is mystifying them and that he is avoiding the "actual[ity]" of which Rosa dreams.

The body of the octoroon woman and not the body of a "pure" black enables Mr. Compson to recognize that there is, supposedly, a "female principle" that preceded "what the white man calls female beauty" (92). Mr. Compson understands this female principle and the "hot equatorial groin of the world" as the nonwhite ancestry of the white, "bleached out" race (92). Mr. Compson also stresses the rarity of this octoroon woman. He imagines Bon, as he fails to admit his own interracialness, telling Henry, "We cannot, perhaps we do not even want to, save all of them; perhaps the thousand we save are not one in a thousand. But we save that one" (92). In the full context of this passage, Mr. Compson imagines Bon arguing to Henry that white men, like himself, "created and produced" the octoroon women and that it was only natural that they would save only selected ones from being "slaves too, laborers, cooks, maybe even field hands" (91). Bon's justification of this selection process, as imaginatively reconstructed by Mr. Compson, is quite compatible with Faulkner's "middle of the road" position on desegregation that James Baldwin critiques as being a mystification of what is simply right and what is simply wrong. As the octoroon women are rendered embodiments of the "middle of the road" position, Faulkner approaches the justification of the status quo that, twenty years later, shapes his views on desegregation.

The Interracial Man's Burden

In contrast to the use of images of the octoroon wife to circle around issues of the white phallus, images of another interracial character, Charles Etienne, are used as Faulkner circles around the black phallus as the "outrageous exaggeration" as opposed to the white phallus as that which marks the unmarked.

Charles Etienne temporarily leaves town, and when he returns he has a "coal black and ape-like woman and an authentic wedding license" (166). After he has returned, Judith meets with Charles Etienne and, according to Mr. Compson, tells him, "That paper is between you and one who is inescapably negro; it can be put aside, no one will anymore dare bring it up than any other prank of a young man in his wild youth" (168). Judith's discounting of the marriage between Charles Etienne and his wife suggests that she herself was able to discount the marriage between Charles Bon and the unnamed octoroon woman. In Mr. Compson's reconstruction of Charles Etienne's return to Jefferson, Judith looks at the skin color of his wife and decides she is "inescapably negro" and "ape-like" (167). There are many reductive images of this woman. How does she invoke the black phallus? As Faulkner feminizes Charles Etienne, his dark-skinned wife emerges as what the phallus really is—the sheer overcompensation for lack. Through the images of this woman, Faulkner begins to subtly demystify the fear of the black phallus—underneath the big black phallus, there is only the grotesque black woman. The fetishism of black virility is, finally, the disavowal of black womanhood, which is rendered grotesque because it is the projected absence that hurts.

Mr. Compson imagines this woman (this deflated phallus) as the burden the feminized Charles Etienne must carry as he protests and attempts to move forward: "he had found her, dragged her out of whatever two dimensional backwater" (166), and as he "thrust" through "a maelstrom of faces and bodies through which the man . . . he dragg[ed] her behind him" (167). Faulkner repeats the word "drag" to emphasize that the woman's pure corporeality and mindlessness is a heavy burden. Charles Etienne's potential for escaping the status of the "pure" Negro is described as "furious and incomprehensible and apparently reasonless moving, progression" (167), whereas his entrapment in the Negro status is signified as "utter mobility like a broken cinema film" (167). Unlike the final image of Jim Bond "howling with human reason" (300) and transcending the status of pure corporeality, Charles Etienne has "reasonless moving" (167). His attachment to the woman reduced to an animal destroys the "sheer desperate will" and reason that he displayed when fighting at the "negro ball" (164).

Judith advises Charles Etienne to revoke the marriage and to pass for white in "the North, the cities, where it will not matter even if—But they will not" (168–69). Charles does not heed the advice of Judith. He remains married to the "ape-like" woman and he does not pass for white. By not revoking the marriage, he becomes tied to what Mr. Compson describes as the "irrevocability" of the "one who is inescapably negro" (168): "a curious and outrageous exaggeration in which was inherent its own irrevocability" (168). This woman is seen as being both overstated and unchangeable; she is an "exaggeration" that Judith and Mr. Compson experience as "irrevocably" actual, as opposed to the abstract, fictional sense of most exaggerations. Faulkner captures the way in which antiblack racism can make the fiction of blackness as pure corporeality and inanimateness be experienced as a concrete and unchangeable truth. The words "curious and outrageous exaggeration" (168) also signal the "othering" of skin color that is much darker than Charles Etienne's "olive" skin. Unlike Charles Etienne, the "white-colored man" (167), whom Judith likens to "some wild bird or beast which might take flight at the expansion and contraction of her nostrils or the movement of her breast" (168), the unnamed wife is "the wild beast" that will never "take flight," even though her "utter immobility" (167) and grotesqueness seems like a "curious and outrageous exaggeration" (168).

Before marrying this woman, Charles Etienne is reared in a "padded silken vacuum cell," the soft and penetrable enclosure used to describe the plaçage society in New Orleans. When these images are read through the lens of James Baldwin's sense of Faulkner's mystification of the middle-of-the-road position, it really matters that there is an explicit focus, in the following passage, on the irrelevancy of "moral value" in these states of interracial suspension. Faulkner writes:

> . . . who could neither have heard yet nor recognised the term "nigger," who even had no word for it in the tongue he knew who had been born and grown up in a padded silken vacuum cell which might have been suspended on a cable a thousand fathoms in a sea, where pigmentation had no more moral value than the silk walls and the scent and the rose-colored candle shades, where the very abstractions which he might have observed—monogamy and fidelity and decorum and gentleness and affection—were as purely rooted in the flesh's offices as the digestive processes. (161)

In this passage, Mr. Compson describes the octoroon society into which Charles Etienne was born. The assertion that Charles Etienne grew up thinking that "pigmentation had no more moral value than the silk walls and the scent and the rose-colored candle shades" is difficult to believe. The men who sought the octoroon women were enticed by their interracial look. The idea of beauty they attributed to this look did have "moral value," because their aesthetic judgment is shown to be a moral judgment. The interracial look of the octoroon women inspires the men to grant them the moral values listed, "monogamy and fidelity and decorum and gentleness and affection."

These values, the "very abstractions which he might have observed," are seemingly "purely rooted" in the flesh. This assertion that the abstractions are experienced as naturally as the "digestive processes" is a compelling image of the idea of "flesh as consciousness." The men's desire for the octoroon women enables them to imagine that the octoroon women are the actual embodiment of these moral values. As a child, Charles Etienne is "suspended" in this place where interracialness is experienced as moral goodness, as opposed to the recurrent images of the moral darkness associated with the problem of race. The "padded silken vacuum cell" is the prophylactic against the ugliness of race that his wife embodies. His wife is entirely separated from this place where femininity is so mystified that, instead of seeming like a site of white male control, it seems as inviolate as the image of the "rich female earth" (162).

The Fear of "It"

Faulkner makes it impossible to separate this interracial fantasy from interracial anxiety. The encounters between Rosa and Clytie foreground this anxiety. In Rosa's narration of this scene when she and Clytie touch on the stairway, she refers to the force created by their bodily contact as "it" in a manner similar to the way in which Mr. Compson refers to "it" while describing Judith's attempted seduction of Charles Etienne. Perhaps, if Judith had touched "it" instead of speaking to "it," she might have experienced the "cumulative over-reach of despair itself" (112) that Rosa cannot avoid when she and Clytie touch in this riveting scene following the murder of Charles Bon. The referent of "it" in the passage describing Judith's attempted seduction of Bon is the "restive light incorrigibility of the free" (169). Instead of speaking to "it" as Judith does, and "not daring" to "actually" touch "it" (169), Rosa is touched by "it" and also speaks to "it." The most explicit referent given for Rosa's "it" is "something monstrous and immobile" that Rosa "seemed to run at blind full tilt into" (112). Judith conflates "it" and Charles Etienne, when she speaks to him as if he were "it," the "restive light incorrigibility of the free." In contrast, in Rosa's recounting of the stairway incident after Bon's murder, she emphasizes to Quentin that she spoke to "it" and not to Clytie. This distinction is crucial, because at the time of the incident, Rosa, unlike Judith, is not trying to blur the distinction between interracials and whites. At the time of the incident, she needs to pretend that her flesh is irrevocably separate from the flesh of Clytie. In retrospect, she can acknowledge the tenuousness of racial hierarchies: "But let flesh touch with flesh, and watch the fall of all the eggshell shibboleth of caste and color too" (112). At the time of the incident, however, she resists the way in which "it" connects her with Clytie. Indeed, when she does speak to "it," her words are, "'Take your hand off me, nigger!'" (112). Rosa stresses, in her narration to Quentin, that "it" cannot be conflated with "the negro, the woman," (112), and yet it is apparent that she does experience Clytie as an embodiment of "it."

Another image of the "it" that overwhelms Rosa, no matter how much she resists, is "bitted bridle-curb to check and guide the furious and unbending will" (112). Before she is "stopped dead" by "it," she is literally being led by the strength of her own convictions. When the "bitted bridle-curb" halts her, her own will is made powerless. The physicality of this metaphor is significant, because Rosa cannot think her way through this "monstrous" and "immobile" force that, as previously analyzed, makes her finally experience the body as "the substance of remembering" (115). The painfully transcendent nature of this experience, the "cumulative over-reach of despair itself" (112), is most apparent when she tells Quentin that "it" had "a shocking impact too soon and too quick to be mere amazement and outrage at that black arresting and untimorous hand on my white woman's flesh" (111).

Rosa feels that she has actually experienced the transcendent when she encounters Clytie on the stairway, whereas Judith only glimpses the transcendent when she sees Charles Etienne as the "restive light incorrigibility of the free." Judith "cajoled the animal" into the "thicket," whereas Rosa herself becomes immobilized by the "bitted bridle-curb." Just as Mr. Compson imagines that Charles Etienne may have been entirely unresponsive when Judith asks him to call her Aunt Judith, there is also no answer when Rosa speaks to "it." Rosa, however, does not expect an answer. She tells Quentin:

> I got none. We just stood there—I motionless in the attitude and action of running, she rigid in that furious immobility, the two of us joined by that hand and arm which held us, like a fierce rigid umbilical cord, twin sistered to the fell darkness which had produced her. (112)

Unlike the image of Charles Etienne walking away from Judith to become a martyr, as he "drag[s]" around his burden, the "ape-like body of his charcoal companion" (167), Rosa and Clytie become "twin sistered." At this moment, Rosa is forced to experience the interracialness of Clytie as a concrete body and also as the abstract and "fell darkness which had produced her."

When Rosa and Clytie are both immobilized by "it," motionlessness is aestheticized and made to signify the transcendent state in which Rosa cannot follow her own "will" and must face the "cumulative over-reach of despair itself" (112). When Faulkner, in "Letter to the North," advocates the slow motion as opposed to forced desegregation, he, like Rosa and Clytie, remains under the spell of a romanticized immobility. The horror, however, of this Southern stasis, for black Southerners, cannot be ignored. As Faulkner depicts the ugliness of Charles Etienne's wife, he is ultimately depicting the ugly underside of the interracial states of suspension. The "woman, who, even a year later and after their son was born, still existed in that aghast and automaton-like state in which she had arrived," is the embodiment of this "utter immobility" (166, 167).

After imagining a motionlessness that is not "un-motion, stasis [or] death," as conveyed when Rosa says that she herself was "motionless in the attitude and action of running" and Clytie was "rigid in that furious immobility" (112), Faulkner then uses Mr. Compson and Judith's imaging of Charles Etienne and his wife as a means of reestablishing a rigid dichotomy between "life as motion" and "stasis as death."[7] The parallel between Judith's attempted seduction of Charles Etienne and the meeting between Rosa and Clytie after Bon's murder underscores the difference between Mr. Compson and Judith's very reductive image of Charles Etienne's wife and the much more complicated images of the interracial Charles Etienne and the interracial Clytie. There is also a parallel between Mr. Compson's and Judith's feeling that Charles Etienne irrationally remains trapped in blackness, although he could have passed for white, and Rosa's feeling that Clytie is "free, yet incapable of freedom" (126). Rosa tells Quentin, "[A]s though presiding aloof upon the new, she deliberately remained to represent to us the threatful portent of the old" (126). This image of the interracial Clytie, being located in the boundary between a future undetermined by the past and a future that is simply a projection of the past, is a strong connection between Clytie and Charles Etienne. Quentin's grandfather and Judith want Charles Etienne to pass for white and thereby, in their eyes, choose a future undetermined by his lineage. In Judith's and Mr. Compson's estimation, Charles Etienne has "deliberately remained" attached to the "ape-like body" and "the threatful portent of the old" (126), even though he could "presid[e]" "upon the new" (126) by passing for white. Rosa imagines Clytie as being located at the point of contact between the new and the old. In a similar sense, when Judith attempts to seduce Charles Etienne, she sees him at a crossroads where he can either choose "the new" and go to the north to pass for white or choose to remain tethered to the "old" South.

In the extended ending of the novel, questions about race and the South become explicitly tied to images of the black phallus and its dilution. At the end of the novel, Shreve asks Quentin why he hates the South, and

Quentin asserts, without being totally convincing, that he does not hate it. When Shreve refers to the "loins of African kings" from which he himself "will [. . .] have sprung" in the future (302), we must remember Quentin's own descriptions of Africa, when Shreve is the listener, as he repeats the stories his grandfather told about the time Sutpen spent in the West Indies. Quentin does not specify Haiti as the particular country in the West Indies, although this specification is made later in the text. When referring to Africa, he does not use the proper noun, but rather refers to "the dark inscrutable continent" (202), which he contrasts with the "cold known land" (202) of whiteness. The West Indies are described as "a little island set in a smiling and fury-linked and incredible indigo sea, which was the halfway point between what we call jungle and what we call civilization" (202). Shreve's assertion that Quentin's and his own descendants will "have sprung from the loins of African kings" must be understood in terms of Quentin's feelings that Africa is "what we call jungle" and the "cold known land" is "what we call civilization" (202). The idea of the wild, jungle-like Africa connects with the image of Sutpen's "band of wild niggers" (4), as well as with the image of the wild, uncontrollable howling of Jim Bond at the end of the novel.

The omniscient narrator in chapter 1 describes Sutpen's "wild blacks" as "beasts half tamed to walk upright like men, in attitudes wild and reposed" (4). Being "half tamed" conveys the idea that, for blackness to be understood by either Rosa or the omniscient narrator as something other than pure corporeality and bestiality, it must be tempered and must not exist in a "pure" state. In contrast to the taming of Sutpen's "wild blacks," the wildness of Jim Bond cannot be tamed: "But they couldn't catch him. They could hear him; he didn't seem to ever get further away but they couldn't get any nearer and maybe in time they could not even locate the direction of the howling anymore" (300–301). In this passage, Shreve imagines how the howling of Jim Bond must have eluded and frustrated Rosa and others. The howling is a type of wildness, uncontrolled abstraction, that cannot be embodied like the other beautified embodiments of abstraction.

When Quentin remembers accompanying Rosa to the Sutpen's Hundred and remembers how disoriented they both were when they saw Henry, he remembers Jim Bond's presence as "a hulking young light-colored negro man in clean faded overalls and shirt, his arms dangling, no surprise, no nothing in the saddle-colored and slack-mouthed idiot face" (296). The howling of Jim Bond is connected to the laughter of the butler; it symbolizes Quentin's sense of the "grand" failure of Sutpen.[8] Sutpen could not strike "it," the real reason why he feels like "trash" as a young boy. Instead, he "dreamed so high," and deluded himself into thinking that he had conquered "it," once he had obtained wealth.[9] But "it" returns through the form of Eulalia Bon. When he learns that she has black ancestry, he begins to defend his "design" against blackness, as if "blackness" really were "it," "what you wanted to hit" (194, 186). He figuratively "hit[s]" both Charles Bon and Eulalia Bon, and the consequence is the uncontrollable howling of Jim Bond, Sutpen's interracial great-grandson. When he treats Charles Bon and his mother as an embodiment of "it," he simply creates another abstraction that he will not be able to actually "hit."

The last words in the novel (Quentin's assertion that "I don't hate it!" when he is asked by Shreve if he hates the South) focus even more attention on the references to "it" in Quentin's descriptions of Sutpen's feelings after the pivotal interaction with the butler. The last words of the novel, as previously explained, can be interpreted as Quentin's reaction to Shreve's image of Jim Bond "bleach[ing] out" and changing his form as he multiplies in number. In contrast to Quentin's denial of feeling hate toward "it," Quentin explains to Shreve that Sutpen does want to hit "it"; whatever "it" is, it represents that which Sutpen needs to "strike" (186) if he is going to escape the status of "cattle, creatures, heavy and without grace" (190). The dehumanizing images of the wife of Charles Etienne and Sutpen's "band of wild niggers" perfectly match this image of weighed-down creatures. When Sutpen's sister is "pumping rhythmic up and down above a washtub in the yard, her back toward him, shapeless in a calico dress and a pair of old man's shoes unlaced and flapping about her ankles and broad in the beam as a cow" (190–91), she is also clearly an image of a creature, "heavy and without grace" (190). Although "they (the niggers) were not it, not what you wanted to hit" (186), they are the most concrete reminders, to Sutpen and Quentin, of the horror of "it." Even as Quentin refuses to make the butler the actual referent of "it," the butler is undeniably tied to the horror of "it" or "what you wanted to hit" (186). Quentin explains to Shreve that if the "balloon face" of the butler is "hit," "roaring waves of mellow laughter meaningless and terrifying and loud" would "overwhelm" one (187–88). The howling of Jim Bond, however, is an expression of "human reason"; it is potentially terrifying, but it is not "meaningless" (188). The potential laughter of the "balloon face" represents meaninglessness and terror. The "balloon face" of the butler is rendered as an inanimate object with an illusory human surface; it is described as a "toy balloon with a face painted on it" (186). The "idiot face" of Jim Bond represents pure corporeality, and his howling represents both terror and the consciousness in the flesh that antiblack racism attempts to deny those interpellated as "black."

After Quentin explains to Shreve that the butler was not what Thomas Sutpen resolved to struggle against once he is told to go to the back door of the plantation house, he imagines Sutpen's father explaining that when he and his peers "whupped one of the Pettibone's niggers" (187), there was "no actual nigger, living creature, living flesh to feel pain and writhe and cry out" (187). The words "no actual nigger" have been interpreted by Thadious Davis and James Snead as a sign that "nigger" is being recognized as a huge abstraction.[10] As Toni Morrison, in *Playing in the Dark*, thinks about the relation between abstractions and embodiment, she refers to *Absalom, Absalom!* as an example of a "literary journe[y] into the forbidden space of blackness" and briefly but provocatively analyzes the final image painted by Shreve of the future "bleach[ed] out" Jim Bonds who will not "show up so sharp against the snow" (58, 302). Morrison wonders if this final image signifies the "eradication of race" (58) and decides that the answer is, "Not quite. Shreve sees himself as the inheritor of the blood of African kings; the snow apparently is the wasteland of unmeaning, unfathomable whiteness" (58). Instead of the "eradication of race," this final image signifies that Shreve predicts a state of "unmeaning" when he will no longer be able to see racial difference and when Africans will become a part of his lineage. Once he begins to think about Jim Bonds conquering the "western hemisphere" and giving birth to future "Shreves," he can no longer understand the concept of whiteness, this abstraction that he thought he embodied. The "bleach[ed] out" Jim Bonds blending with the snow emphasize that Faulkner's "literary journey into the forbidden space of blackness" is actually a "literary journey into the forbidden space" of whiteness (58). The great abstraction of interracialness throughout the novel and the rendering of "pure" blackness as grotesque are both distractions from the Southern white postbellum fear and anxiety over the precariousness of whiteness and the "long dead South."

Blackness and Temporality

In *The Sound and the Fury* (1929), Faulkner captures the racialized stasis, the issues of race, time, and space, at the heart of his images of blackness. When Quentin breaks his watch, the broken glass cuts him, and he then "paint[s] the cut" with iodine (80). The confusion and sheer disorientation of time, represented by the broken watch, is contrasted with the stasis of the "negro" when Quentin throws a quarter to a "negro" from his own position on a moving train. Interracialness, in *Absalom, Absalom!*, in contrast to both the stasis of the imagined "pure negro" and the frustrated, stalled movement tied to whiteness, is the state of becoming, the movement that is never, seemingly, defined by the sense of linear, mechanical time created by the clocks of biological race. In *The Sound and the Fury*, when Faulkner writes, "Because Father says clocks slay time. He said time is dead as long as it is being clicked off by little wheels; only when the clock stops does time come to life" (85), he could be describing the sense of time tied to interracial bodies in *Absalom, Absalom!* Moving while standing still appears to be the most seductive option for Quentin and his father, in *Absalom, Absalom!*, when they are enamored by the lovely state of suspension of Charles Etienne and his mother (the octoroon mistress). As they muse about the metamorphosis that these interracial bodies are imagined as embodying, Quentin and Mr. Compson contemplate their options in relation to the "long dead" South: abandoning their white heritage or somehow gaining distance even as they remain faithful sons. As they fully indulge in the image of the octoroon butterfly, who "carr[ies] nothing of what was into what is, leaving nothing of what is behind but elide[s] complete and intact" (159), they wish that their frustrating relation to the "long dead" South would allow such utter transcendence.

We must, however, remember the blood on Quentin's broken watch. It evokes the "wounded, bleeding body" that, as Laura Mulvey reminds us, is the "bloody truth" underneath the beauty of the fetish object.[11] In *Fetishism and Curiosity*, Mulvey writes, "The fetish object acts as a sign in that it substitutes for the thing thought to be missing, the maternal penis. The substitute also functions as a mask, covering over and disavowing the traumatic sight of absence, especially if the 'absence' sets off associations with the wounded, bleeding body. The psyche constructs a phantasmatic topography, a surface, a carapace, which hides ugliness and anxiety with beauty and desire" (5). As Faulkner situates interracialness as the mark of the unmarked, the fetishized bodies (the interracial bodies) are seemingly without a skin color "cover." The fetishism of interracialness in *Absalom, Absalom!* is the fetishism of lighter-skinned blackness as a sign of moving from "what was into what is" (159). Images of lighter-skinned blackness (particularly the images of the octoroon mistress and Charles Etienne) aestheticize the "wounded, bleeding body" of "what was" (the bodily pain inflicted on black bodies during slavery and its aftermath). Faulkner separates the "what is" from the woman described as a "coal black and ape-like woman" and the "charcoal companion" of Charles Etienne (166, 167); the novel reveals the temporality often at the core of colorism.

A contemporary, mixed-media assemblage, *Colored* (2002), created by

Betye Saar, underscores the ways in which a timeline is often imagined between shades of blackness.[12] Saar imagines a lateral twist to the vertical timeline between light- and dark-skinned blackness. There are four women in this horizontal chart ranging from lighter to darker skin or darker to lighter skin, depending on the direction through which viewers read the progression. In the center of the horizontal bar, Saar includes the words, "Light is alright [*sic*] / Yellow is mellow / Brown, stick around / Black, get back (but black don't crack)." This is a popular saying in African American expressive culture and folklore. The parenthetical statement "but black don't crack" is also a part of African American expressive culture. "Black don't crack" describes a black gaze that views white people as aging much earlier than black people. Within this black gaze, the celebratory imperviousness of blackness to time begs to be compared to the beautifying, in *Absalom, Absalom!,* of light-skinned blackness and the ugly, "living fossil" images of dark-skinned blackness. Saar's visualization of the embodiment of time and the confusions of time and space greatly illuminate the representation of the fetishism of interracialness in *Absalom, Absalom!* Faulkner does not undermine antiblack racism, but he does expose the issues of temporality at the core of colorism. *Absalom, Absalom!* demonstrates that any undoing of the fetishism of shades of blackness must also be a fight against the blackening of the primitive and the fetishism of interracialness as a state of *becoming* set apart from dark-skinned stasis.

The continued contemporary investment in this aura of oldness tied to dark skin versus newness and youthfulness tied to lighter skin is dramatized in an advertisement for Lumedia Facial Brightener, which first appeared in 2006 issues of *Vogue* magazine.[13] The advertisement includes the words "I used to think looking old was all about wrinkles . . . but I was wrong. It turns out that looking young has more to do with skin color and something called 'brightness scale' or 'full-spectrum reflectivity' than it does with wrinkles. That's why Facial Brighteners (not the old-time 'age-spot' removers, but new formulations designed to brighten skin all over your face) are replacing wrinkle creams [. . .] Facial Brighteners make you look younger . . . much younger." This advertisement is marketing, in effect, a bleaching cream for white people. *Absalom, Absalom!* ends with Quentin's conflicted feelings about the possibility that "bleached" Jim Bonds will "conquer the western hemisphere" (302). Faulkner's use of this final image of bleaching as he ends with this representation of the threatening, violent black phallus signals that which this contemporary advertisement brings to the surface: the naturalizing of white power as an aesthetic, not a violent ideology. In this advertisement, the references to the "brightness scale" and "how light is reflected" are seemingly just descriptions of the aging skin, not racially informed ways of seeing light and dark. As Faulkner connects the Civil War, in one telling passage, to the "very pigmentation" of Clytie's "in between" skin color, the "threatful portent of the old" is darker skin; the "diluted" darkness "presid[es] aloof upon the *new*," which, in spite of the mystification, remains the sign of white power (126).

As she inveighs against this connection of blackness with oldness, Josephine Baker insists, in response to a description of her primitive nature in *La Revue Negre,* "What are you trying to say? I was born in 1906 in the twentieth century."[14] In *Absalom, Absalom!* as Faulkner plays with issues of temporality while depicting lighter- and darker-skinned black characters, he enters, partially but tellingly, into the larger modernist discourse of racialized primitivism.

The black primitive within modernist primitivism was clearly a fantasy of a white gaze.[15] Primitivism, in art history, is the study of a Western aesthetic shaped around a celebration of what is imagined as the purity, freedom, and naturalness of the non-Western. Modernist primitivism, as a *relation,* as opposed to a more fixed object of study, is now in the process of being analyzed in an interdisciplinary manner as we begin to gain a fuller sense of the relation between the primitivist sensibility in literary texts and the primitivist aesthetic in visual culture. Primitivist visual art often is the conscious response to non-Western art. Picasso's primitivism, for example, is the "elevation" of the African mask as the very core of the new modernist aesthetic. This definition works for art history in a way that it would not necessarily work in literary history. In literary studies, the most productive working definition of primitivism is the representation of the blurring of the boundaries between the new and the old in a wide range of love affairs with a non-Western veritable playground for the imagination. Primitivist modernism can be best understood, in its full complexity, by remembering the ways in which it was conceptualized, at its height, by modernist writers and visual artists. In 1902, Paul Klee admits the imagined rebirth at the heart of the primitivist fantasy. He asserts, "I want to be as though newborn, knowing nothing absolutely about Europe; ignoring poets and fashion, to be almost primitive."[16] With a real self-consciousness about the primitivist agenda, in 1911 Wilhelm Worringer explains, "This modern primitivism should not be a final goal. The pendulum never remains fixed at the broadest sweep. This primitivism should be seen much more as a means of passage, as a great long drawing of breath, before the new and decisive language of the future is pronounced."[17] When the African American artist Hale Woodruff, in 1972, explains that his encounter with primitivism was "a real turning point" in his journey to see through white-dominated art, it is clear that primitivism was partially a subversion of antiblack racism.[18] The racialized issues of time and space, at the core of primitivism, were reiterations of a normative racial discourse as well as experimentation with new ways of thinking about the very binaries undergirding the production of racial otherness.

Images of blackness in white modernist primitivism and African American primitivism hinge on the critique or lack of critique of anachronistic blackness (blackness that is constructed as representing the lingering signs of the past in the present). Whereas Gertrude Stein encapsulates primitivism as "the wide, abandoned laughter that makes the warm broad glow of negro sunshine" and William Faulkner bends it to his purpose when he imagines Africa as the "hot equatorial groin of the world" set apart from the "cold known land," the African American painter William Johnson, in 1930, both absorbs and rewrites the white gaze of primitivism when he insists, "All of the darker races are far more primitive—these are the people who are closer to the sun . . . My aim is to express in a natural way what I feel, what is in me, both rhythmically and spiritually, all that which in time has been saved up in my family of primitiveness and tradition, and which is now concentrated in me."[19] Johnson's reference to the "family of primitiveness" is a sign of a complicated African American response to the long history of Africa being imagined as the "quintessential locus of the primitive."[20] Johnson's celebration of the black primitive leads him to a celebration of race as kinship. As African American artists and writers respond to the blackened primitive in the white modernist gaze embedded in texts such as *Absalom, Absalom!*, they often, in the process of reclaiming the primitive as a positive value, beautify the very images that in *Absalom, Absalom!* remain the ugly, nonromanticized, dark-skinned counterpart to the beautified images of light-skinned blackness.

three

The Black Arts Phallus

AFRICAN American attempts to subvert the idea that the very body of the black person is primitive begin as early as 1906, in "The Health and Physique of the Negro American," when Du Bois presents his photographs of different "negro types" and adds his own reading of black bodies to the school of scientific racism and phrenology. There is a transition, in Du Bois' photographs, from these darker shades of blackness to lighter ones, but his commentaries on each body type aim to defy the racist associations of lighter skin with racial progress. Nonetheless, when Du Bois explains the significance of the photographs by presenting a genealogy chart that demonstrates that whiteness can be produced from black bodies, we see the complication of the idea of bloodlines as well as the presentation of whiteness as an end result in a teleology that may not be entirely different from the timeline created by the schools of scientific racism. Du Bois' focus on the whiteness that can be produced from blackness may reinforce the idea that lighter-skinned blackness is the novelty, the signifying difference, as opposed to the original sign of darker-skinned blackness.

The acknowledgment that miscegenation happened is the historical truth that is naturalized and written indelibly on the body when dark-skinned blackness is viewed as "old" and light-skinned blackness as "new." In "Du Bois's Anthropological Notion of Race" (2000), Tommy Lott explains that Du Bois "rejected the notion of pure unmixed races, yet in his

Atlanta University study of the health and physique of African Americans, he not only distinguished mixed and unmixed, but within the mixed group he distinguished between mulatto, quadroon, and, especially important for his theory of racial origin, 'white types with Negro blood.'"[1] This contradiction, the rejection and reliance on the categories "mixed" and "unmixed," emerges as Du Bois wrestles to present a science that would defy the racist claims of those working in phrenology (the field connecting skull measurements and intelligence and character traits), what Lott aptly refers to as "racist science." Lott explores Du Bois' vacillation between blackness as a cultural identity and lived experience and blackness as a bodily essence. When Du Bois moves from the photographs of "negro types" to quoting phrenologists, he continues an African American tradition of engaging with the "racist science."[2]

Whereas Du Bois presents a temporal progression from dark-skinned blackness to the lighter skin colors when he engages with racist phrenology in "The Health and Physique of the Negro American," 1960s and 70s Black Arts movement literature often celebrated the black primitive as Black Power. In the poem "Black People: This is Our Destiny" (1966), for example, Amiri Baraka celebrates the "black primitive" when he insists on a "rhythm a playing re-understood now by one of the 1st race / the primitives the first men who evolve again to civilize the world."[3] In this poem, Baraka reclaims the very word "primitive" (countering its use, in antiblack racism, to describe the supposed backwardness of black people).

The Black Arts movement often connected the reclamation of the black primitive and the reclamation of the beauty of dark-skinned blackness. Baraka, for example, in *In Our Terribleness,* responds to one of Fundi Abernathy's photographs of a dark-skinned young man with the following words: "You shd been there man / like you shda been eatin sun" (17). Abernathy entitles this photograph "Abshalom." There is a striking contrast between the fetishism of light-skinned interracialness in *Absalom, Absalom!* and Abernathy's desire to create a black gaze that makes room for a subversive fetishism of dark-skinned blackness. The reclamation of racial primitivism embedded in Baraka's celebration of the black "sun people" leads Baraka to fetishize the darkest shades of blackness. If fetishism is always the huge overcompensation for a notion of lack that has often been naturalized, the dark skin tone of the subject photographed in the image that accompanies the words "you shda been eatin sun" is the huge overcompensation for the lack of whiteness. The photograph is a "close-up" that accentuates all the features that antiblack racism has vilified. Dark-skinned blackness, in so many Black Arts movement texts, becomes an embodiment of the "black light" that many of the poets and visual artists were discovering.

Black Light

The fight against the insidious aestheticizing of light skin color led many Black Arts writers and visual artists to circulate the new paradigm of "black light." In the poem "The Negro" (1968), Haki Madhubuti muses on the possibility of "black light" as he thinks about the racist underpinnings of the associations of light with enlightenment. Madhubuti writes, "Swinging, Swinging, / into aberration where there is a black light trying to penetrate that whiteness called mr. clean" (65). In the seminal Black Arts movement anthology *Black Fire* (1968), Larry Neal unpacks this "black light." He explains, "We know who we are, and we are not invisible, at least not to each other. We are not Kafkaesque creatures stumbling through a white light of confusion and absurdity. The light is black (now, get that!) as are most of the meaningful tendencies in the world."[4] Neal denaturalizes "white light" as he reveals that optics itself has been tainted by the racist privileging of whiteness. This discussion of white versus black light is omnipresent in *Black Fire*. In "Pome. For Wierd. Hearts. & All you mothers" (1968), Ahmed Alhamisi refers to "white light" as that which teaches black people to hate themselves (428). In "The Tide Inside, It Rages!" one of the essays in *Black Fire*, the novelist Lindsay Barrett theorizes about black light in the following manner: "Today, what the artistic sensibility of the black man spreads before the world as evidence of his social and historic dilemma, is really the articulation of a protest against the white denial of the possibility or existence of black light, and the superimposition, on his knowledge of this black light, of the hostile white light of Western history" (150). Barrett recognizes that the very "possibility" and "existence" of black light is hard to imagine because of the glare of white light.

Black light became the movement's trope for an imagined resolution of an imagined contradiction. Black Arts movement poets, visual artists, and theorists wrestled to imagine new aesthetic experiences of light itself. In the poem "An Aspect of Love, Alive in the Ice and Fire" (1971), Brooks describes a "Black is Beautiful" sensibility that experiences "Afrikan velvet" skin as "a physical light in the room" (479). The idea that "Afrikan velvet" skin is the embodiment of light subverts the deep-seated connection of light and whiteness. In "Intermission" (1949), one of Brooks's pre–Black Arts movement poems, the speaker admits, "It is plausible. The sun is a lode," after she implores the "daughter of the dusk" to "[s]tand off . . . / And do not wince when the bronzy lads / Hurry to cream-yellow shining" (137). The use of the word "lode" conveys the idea of the sun being akin to a layer of minerals in the body, perhaps just underneath the surface skin, making some skin tones "bright." The word "lode" can also signify a rich supply. As demonstrated by Baraka's reference to the "sun people," dark-skinned blackness is often imagined as "having" the most sun. As the speaker of the poem confesses that desire for light-skinned blackness is not surprising, we hear Brooks herself wince as she realizes that if the sun is a rich supply, desire for dark-skinned blackness should be just as "plausible" as desire for "cream-yellow shining." In "Ballad of Pearl May Lee" (1945), Brooks fully unveils the pain light-skinned privilege causes dark-skinned black women. In one of the most scathing stanzas, the speaker taunts Sammy with the following words: "At school, your girls were the bright little girls. / You couldn't abide dark meat. / Yellow was for to look at, / Black for the famished to eat. / Yellow was for to look at, / Black for the famished to eat" (61). Brooks critiques the sexual "consumption" of dark-skinned blackness and the beauty attributed to light-skinned blackness. In *The Sexual Politics of Meat* (1990), feminist critic Carol Adams argues that, when people consume meat, what they are eating is an "absent referent" (14–15), the reality of blood and slaughter sanitized by the supermarket packaging of meat. Brooks imagines the horror of "yellow" women becoming the "absent referent" as dark-skinned blackness is consumed, the horror of a black male gaze that places "yellow" women on a beauty standard pedestal and views dark-skinned black women as sexual prey ("black for the famished to eat" [61]).

In a post–Black Arts movement essay, "Race, Rage, and Intellectual Development: A Personal Journey" (1995), as Madhubuti explains the insidiousness of colorism (the privileging of lighter shades of blackness within the palette of shades of blackness), he remembers his mother's beauty as "illuminated by very light skin color that attracted the darkest of black men" (249). It is significant that Madhubuti muses on this "yellow light" three decades after the Black Arts movement. He and other Black Arts poets focused on the possibility of a "black light" illuminating the beauty of dark-skinned blackness. The very words "black light" circulated between writers such as Madhubuti and Larry Neal and visual artists such as Faith Ringgold.[5]

In one of the most furious Black Power texts, *Die Nigger Die!* (1969), written by H. Rap Brown, the idea of black light is presented in a collage that includes an overexposed image of one of the core bleaching cream advertisements that appeared in many 1960s issues of *Ebony* magazine (figure 4).[6] When H. Rap Brown juxtaposes the overexposed image of a woman's face and the actual light-skinned image used to sell the bleaching cream, he anticipates Kobena Mercer's recognition that black-and-white photography is indeed racial fetishism, the fetishism of the contrast between whiteness and blackness. Since dark skin absorbs light, the blackened subject of black-and-white photography, depending on the amount of light used, can be lightened or darkened. To force readers to visualize the violent ideology that shapes this fetishism of the lightening of dark skin, H. Rap Brown includes (underneath the two frames of the original and darkened bleaching cream advertisement) two images of a white police officer fighting a civilian. An overexposed image of the police officer with darkened skin appears directly underneath the overexposed image that darkens the light skin of the model in the bleaching cream advertisement. The same image, without the overexposure and the darkened white police officer, appears directly underneath the original, nonmanipulated bleaching cream advertisement. H. Rap Brown, in this collage, visualizes the connections between the violence of the dominant ideology's fetishism of light-skinned blackness and the violence of the dominant power structure that often makes black men victims of police brutality. By using these different layers in the collage and the technique of overexposure, H. Rap Brown insists that "black light" is the only way to fight back against the naturalization of the "white light."

In the poem "Judy-One" (1970), Haki Madhubuti reveals that, during the Black Arts movement, black-and-white photography was reclaimed as the process of embodying darkness as opposed to entering light, the racially inflected understanding of photography crystallized in the following passage written by Lacan (cited earlier, in the analysis of Stein and Thurman): "It is through the gaze that I enter light and it is from the gaze that I receive its effects. Hence it comes about that the gaze is the instrument through which light is embodied and through which—if you will allow me to use a word, as I often do, in a fragmented form—I am *photo-graphed*" (106). In the first two stanzas of "Judy-One," Madhubuti writes, "She's the camera's / subject: / the sun for colored film / her smile is like / clear light bouncing off / the darkness of the / mediterranean at nighttime" (75). As opposed to dark skin absorbing light, our normal understanding of what happens when dark skin is photographed, Madhubuti imagines "light bouncing off / the darkness," as if the skin itself becomes a projector instead of an absorbent of a white gaze. When Madhubuti begins the poem by announcing that Judy is the "sun for colored film," it is clear that there is a conscious

Figure 4. Die Nigger Die! *(H. Rap Brown, 1969)*

assumption of a new metaphysics of darkness, one in which darkness is a "way of seeing and being seen," and dark skin when photographed is not "captured" by light but, rather, a projector of light—black light.[7]

In "Natural Black Beauty" (1969), an essay in *Black Arts: An Anthology of Black Creations,* poet and editor Joe Goncalves explains the "Black is Beautiful" ideology of the 1960s in the following manner: "As for our natural beauty: Our lips complement our noses, our noses 'go with' our eyes and they all bless our skin, which is black. If your face does not complement itself, you are in a degree of trouble. . . . The real geometry of our faces, the natural geometry in terms of art is found, among other places, in African sculpture. Our natural architecture, our natural rhythm."[8] The idea of natural black beauty was a key part of the body politics of the Black Arts movement. Black Arts participants often imagined that the black body was the most local site of the black nation that needed to be protected from dominant beauty standards. The new physical beauty standards privileged looking "natural" and looking "African." "Africa" signified nature, roots, authenticity, and purity within this Black Arts imagination. Clothing and hairstyles that were deemed "African" became signs of this natural black beauty. The short "afro" hairstyle began to be named the "natural." The cover story of a 1967 issue of *Ebony* magazine celebrates the "afro" as the "natural" hairstyle.[9] In addition to "natural" hair, dark-skinned blackness was embraced, in the Black Arts gaze, as the epitome of natural beauty. In a 1969 issue of *Ebony* magazine, Larry Neal crystallizes the body politics of the Black Arts movement when he proclaims, "The new references of clothing and hair are essentially visions of ourselves perfected; they are sign posts on the road to eventual Self-Determination. For a Sister to wear her hair natural asserts the sacred and essentially holy nature of her body. The natural, in its most positive sense, symbolizes the Sister's willingness to determine her own destiny. It is an act of love for herself and her people. The natural helps to psychologically liberate the Sister. It prepares her for the message of a Rap Brown, a Robert Williams, a Huey Newton, a Maulana Karenga."[10] Unfortunately, Neal does not imagine that the "Sister with the Natural" might be more drawn to Audre Lorde's poem "Naturally" (1970). This poem fully unveils the male gaze that often shaped Black Arts movement formulations of "natural black beauty" and the Black Arts movement equation of "natural" beauty and dark-skinned blackness. The speaker in this poem skeptically proclaims, "Since Naturally Black is Naturally Beautiful / I must be proud / And, naturally, / Black and / Beautiful / Who always was a trifle / Yellow / And plain though proud / Before."[11] Lorde muses on yellow skin, light-skinned blackness, becoming a badge of shame in the "Black is Beautiful" lens that fought against the fetishism of light-skinned blackness in the advertising industry of bleaching creams and hair-straightening products.[12]

Reclaiming the Black Phallus

With Audre Lorde's poem "Naturally," the 1970 anthology *The Black Woman* begins, in the very first pages, with an emphasis on the difference between "black bread" (the real changes that will improve lives) and the abstractions tied to black cultural nationalism. *The Black Woman* has more radical perspectives than the male-oriented anthology *Black Fire* (1968) on the question of how to fight the historical (forced) non-normative gender structure of black Americans. As opposed to the opening essays in *Black Fire, The Black Woman* opens with poetry. By deciding to make the first poem "Woman Poem," by Nikki Giovanni, the editor Toni Cade Bambara immediately makes the anthology a response to the castrated black men narrative, which gains widespread attention through Daniel Patrick Moynihan's 1965 report "The Negro Family: The Case For National Action" (produced while he was Assistant Secretary of Labor during Lyndon Johnson's administration). Whereas Moynihan argues that black men have been castrated by black matriarchs, in this opening poem in *The Black Woman,* Giovanni writes, "it's having a job / they won't let you work / or no work at all / castrating me / (yes it happens to women too)" (13). The radical edge of this poem is Giovanni's insistence on this unacknowledged castration that happens to black women.

As Black Arts movement writers attempted to castrate white power and render it feminine, black women were often objectified as the embodiments of black beauty ("African Queens" and "natural black beauty"). In addition to the rampant references to black male genitalia in Black Arts poetry, the word "castrated" is directly used in the anthology *The Black Woman* (1970) in the title of the essay "Is the Black Male Castrated?" written by Jean Carey Bond and Patricia Peery, and the word "impotent" is used in the title of the first essay in the 1971 special issue "The Black Male" of *The Black Scholar*—"The Myth of the Impotent Black Male," written by Robert Staples. As Black Arts men reclaimed the black phallus, they often objectified black women even as they engaged in the laudable attempt to remove black women from the dominant visual culture that continues to define quintessential femininity through the sign of the white woman's body. The body of the black woman was often imagined as the motherland, the receptacle for the black (male-dominated) nation, and this black motherland became the ambiguously gendered space between the black phallus (the male position in the Black Arts ethos) and feminized whiteness.

In "Is the Black Male Castrated?" Bond and Peery argue that, contrary to Daniel Patrick Moynihan's insistence on "Black male emasculation" and "Black female matriarchy," black women have never had the power to castrate, and black men have never truly become victims of the "white man's" attempts to castrate them (143). Bond and Perry assert, "Indeed, the Black man always surfaces with his manhood not only intact, but much more intact than that of his oppressor, which brings us to the question: just who is the emasculated person in this society? Surely, it is the white man, whose dazzling symbols of power—his goods, his technology—have all but consumed his human essence" (147). Keorapetse Kgositsile's poem "The

Awakening" may be the most explicit rendering (among many similar representations in *The Black Fire*) of the reclamation of the black phallus. He screams, "Retrieving Black balls cowering in glib Uncle Tomism / Forcing me to grow up ten feet tall and Black / My crotch too high / For the pedestal of Greco-Roman Anglo-Saxon / adolescent Fascist myth."[13] Larry Neal echoes this imagery in "The Baroness and the Black Musician," another poem in *Black Fire,* when he writes, "[T]he icy ride of her touch up toward / the place where your penis once was" (309). In a similar manner, A. B. Spellman recalls, in the manifesto "Big Bushy Afros" (1998), the afro hairstyle as a phallic symbol: "Hair was pride you could grow. Pride that filled the eye" (53).

The Black Arts reclamation of the black phallus is inseparable from the theorizing about race and gender that occurs during this movement. In *Soul on Ice,* for example, Eldridge Cleaver insists:

> The Amazon [black woman] is in a peculiar position. Just as her man has been deprived of his manhood, so she has been deprived of her full womanhood. Society has decreed that the Ultrafeminine, the woman of the elite, is the goddess on the pedestal. The Amazon is the personification of the rejected domestic component, the woman on whom "dishpan hands" seem not out of character." (218)

The real connection between the Black Power men's movement and the Black Power women's movement may be the insistence, respectively, on *black* masculinity and *black* womanhood. Both movements, then, not just the Black Power women's movement, use a politics of location that is a politics of intersectionality. As critics and historians aptly recognize the male-dominated discourse of the Black Power movement, we also need to remember the intersectional emphasis in these acts of black patriarchy. This focus on the common thread of intersectionality accentuates what is really at the core of the sexism of the Black Power movement. It is not simply the fact that the male-dominated discourse could not recognize both race and gender. The most pernicious act was the lapse, by many Black Power male leaders and writers, into a normative gender script (entrenched ideas of the sheer difference between men and women) as a means to fight against the gender confusion that has emerged from and aided the oppression of African Americans.

Any focus on the gender and race analyses during the Black Arts and Black Power movements must consider the full impact of Moynihan's 1965 report. This report helped naturalize the idea of the emasculated black man and the castrating black matriarch. Moynihan's images of this emasculated male figure and castrating female figure are key signs of the dominant race and gender script that many men in the Black Power movement were attempting to subvert. The nature of this subversion included the move from the black woman as the castrating figure to the insistence on the white power that has debilitated black men. Moynihan's report brought the African American family crisis into the dominant culture spotlight. As Moynihan insisted on the connections between the economic troubles of black Americans and the lack, in many cases, of a nuclear family structure, he reinforced the idea that families with unwed mothers as head of the household are pathological. African American men are rendered impotent as he argues that there is a pathological matriarchy of unwed black mothers. In addition to the important work that has been done as scholars recognize the pathologizing impulses reverberating from this report, we can also use this report to more fully appreciate the reasons why investments in family structure played such a huge role in the Black Power discourse. Moynihan and many Black Power writers agree that the family crisis must be corrected in order to improve the quality of life for black Americans. Whereas Moynihan is mobilized by a belief in assimilation as the means of economic mobility, the Black Power writers focus on ideal family relations as they often express their fear of black genocide and their desire for black self-determination. The brother and sister language and the images of black women as queens were attempts to repair the fractured family ties caused by the historical trauma that made some of the normative family roles irrelevant.

This family trauma, the besieged black masculinity and black femininity, must be placed within the larger context of the rise, in the 1960s and 70s, of black psychologists studying the crisis of the black family and the blurring of gender roles. William Grier and Price Cobbs' *Black Rage* (1968) set the stage for this school of black psychology. Nathan and Julia Hare's *The Endangered Black Family: Coping with the Unisexualization and Coming Extinction of the Black Race* (1984) is an extension of their Black Power movement analyses of the black family crisis and gender confusion. Compared to Nathan and Julia Hare's naturalization of the idea that African American men have been castrated, Bond and Peery, in the essay "Is the Black Male Castrated?" in *The Black Woman,* pose the necessary questions about the usefulness of this trope of castration. They ask:

> What is emasculation? In a broad sense, an emasculated people (cultural group) are a broken people, a people whose spirit, strength, and vigor have

> been destroyed, who have been reduced to a state of almost total ineffectuality. [. . .] And notwithstanding the often literal but more often symbolic castration of hundreds of thousands of Black individuals throughout our sojourn in the wilderness, have Black men really been stripped of their virility? (115)

Black women's critique of *and* participation in the Black Arts reclamation of the phallus must be acknowledged when this questioning is contrasted with the images of the black phallus in some of the poetry written by women poets in the Black Arts movement.

In the poem "Black Music Man" (1968), Lethonia Gee, one of the select group of women poets chosen for *Black Fire,* begins with the words "As a Masai warrior / With his Burning Spear / Blessed by the Gods / The epitome of man" and ends with the confession "Never once do you know / That behind you I walk / And in my arms / I carry your soul" (222–23). This poem parallels the confession to "my Queen" that Eldridge Cleaver makes, in *Soul on Ice,* when he writes, "Across the naked abyss of negated masculinity, of four hundred years minus my Balls, we face each other today, my Queen. I feel a deep, terrifying hurt, the pain of humiliation of the vanquished warrior" (237). By 1970 when Toni Cade Bambara edits *The Black Woman,* she, unlike some of the women poets who reiterate images of the black phallus, is entirely convinced of the limitations of this prime trope. She muses, in the essay "On the Issue of Roles":

> And I wonder if the dudes who keep hollering about their lost balls realize that they probably surrendered them either to Mr. Charlie in the marketplace, trying to get that El Dorado, or to Miss Anne in bed, trying to bang out some sick notion of love and freedom. It seems to me you find your Self in destroying illusions, smashing myths, laundering the head of whitewash, being responsible to some truth, to the struggle. That entails at the very least cracking through the veneer of this sick society's definition of "masculine" and "feminine." (108)

An unsettling of gender clearly occurs when men are emasculated. Bambara worries that the Black Power reliance on castration images and the conscious attempt to assert manhood necessarily reinforce a "sick society's" gender script.

In addition to the focus on the reclamation of the black phallus, the Black Arts movement often revolved around the idea of new mirrors. In "Big Bushy Afros," Spellman remembers the new mirrors that the Black

Arts movement attempted to create. He muses, "Some called it a new mimesis because it made a mirror that affirmed us. But I thought it was an anti-mimetic art, for it was art beyond the probable, [. . .] Not to say it was all figures and forms. Abstraction didn't cost consciousness."[14] How did the desire for black mirrors, for mimesis, within the 1960s and 70s Black Arts movement relate to the desire for "art beyond the probable," the art that would shatter any mirror aiming to "fix" blackness? At the end of this manifesto, Spellman confesses, "I do regret the culture cops who tried to legislate a single vision." The policing of blackness during this movement somehow did not cancel out images of blackness as sheer fluidity, that which Spellman describes as a "Negritudinous surreal dream of universal Africa." How did this fluidity coexist with the attempts to "fix" blackness? We need to begin with the Black Arts images of the black mirror stage. This mirror stage (the mimetic, the claim for representation) is fully evoked when Baraka insists, in *In Our Terribleness* (1970), that "each of these images is, (not represents, but *is*)" (114). The move away from representation to an imagined transparent, unmediated relation to "blackness," signaled by the very presence of the full-page mirror at the beginning of *In Our Terribleness,* is a move to self-representation. The complexity fully emerges when this self-representation is situated as a nonrepresentation, an essence ("not represents, but *is*").

The Call Itself Is Beautiful

The conversion narrative surrounding Gwendolyn Brooks fully unveils the Black Arts dramatization of the imagined concrete event or moment of interpellation and the attempts to embody the abstract signs of blackness. In *Report from Part One* (1972), Gwendolyn Brooks recounts, "The real turning point came in 1967, when I went to the Second Black Writers' Conference at Fisk University."[15] The idea of the 1967 conversion, at the height of the Black Arts movement, creates a dramatic before and after that should be questioned when we recognize that the boundaries between the pre-1967 poems and the later ones are often blurred. The literal nature of the conversion emerges when we recognize the direct references to hypnotism during the Black Arts movement. In Brooks's prose poem "Requiem before Revival" (1980), she explicitly discusses the hypnotic effects of hegemonic whiteness ("we have allowed ourselves to be hypnotized by its shine" [6]) and the need for black people to "imitate the efficacy of Iteration" (7). The full discussion of "Iteration" reveals Brooks's interest in imagining a type of counter-interpellation, a type of interpellation that would be a decolonization of the mind. Brooks writes:

> Swarms of Blacks have not understood the mechanics of the proceeding, and they trot along to the rear of Pied Piper whites, their strange gazes fixed on, and worshiping, each switch of the white rear, their mesmerized mentalities fervently and firmly convinced that there is nothing better than quaking in that tail's wake. [. . .] They have not seen some Announcements register just *because* they are iterated and iterated and iterated—the oppressed consciousness finally sinking back accepting the burden of relentless assault. (7)

In the late 1960s when Brooks began to lead workshops with the young black Chicago poets, she was introduced to poems that were "Announcements" that presented a counter-iteration. A prime example of these "announcements" is Haki Madhubuti's poem "Awareness" (1966):

BLACK PEOPLE THINK
PEOPLE BLACK PEOPLE
THINK PEOPLE THINK
BLACK PEOPLE THINK—
THINK BLACK.[16]

Every letter in this poem is capitalized, and the words are graphically displayed as if the poem were a sign within a protest demonstration or even on the wall of a doctor's office. Since the conditioning process of antiblack racism has been so thorough and naturalized, the Black Arts practitioners decide that this collective therapy and hypnotism is necessary.

The poem "SOS" (1966), written by Baraka, epitomizes this conscious interpellation of new black subjects. The first lines of the poem are "Calling black people / Calling all black people, man woman child / Wherever you are."[17] Hypnotism is also at the core of Baraka's aesthetic warfare in *In Our Terribleness.* Baraka asks his readers to "Look into my eyes. (These flicks.) Look into your own eyes [. . .] Look into our eyes. Visualize yr own face, when you close yr eyes. Can you do that? Can you see your own image?" (150). When Baraka and Madhubuti become hypnotists, they imagine that they can be the mediums through which their subjects can find a self-definition.

The move from the "individual" to the "subject," in Black Arts interpellation, often takes the shape of the move from "Negro" to "Black." In Terry Eagleton's interpretation of Althusser's understanding of ideology and interpellation, the key issue becomes the possible contradiction between the idea that the subject is always already a subject and the very definition of interpellation as the transformation of individuals into subjects. Eagleton writes, "If Althusser's subject were as split, desirous and unstable as Lacan's, then the process of interpellation might figure as a more chancy, contradictory affair."[18] As Eagleton tries to make sense of Althusser's "insistence on the moment of interpellation," he wonders, "How can the subject recognize its image in the mirror as itself, if it does not somehow recognize itself already?" (215). When Brooks, in *Report from Part One,* insists on the "moment of interpellation," the 1967 Fisk Conference, we must consider the possibility that she, like Althusser, like so many Black Arts practitioners, creates this "moment of interpellation." Althusser may focus on this moment to emphasize the sheer drama of the transformation of individuals into subjects. Black Arts practitioners often emphasize the moment of interpellation in order to emphasize the drama of the veritable decolonization of the mind that must occur if Black is to be Beautiful. But just as Althusser presents the "always already subject" in addition to the "moment of interpellation," Black Arts practitioners present the necessary transformation of the Negro into the black and Karenga's idea that "We were Black before we were born," blackness as the prenatal template, the "always already" subject.[19]

Many Black Arts writers foreground a "mirror stage" of blackness in addition to the hailing of new black subjects. Black Arts literature is an ideal lens for an analysis of this Althusser and Lacan connection. Eagleton writes:

> What if we fail to recognize and respond to the call of the Subject? What if we return the reply: "Sorry, you've got the wrong person"? That we have to be interpellated as *some* kind of subject is clear: the alternative, for Lacan, would be to fall outside the symbolic order altogether into psychosis. But there is no reason why we should always accept society's identification of us as this *particular* sort of subject. Althusser simply runs together the necessity of some "general" identification without submission to specific social roles. There are, after all, many different ways in which we can be "hailed," and some cheery cries, whoops, and whistles may strike us as more appealing than some others. (217)

As Black Arts practitioners engage in ideological warfare, they often represent the reply "Sorry, you've got the wrong person." Indeed, Madhubuti ends the poem "Gwendolyn Brooks" with the insistence "bro, they been calling that sister by the wrong name" (90). This poem appears in a volume entitled "Don't Cry, Scream" (1968).[20] Madhubuti's separation of the cry and the scream, like Eagleton's focus on the "cheery cries, whoops, and whistles," illuminates the connections between Black Arts rhetoric and theories of interpellation. In the pre-1967 years, Brooks's "whoops" (that which the poet Eamon Grennan refers to as her "chewiness") sometimes differed from what was viewed as the sounds of "blackness."[21] Her consummate use of the sonnet, of course, becomes the consummate deformation of mastery. And yet Brooks herself, in a 1977 interview, remains convinced and worried that "We Real Cool" (1960) was the only example of a poem that was "significant for the unique word and still accessible to all manner of life."[22] Brooks, after 1967, expresses her desire for a "newish" voice that would "successfully call (see Imamu Baraka's 'SOS') all black people."[23] It is significant that "SOS" (1966) is the poem that, in Brooks's estimation, exemplifies the nature of her conversion. As opposed to other poems by Baraka, this poem is a pure state of address that does not include any explanations of blackness. The poem simply and powerfully calls black people as if the call itself is the goal, the creation of the desire *to answer* this call.

Visualizing the Black Arts Phallus

When studying the 1960s and 70s Black Arts movement from a contemporary vantage point, we must remember the aesthetic overhaul that the "Black is Beautiful" sensibility represented. Black Arts movement photography illuminates how this "collective consciousness" was visualized. In *In Our Terribleness* (1970), as Amiri Baraka responds to the photography of Fundi Abernathy, a Chicago Black Arts movement photographer, he announces, "I can take off these clothes and wear some others."[24] Like *In Our Terribleness,* the photography of Bob Crawford, another Chicago Black Arts movement photographer, presents the "clothing" of black cultural nationalism.[25] In the photograph entitled "The Middle Passage" (figure 5), the lack of clothing, the bare chest of the young boy, is overcompensated for by the expanse of water that recalls the middle passage, although it is, in actuality, the shores of Lake Michigan in Chicago. The title of the photograph emphasizes the huge signifying power that "Africa" has in the African American imagination. The bare chest of the photographed subject makes the title "The Middle Passage" even more intriguing. Crawford's photographic lens imagines an undressing of the African American body in order to locate the lost origin, Africa.

Figure 5. *"The Middle Passage" (Bob Crawford, 1968)*

In Crawford's photograph entitled "Beauty Culture" (figure 6), the beauty salon, the "College of Beauty Culture" that straightens "natural" black hair, is figured as the background against which signs of black nationalism (the clothing of the Nation of Islam) emerge. The rage in the face of the gesticulating woman is imagined, within this photographer's frame, as rage against the "College of Beauty Culture." The erectness of the young man wearing the Fruit of Islam uniform represents the bold efforts of the newly emergent black aesthetic to combat this dominant white "beauty culture." In *In Our Terribleness,* Baraka crystallizes the *body* politics of the Black Arts movement:

> So we are parts of a body. And this is what you see. The energy revealed. Its slow parts for you baby. And what is the changing same for us, the reality beneath illusion that binds us, as the body is bound by its motion its intent. From the kids the simbas to the old folks, sweet sisters in between, what will hold us in motion, with the content of the black chemist the black magician, the changers of what is to what must be, what but our selves. (133)

The words "changing same" place such a transcendent emphasis on the simultaneous evanescence and durability of "blackness." The notion of "sweet sisters in between" reveals that the black woman's body is objecti-

Figure 6. *"Beauty Culture" (Bob Crawford, 1967)*

fied as a medium through which black male nationalism is articulated. The words "we are parts of a body" recall Baraka's insistence, earlier in *In Our Terribleness,* that "we are trying literally to get our selves back together" (43).

As opposed to Baraka's sense that African Americans are "parts of a body," theorist Judith Butler argues that "one does one's body" in the sense that gender is a performance, a "stylized repetition of acts."[26] Baraka's understanding of culture and the body is not entirely different from Butler's understanding of gender and the body. Baraka theorizes about the performance of African American culture even as he lapses into racial essentialism. His focus on the "changing same," as Houston Baker has shown, is a dazzling definition of African American modernism.[27] The assertion "we are parts of a body" and the idea that "faces collect the change" demonstrate that Baraka is attempting to visualize the elusive "changing same."[28] The "collection" of change belies the evanescence of the "changing same." This attempt to capture the elusive essence of blackness was a core component of the Black Arts ethos.

As Baraka responds, in *In Our Terribleness,* to Abernathy's photographs, he insists, "not represents, but *is*" (114). Crawford's photograph "Culture"

Figure 7. *"Culture" (Bob Crawford, 1969)*

(1969) (figure 7) is an explicit rendering of how the Black Arts ethos often imagined representations of blackness as more than representations. The subject in this photograph holds two texts in a manner of exhibition, as if she is either posing for the camera or selling these texts on the city street, her own body becoming the display shelf. One of the texts she holds is entitled "American Negro in Bible Prophecy." The word "negro" in this title is one of the signifiers that the photographer's Black Arts gaze is aiming to subvert. The camera focuses on the features of the woman's face that is framed by the texts. As we read her body through the Black Arts lens, she is the "American Negro" in the process of being transformed into the Black Arts "prophecy"; the "negroness" of her body and the texts she holds are transformed into the "blackness" celebrated in Crawford's photographic gaze. The title of the second text announces, "Return to Africa Her Stolen Children." The woman displaying these books is positioned, in this photograph, as the "motherland" through which this "return to Africa" might occur.

What if the woman in this photograph displayed James Baldwin's *Tell Me How Long the Train's Been Gone,* a novel published in 1968, the heyday of the Black Arts movement? How does *Tell Me* complicate a quick and easy packaging and display of the Black Arts ethos? In *Tell Me,* James Baldwin connects the Black Power movement and gay black male identity. In the documentary *James Baldwin: The Price of the Ticket* (1989), Baraka asserts, "Jimmy Baldwin was neither in the closet about his homosexuality nor was he running around proclaiming homosexuality."[29] In *Tell Me,* he "proclaims" homosexuality as he "proclaims" that "Black is Beautiful." Baldwin insists that there is no rift between "Black is Beautiful" and "black is gay." Theorist Eve Sedgwick remembers, in *The Epistemology of the Closet,* a National Public Radio discussion of the 1960s as "the decade when Black people came out of the closet."[30] Baldwin makes "coming out of the closet" much more than a trope for the Black Power movement when he explores, in *Tell Me,* the inseparability of the "racial closet" and the "sexual closet."

Early in the novel, Baldwin presents the "long career of blackmail" of the central character, Leo Proudhammer—a "blackmail" rendered explicitly as the "blackmail" of his "imperious bit of flesh," his penis.[31] Black Christopher, Leo's lover, emerges as the black phallus, the "black male" as opposed to Leo's affliction by "blackmail" (6). Baldwin imagines the emergence of the black phallus in the scene when Leo and his brother, Caleb, become physically intimate. Leo wrestles with the "god of the flesh" (210), as Baldwin invokes the biblical image of Jacob wrestling with the angel. As Leo curses "God," he proclaims his love of the blackness of his brother. The phallus ("God") is resisted as a black phallus is imagined. Gaining sexual access to the brother's body enables Leo to discover "black power." When his love affair with Black Christopher begins, he fully realizes the erotic nature of "Black Power." The darkness of Black Christopher's skin reminds Leo of "Africa" (107). Leo connects his brother, Caleb, and Christopher to "undiluted blackness." In the scene when Leo and Caleb become physically intimate, the celebration of "undiluted blackness" adds a new twist to the infamous comparison of incest and miscegenation in *Absalom, Absalom!* (1936): "So it's the miscegenation, not the incest, which you [Henry] can't bear."[32] When Leo curses "God," he embraces black incest and curses the white phallus. As he refers to the black "balls" (210), he reclaims the "undiluted blackness" of his brother as the phallus.[33]

Baldwin places the Black Power movement and the sexual revolution of the 1960s in close proximity. In the penultimate scene of the novel, immediately prior to Black Christopher's succinct explanation of his understanding of black power—"We need guns"(482)—Baldwin describes a dance party that reflects the sexual revolution of the 1960s. Leo thinks, "It was a rite that I was witnessing—witnessing, not sharing . . . The music drove and drove, into the past—into the future. It sounded like an attempt to make a great hole in the world, and bring up what was buried. And the dancers seemed, nearly, in the flickering, violent light, with their beads flashing, their long hair flying, their robes whirling—or their tight skirts, tight pants signifying—and with the music assaulting them like the last, last trumpet, to be dancing in their grave-clothes, raised from the dead" (368–69). Black Christopher takes Leo Proudhammer to this dance party. Christopher is the embodiment, for Leo, of Black Power and "Black is Beautiful." As if rewriting the heterosexist, homophobic images produced by some of the key black male leaders of the Black Power and Black Arts movements, Baldwin presents Black Christopher as "macho" and gay. Leo Proudhammer falls in love with the seemingly authentic, unadulterated blackness of Black Christopher. The older Leo is also enchanted with the fearlessness of Black Christopher's generation; he marvels at the ability of young gay men to "dar[e] to embrace another in the sight of all the world" (368). At the height of the "Black is Beautiful" and Black Power movement, Baldwin presents the subversive image of Black Christopher.

Leo admires the aesthetic of Black Christopher and his friends: "[T]heir beautiful black kinky hair spinning around their heads like fire and prophecy—this hair putting me in mind, somehow, of the extravagant beauty of rain-forests—and with Camus or Fanon or Mao on their person, or with *Muhammad Speaks* under their arms" (454). Leo, the central character in the novel, is a consummate performer who believes that the "dressing room [is his] only home" (11). The novel is an intense meditation on the relation between performance and identity. Leo understands that identity is performative, but he also views acting as an "impossibility" given the way that people are trapped by the ideologies written on their bodies (82). When he decides to become an actor, Leo "commit[s] [himself] to this impossibility" (82). The interracial love affair between Leo and Barbara and the homosexual love affair between Leo and Black Christopher do not fit in the politics of the Black Power movement. Baldwin's position in the Black Power and Black Arts movements was tenuous due to his depictions of homosexuality and bisexuality. Eldridge Cleaver, in *Soul on Ice* (1968), published the same year as *Tell Me*, attributes Baldwin's homosexuality to "self-hatred." When Cleaver articulates his own dilution anxiety, fear of loss of "authentic" blackness, it is clear that Cleaver views black homosexuality as a dilution of "blackness" and erasure of black power.[34] Baldwin subverts this dominant discourse of the Black Power movement when he writes unflinchingly about the urgency for black power and a "Black is Beautiful" gaze even as he places homosexuality and interracial love in the center of the text. We often quickly define the Black Arts movement as the artistic counterpart of the Black Power movement. When we think about the significance of the publication of *Tell Me* in 1968 and Baldwin's insider/outsider status in the Black Power movement compared to his key presence in the Civil Rights movement, *Tell Me* complicates a quick definition of Black Arts movement literature. If we place *Tell Me* in a canon of Black Arts movement literature, we need to define the Black Arts movement as the artistic complication of the Black Power movement, as opposed to the artistic counterpart or bedfellow.

Like *Tell Me,* Bob Crawford's photographs of a black crossdressing Halloween ball in 1969, in Chicago, complicate a quick and easy definition of the Black Arts ethos (figure 8). When Crawford photographed the crossdressing ball, he departed from his usual imaging of street life in black Chicago.[35] In contrast to the celebration of dark-skinned blackness, afro hair styles, black power fists, Nation of Islam clothing, and Black Panther images in Crawford's typical Black Arts photography, the photographs of the gay crossdressing ball place new subjects within his "Black is Beautiful" gaze. Crawford remembers being amused by the outlandishness of the crossdressers. The representation of crossdressing as a spectacle is overshadowed, however, by the "Black is Beautiful" sensibility that overdetermines his photographic gaze. In the photographs of the crossdressers, blond wigs, straight-haired wigs, and skin lightened with makeup become part of the performance of "Black is Beautiful." Typical Black Arts photography inveighs against these signs of "whiteness." Like *Tell Me,* the photographs of the crossdressers present new signs of "Black is Beautiful." The photographer's memories of his amused spectatorship at the ball naturalize the conflict of signs between "Black is Beautiful" and black drag. The photographs themselves, however, might reveal that black drag, for the crossdressers, is black power.

Crawford's camera captures the sense of empowerment the men achieve through crossdressing. The crossdressers' wigs beg to be compared to Crawford's photograph entitled "Wigs," which confronts mammy and Aunt Jemima stereotypes (figure 9). The wigs on the maternal black women, domesticated in the photograph by the background of the rural-looking home on Chicago's South Side, may be read as signs of racial self-hatred and a desire for white femininity; however, upon comparison with the crossdressers' wigs, they can also be read as signs of empowerment, a bold sense of style. In the photograph "Batman" (figure 10), we see Crawford's explicit attempt to subversively objectify the white crossdressers at the ball. The Batman suit can be interpreted as the racialized "darkness of sexuality" worn by the white man. The "Black is Beautiful" photographer laughs at the

Figure 8. *Untitled (Bob Crawford, 1969)*

Figure 9. *"Wigs" (Bob Crawford, 1970)*

Figure 10. "Batman" (Bob Crawford, 1969)

ridiculousness of this "dark suit of sexuality." The photograph can be read as a response to Frantz Fanon's recognition that the black man has become "the genital" in the white imagination.[36] The white phallus is demystified in this photograph. The white male is reduced to a body part. The psychoanalytic understanding of the fetish as the covering or masking of lack gains real meaning in this photograph. The dark Batman mask covers the white face and may allow the performer to feel connected to the potent sexuality attributed to black men.

How does this subversive fetishism of the white male body compare to the imaging of the women in the photograph entitled "Wigs"? The wigs do not match the "Black is Beautiful" aesthetic of unstraightened hair. In

In Our Terribleness, Baraka writes, "So the blood with the Agbada (robe) and the sisters with the natural must also represent the consciousness that change symbolizes."[37] The very word "natural" as a reference to the afro hairstyle fully displays the way that the "Black is Beautiful" ideology often led to a belief in the embodiment of abstraction—seemingly, the "natural," the hairstyle, embodies a blessed state of "nature." The fetishism of the afro as "natural" during the Black Arts movement was comparable to the fetishism of dark-skinned blackness as "naturally" beautiful. In the photograph "Wigs" and the photographs of the black male crossdressers wearing wigs, Crawford's normal fetishism of the "natural" is forced to confront the fetishism of the "unnatural"—the blond wigs, the makeup, the female clothing on male bodies. The juxtaposition of these photographs and Crawford's "Black is Beautiful" images reveals connections between black drag and the cultural nationalism of the Black Arts movement. As we look at these photographs, we hear Baraka's insistence that "I can take off these clothes and wear some others."[38]

In *Tell Me,* Leo Proudhammer often feels that his acting career becomes black drag, whereas Black Christopher is figured as the embodiment of "Black is Beautiful." Leo becomes a consummate racial crossdresser as he plays roles that have been imagined as "white" roles. He "commit[s] [himself] to [the] impossibility" of acting because genuine acting, as opposed to the body of the actor being read through the lens of racial stereotypes, seems impossible to Leo.[39] He becomes painfully aware that any performance that does not cater to stereotypical, racist notions of blackness is liable to be interpreted as black drag. Once he becomes a famous actor, he yearns to take off the mask that may be the real cause of the heart attack described in the opening scene. Black Christopher is potentially the antidote for the pain of the black drag. Leo's love affair with "Black is Beautiful" begins at the end of a "long career" of black drag.[40] The beauty of Black Christopher is described as "black in color, black in pride, black in rage" (73). Leo tells Christopher that "he [is] certainly black enough to be an African, and even . . . that the structure of his face reminded [him] of faces [he] had seen in Dakar" (107). In the Black Arts movement, the words "Black is Beautiful" and "African" often became synonymous. The recurring references to "Africa" in *Tell Me* reveal Baldwin's interest in the meaning of "Africa" in the African American imagination.[41]

There is a rift between Leo's black drag and Black Christopher's "African essence." Even as Baldwin thinks deeply, through the representations of Leo and Barbara, about identity itself as performative, he removes Black Christopher from the realm of the performative. In a key scene in the first of the three sections of the novel, Baldwin muses on the difficult but necessary task of making sure that public expressions of black power do not become cathartic performances. In this scene, it becomes abundantly clear that Leo Proudhammer, the famous actor, has much in common with James Baldwin, the famous novelist. Like Baldwin, once Leo gains fame, he is invited to speak in public forums and at rallies. In this scene of the novel, Leo is waiting to deliver his speech at a rally. As he waits and listens to a little girl singing, he wonders if he can deliver an uplifting speech without reducing black power to a cathartic performance. He wonders about the "price of the song": "No song could possibly be worth the trap in which so many thousands, undelivered, perished every day. No song could be worth what this singing little girl had already paid for it, and was paying, and would continue to pay. And yet—without a song?" (111). Baldwin refuses to give his reader any cathartic moment in the scene when Leo and his brother Caleb become physically intimate and Leo curses a white God as he imagines a black God. In a manner comparable to his way of seeing Black Christopher, as Leo becomes physically intimate with Caleb, he imagines Caleb as the embodiment of black power. This scene is an explicit rendering of how the equation of the phallus and the penis is transmuted into the phallus as God, the phallus as cultural power. The black crossdressers, in Crawford's photographs, fight against the white phallus by putting on that which is interpreted, through the Black Arts lens, as signs of white femininity, described by Baraka, in "Black Art" (1968), as "girdlemamma mulatto bitches whose brains are red jelly stuck between 'lizabeth taylor's toes."[42] The social construct "white woman" is the clothing that the black male crossdressers put on. Barbara, in *Tell Me,* argues that white women have been conditioned to believe that they can be transformed through sexual intimacy with black men. According to Barbara, "everybody wants to be changed" (278). In Crawford's photographs of the black crossdressers wearing blond wigs, signs of white femininity are the means through which black men "change."

In *Soul on Ice,* Cleaver feminizes Baldwin. In a metanarrative moment in *Tell Me,* Baldwin expresses his own awareness of the homophobia that led to mixed opinions of his work: "Some people considered me a fagot, for some I was a hero, for some I was a whore, for some I was a devious cocks-man, for some I was an Uncle Tom. My eminence hurt me sometimes . . . , but I tried not to think too much about it. I certainly couldn't blame the people if they didn't trust me—why should they?" (454). Baldwin was aware that he was viewed by some as "Martin Luther Queen."[43] Huey Newton explains, in "On Eldridge Cleaver: He is No James Baldwin," that Baldwin did not respond publicly to Cleaver's accusations. When Newton recounts a kiss exchanged between Cleaver and Baldwin, Cleaver's homophobia emerges as a form of drag, a disguising of his real feelings toward Baldwin: "When we arrived, Cleaver and Baldwin walked into each other, and the giant, six-foot-three-inch Cleaver bent down and engaged in a long, passionate french kiss with the tiny (barely five feet) Baldwin . . . I later expressed my surprise to Cleaver, who pleaded that I not relay this incident to anyone."[44] The release of tension and overcoming of boundaries described in this anecdote is comparable to the merging, in Crawford's photographs of the Halloween ball, of the signs of "Black is Beautiful" and black drag.

The "Black is Beautiful" ideology of the Black Arts movement inveighed against the transformed black body. Haki Madhubuti provides a prime example of this protest in the poem "On Seeing Diana Go Madddddddddd" (1970). As the speaker in this poem begs Diana Ross to resist being co-opted by a white power structure, to "stop! in the name of love before [she] break[s] [black] heart[s]," he highlights her position as "the wearer of other people's hair" as one prime example of her co-option.[45] In Madhubuti's "Black is Beautiful" gaze, a black woman wearing a straight-haired wig is wearing something that does not conform to her "nature"—she is in drag. In the poem "To Those of My Sisters Who Kept Their Naturals" (1969), Gwendolyn Brooks reveals that signs of "Black is Beautiful" were imagined, during the Black Arts movement, as transcendence of black imitation of whiteness. The speaker in this poem asserts, "Farrah's hair is hers."[46] The images of the empowerment of the black crossdressers, in the Halloween ball Crawford photographed in 1969, deliver the message "Farrah's hair is ours." The speaker in "To Those of My Sisters" pays homage to the black women wearing "naturals" who "never worshipped Marilyn Monroe."[47] Through the character Leo Proudhammer, who views the "dressing room as his only home" and his "natural" hair as a "vile plantation," Baldwin imagines that performance and crossdressing may be a way of changing the script that has constructed kinky black hair as a "vile plantation."[48] Baldwin's use of these words underscores that black bodies themselves have become the most local site of post-slavery trauma.

When Baraka, in *In Our Terribleness,* insists that African Americans must wear "new clothes," we see that the "Black is Beautiful" ideology of the Black Arts movement often took the shape of revolutionary crossdressing.[49] The vitriolic images of transgendering in *Black Fire* demonstrate why it is so important that 1969 Black Arts photographs of a crossdressing ball be included in the archive of the Black Arts movement. The striking images of this transgendering include the poet Welton Smith's rage against the "nigga," an unenlightened black person, who has "made [his[women / to grow huge dicks."[50] The black male crossdressers in Crawford's photographs put on signs of femininity even as the legacies of American slavery continued to defeminize black womanhood. The many references to "black queens" in *Black Fire* can be viewed as black male nationalists' huge objectification of black women, as well as their strident attempt to counter the lie that beauty and femininity are the natural properties of white womanhood. In "Special Section for the Niggas on the Lower Eastside or: Invert the Divisor and Multiply," one of the poems in *Black Fire,* Welton Smith presents another recurrent image of crossdressing in Black Arts movement literature, the black "sell-out" wearing the clothing of the black revolutionary. Smith attacks this type of crossdressing by accusing the "sell-out" who wears the "wire-rim glasses" (a visual sign of the black male nationalist) of desiring to be a white woman: "you don't just want a white woman / you want to be a white woman / you are concubines of a beast / you want to be lois lane, audrey hepburn, ma perkins, lana turner."[51] Can the performance of the black male crossdressers, photographed through the Black Arts lens, defy this claim "you want to be a white woman"? Considering that the afro and "natural" are not hairstyles that are coded as exclusively female, if the black male crossdressers were consciously performing black femininity as opposed to white femininity, what type of hair would they wear, if straight-haired wigs are signs of white femininity?

Within contemporary black queer culture, the short "natural," the short version of the "afro" hairstyle, is both embraced and contested as a sign of "black butch" identity. When the short "natural" is read as a sign of the "black butch," are we witnessing the transformation of "natural black beauty" into a particular gender identity, the gender identity of black women who have no desire to be the "earth" of the particular black male nationalism exemplified in "Earth," one of Rolland Snellings' poems in *Black Fire?* After reiterating the classic nationalist images of the male soldier and the feminized territory that needs protection, Snellings pays homage to "Mother of the World! / Fecund, Beating Heart! / Enduring Earth!"[52] Snellings differentiates between the castration of the black male soldier by the white "snow queen" and the home the black woman's "Womb" provides. Like this image of the black male appropriation of the womb, Baraka's reference, in *In Our Terribleness,* to the black "male tits" (as opposed to the images of the penis which abound in *Black Fire*) may be the real sign of the black phallus imagined during the Black Arts movement. Baraka refers to the "male tits," in *In Our Terribleness,* as he presents the black male body as the black mind. He writes, "The two male tits and navel and the penis are a big face."[53] In a manner that is comparable to drag, the masculinist discourse of the Black Arts movement often gained "male tits" as it used images of black women as a means to express black male fraternity (brotherly love). This latent black male homoeroticism in the black male cultural nationalism of the Black Arts movement is brought to the surface in *Tell Me How Long the Train's Been Gone,* Baldwin's liminal, long-lost Black Arts novel.

four

The Surreal Aesthetic and the Sticky Racial Fetish

The Bluest Eye and *Tar Baby*

LIKE James Baldwin's *Tell Me How Long the Train's Been Gone,* Toni Morrison's *The Bluest Eye* is a peculiar type of Black Arts novel. She completed this first novel between 1962 and 1970, during the height of the Black Arts movement. In the 1993 afterword she explains that as she wrote this novel, she was thinking deeply about the black aesthetic that emerged with such force in the 1960s. She writes, "The reclamation of racial beauty in the sixties stirred these thoughts, made me think about the necessity for the claim" (210). Morrison began her literary career as the Black Arts movement was emerging. The body politics of the Black Arts movement is reflected and deflected in this first novel. Within the abundant amount of criticism on Toni Morrison's novels, there are few sustained analyses of the Black Arts movement backdrop of *The Bluest Eye* and the post–Black Arts movement sensibility of later novels such as *Tar Baby* and more contemporary ones such as *Paradise.*[1]

One of the central images in *The Bluest Eye,* the dismemberment of a white doll by a young black girl, is a vivid portrayal of the consequences of the violent whitening of feminine beauty. The phallus in *The Bluest Eye* becomes whiteness. As the child Claudia takes the doll apart, she looks in vain for the part of the doll's body that gives it the ability to enchant. She does not understand this beauty (she "cannot love it"). She "dismembers" the doll as she searches for the secret of its beauty and power. When we place *The Bluest Eye* in the context of the Black Arts movement, this dismemberment gains even more significance. In *In Our Terribleness,* published the same year as *The Bluest Eye,* Amiri Baraka presents the dismemberment of the black race as the Middle Passage itself and the healing of this dismemberment as the collective black body. In *Tar Baby* Morrison, like Hortense Spillers' groundbreaking theories of black masculinity and black femininity, fully confronts the "middle passage" of gender confusion in which the very categories "man" and "woman" become inadequate ways of thinking about the gender positions emerging from slavery and post-slavery trauma.[2] In Morrison's trajectory from *The Bluest Eye* (1970) to *Tar Baby* (1981), she shows how black nationalist fetishism of a collective black body, in the absence of a viable concrete nation-state, makes the body the most local site of the nation, a displaced nation overdetermined by racialized gender trauma. In "Black Nationalism and Black Common Sense: Policing Ourselves and Others," Wahneema Lubiano asserts that "[b]lack identity is also a sign for remembering our specificity and aestheticizing our resistance to racist trauma."[3] Morrison's path from *The Bluest Eye* to *Tar Baby* captures the aestheticizing of resistance to racial self-hatred.

In *The Bluest Eye* dominant standards of beauty traumatize Pecola. She idealizes visions of white femininity and dreams of blue eyes. Feminine beauty, in Pecola's absorption of antiblack racism, seems to be "white." The more limiting and reductive her own body feels, the more she exaggerates the power of white feminine beauty. In an interview conducted in 1983, Morrison explains that aesthetic experiences are difficult to interpret because one must "get underneath them" and "see what they mean": "The concepts of beauty and ugliness are mysterious to me. Many people write about them. In mulling over them, I try to get underneath them and see what they mean, understand the impact they have on what people do."[4] In *The Bluest Eye,* Claudia literally attempts to "get underneath" the concept of beauty when she considers the dismemberment of her white doll. The white doll puzzles Claudia, an African American youth who has witnessed the exaltation of the doll's image by "[a]dults, older girls, shops, magazines, newspapers, window signs."[5] In her effort to demystify the beauty attributed to the doll, she takes the doll apart in order to find the essence of its beauty: "I had only one desire: to dismember it. To see of what it was made, to discover the dearness, to find the beauty, the desirability that had escaped me, but apparently only me" (20).

As this passage progresses, it becomes apparent that white femininity is being represented as the phallus and Claudia is imagining the castration of this phallus. Claudia explains:

> I could not love it. But I could examine it to see what it was that all the world said was lovable. Break off the tiny fingers, bend the flat feet, loosen the hair, twist the head around, and the thing made one sound—a sound they said was the sweet and plaintive cry "Mama," but which sounded to me like the bleat of a dying lamb, or, more precisely, our icebox door opening on rusty hinges in July. (21)

This image of the violent nature of the breaking, bending, loosening, and twisting of the doll is strikingly comparable to the Black Arts reaction to the violence of white aesthetics. The Black Arts move to explicit images of castrated whiteness include Keorapetse Kgositsile's image of the "ball of transparent pus where the manhood used to be" in the poem "For Sons of Sonless Fathers" (1971). Morrison's rendering, in *The Bluest Eye,* of the dismemberment of the white doll is the pivotal part of the novel that explains the real influence of the Black Arts and Black Power movements on this novel. The novel's central focus on black self-hatred is simply the surface; on the deepest registers Morrison confronts the role of the phallus in constructions of dominant white aesthetics and black aesthetic warfare. Claudia hears the "bleat of a dying lamb," instead of the word "Mama," as if to underscore how alienated she is from other children's way of understanding this doll. Unlike Pecola, who is simply seduced by the "sweet and plaintive cry" of the constructs of white feminine beauty to such an extent that she loves an image of white beauty and despises her bodily image of self, Claudia has much more ambivalent feelings about the doll and what it represents. Initially, she wants to dismember the doll violently, because she wants to understand what makes it beautiful. This violence is "disinterested," in the sense that it is not spurred by hateful feelings toward the doll. Once she "learn[s] how repulsive this disinterested violence was," she begins to feel a "fabricated hatred" of the doll, which finally evolves into a "fraudulent love" (23).

The love of the doll is "fraudulent" in the sense that Claudia is fully aware that the love is an internalization of a dominant ideology. Morrison begins the novel with the elementary school primer in order to frame the entire story with the invisibility of a dominant white aesthetic. Morrison moves from the different print type of the primers, moving from the normal space between words to wider spaces between words and no punctuation, to the collapsing of the space between words ("Hereisthehouseitis-greenandwhite" [2]), in a final representation of the same "Dick and Jane" story. When Morrison makes the words merge, she blurs the script of the dominant white aesthetic. Morrison's use of the primer as the very frame of *The Bluest Eye* sheds more light on her own sense that this first novel was deeply affected by the 1960s "Black is Beautiful" movement. In 1969 the poet Mari Evans published an alternative elementary school primer, *I Look at Me!* The language in this alternative primer aims to teach self-love. As children color the images, they read announcements such as "You are beautiful" and "Nation Time!"[6] At the same time as this type of reconditioning, this attempt to teach self-love, shaped the Black Arts movement, Morrison, in *The Bluest Eye,* used the standard primer as a means of exploring the ways in which racial self-hatred is consciously taught through the lack of visual images of blackness. *The Bluest Eye* captures the underside of Black Arts ideological warfare: the conscious tutelage of "White is Beautiful."

Claudia desires to dismember the doll because she realizes, with the raw insight of a child's impulse to love self, that the doll's beauty is an ideological construct. Morrison emphasizes the young girl's attempt to separate the metaphysical and the physical. The terms "metaphysical" and "physical" themselves are included in one of Claudia's narrations when she thinks about the temporary homelessness of Pecola's family. Morrison writes:

> There is a difference between being put out and being put outdoors. If you are put out, you go somewhere else; if you are outdoors, there is no place to go. The distinction was subtle but final. Outdoors was the end of something, an irrevocable, physical fact, defining and complementing our metaphysical condition. Being a minority in both caste and class, we moved about anyway on the hem of life, struggling to consolidate our weaknesses and hang on, or to creep singly up into the major folds of the garment. Our peripheral existence, however, was something we had learned to deal with—probably because it was abstract. But the concreteness of being outdoors was another matter—like the difference between the concept of death and being, in fact, dead. (17–18)

As the novel progresses, the words "an irrevocable, physical fact, defining and complementing our metaphysical condition" gain more and more significance.

The emphasis on the confusion of the physical and the metaphysical is most pronounced when Pecola imagines that the metaphysical escape from her trauma could occur only through an alteration of her "physical fact[s]"—if she gained blue eyes. When this layer is connected to the Black Arts/Black Power emphasis on the assumption of a new way of appearing (natural hair and African clothing) as inseparable from a new way of thinking, it is clear that Morrison continues to use the theme of black self-hatred as a means of indirectly thinking about the Black Arts and Black Power movements.[7]

The deflection of the Black Arts movement in *The Bluest Eye* can be visualized through the striking similarities and contrasts between *The Bluest Eye* and *In Our Terribleness.* In a key passage in *The Bluest Eye,* Morrison describes Pecola as trapped in "her blackness [that] is static and dread" (49), when the gaze of the store owner, Mr. Yacobowski, cannot focus on her and "hover[s]" "[s]omewhere between retina and object, between vision and view" (48). This very idea of blackness being "static and dread" is the black motionlessness that Baraka seeks to reshape into blackness as a "long image story in motion" in *In Our Terribleness.* The explicit focus on the hailing of new black subjects and the hypnotism needed to recondition the mind of the new black subject parallels Morrison's explicit focus on the interpellation that produces black self-hatred.

Hypnotism is represented directly in *In Our Terribleness,* when Baraka writes, "Look into my eyes. (These flicks.) Look into your own eyes [. . .] Look into our eyes. Visualize yr own face, when you close yr eyes. Can you do that? Can you see your own image?" (150). Morrison begins *The Bluest Eye* with the horror of the veritable hypnotism, created by a dominant white aesthetic, in children's literature: "Here is the house. It is green and white. It has a red door. It is very pretty. Here is the family. Mother, Father, Dick, and Jane live in the green-and-white house. They are very happy. See Jane. She has a red dress. She wants to play" (1). In *The Bluest Eye,* as Sally plays, blackness remains "static and dread" as Pecola sinks under the weight of her internalized antiblack racism.

In contrast to the motionlessness of Mr. Yacobowski's gaze, Pecola's wishes and desires, "all things in her" (49), are "flux and anticipation" (49). Unfortunately, this "flux and anticipation" becomes a "craving for things" antiblack racism has constructed as beautiful (165). Morrison uses Soaphead Church to introduce directly the idea that Pecola begins to experience objects and surfaces as sites of consciousness and "human spirit" (165). Morrison writes, "All his life he had a fondness for things—not the acquisition of wealth or beautiful objects, but a genuine love of worn objects: a coffee pot that had been his mother's, a welcome mat from the door of a rooming house he once lived in, a quilt from a Salvation Army store counter. It was as though his disdain of human contact had converted itself into a craving for things humans had touched. The residue of the human spirit smeared on inanimate objects was all he could withstand of humanity" (165). Soaphead calls himself a "spiritualist," but the only inwardness he can tolerate is that which is present in its absence. His cherished objects become surfaces with depth. When Pecola comes to ask him to give her blue eyes, he "looked at that ugly little black girl" and "loved her," because she is yet another worn object that he can use as a means of approaching humanity from afar (182). In this passage, Morrison provides a vivid image of the identity formation and sheer objectification that occur when race is inscribed on bodies: "the residue of the human spirit smeared on inanimate objects."

The tension between race as the "smearing of the spirit" (race as embodied consciousness) and race as the coloring of an inanimate object is one of the "splintered mirrors" in *The Bluest Eye*. In "Memory, Creation, and Writing" (1984), Morrison explains that "[t]he visual image of a splintered mirror, or the corridor of split mirrors in blue eyes, is the form as well as the content of *The Bluest Eye*."[8] Her description of the "corridor of split mirrors in blue eyes" presents the image of Pecola entering a world of fragmented pictures of "self" that are as disturbing to Morrison as the picture that was the impetus of the novel, the picture of what Morrison's friend wanted, "very blue eyes in a very black skin" (211). The "splintered mirror" signifies mediated perception: the ideologies of race, gender, and class that shape Pecola's negative ways of seeing herself. The idea of the "split mirror" also illuminates the relation between Claudia's evolving feelings of "pristine sadism" toward the doll, then "fabricated hatred" of it, and, finally, "fraudulent love" (23). Claudia does not simply look through the "blue eyes," the gaze of the dominant ideology that has exalted white feminine beauty. Instead, the confusing "split mirrors" of sadism, hatred, and love are the lenses through which Claudia looks at the "blue eyes."

In *Tar Baby*, Morrison continues to explore the trauma of the "splintered mirror" and "fraudulent love" generated by constructs of beauty and race. In *Tar Baby*, unlike *The Bluest Eye*, there is a dramatization of differences between aesthetic experiences and skin-color fetishism. As Morrison overtly depicts the aesthetic experience, through her focus on Jadine as an art history student, she focuses on the excessiveness of the aesthetic versus the reduction of the fetish. Son becomes the work of art Jadine wishes she knew how to draw, how to "lay down" (158): "He was still life, babies, cut glass, indigo, hand spears, dew, cadmium yellow, Hansa red, moss green and the recollection of a tree that wanted to dance with her" (230). Jadine's fascination with the excessiveness of his presence is underscored in the following passage:

> Spaces, mountains, savannas—all those were in his forehead and eyes. Too many art history courses, she thought, had made her not perceptive but simpleminded. She saw planes and angles and missed character. Like the vision in yellow—she should have known that bitch would be the kind to spit at somebody, and now this man with savannas in his eyes was distracting her from the original insult. She wanted to sketch him and get it over with, but when she thought of trying to lay down that space and get the eagle beak of his nose, she got annoyed with herself. (158)

Son keeps escaping the terms that Jadine finds to represent him. Morrison demonstrates that the aestheticizing of human beings is problematic because the "space" of human beings cannot be "la[id] down" (158). Her urge to "lay down" the face is an urge to experience him as an object, an embodiment of the hidden "spaces, mountains, [and] savannas" (158). It is significant that she is not able to simply enjoy her aesthetic perception of him. She feels the acute need to create an external image of her mental image.

Jadine is an aspiring artist who has studied art history at the Sorbonne. Like the presumably white voyeurs in the Paris store, she is "transfixed" (45) by the unconventional beauty of the "woman in yellow" (48, 49). Her reaction to the African woman is similar to white modernist primitivists. Jadine, however, is very skeptical of efforts to reclaim the value of African art. As she agrees with Valerian's contempt for the "falseness and fraudulence of the anthropological position" and those who are "purveyor[s] of exotics" (145), she asserts, "Picasso is better than an Itumba mask. The fact that he was intrigued by them is proof of his genius, not the mask-maskers" (74). Jadine explicitly connects "primitivism" to Son when she refers to "his white-folks-black-folks primitivism" (275). She believes his narrow notions of "black culture" and "white culture" make him a "cultural throwback" (275). Nonetheless, Jadine is seduced by the images of "Hansa red" and other vibrant colors that Son seemingly evokes. The vibrant, exotic colors she connects to Son (such as Hansa red and cadmium yellow) convey the idea that Jadine, like Valerian's son, is also a "purveyor of exotics" (145). Valerian critiques his son's love of the exotic as "fraudulen[t]" (145), but Jadine initially does not recognize the falseness of the exoticism shaping her way of seeing the African "woman in yellow" (48, 49). She believes that she has simply and purely "fallen in love": "When you have fallen in love, rage is superfluous; insult impossible. You mumble 'bitch,' but the hunger never moves, never closes. It is placed, open and always ready for another canary-yellow dress, other tar-baby fingers holding three white eggs; or eyes whose force has burnt away their lashes" (46).

When Jadine contemplates what "fall[ing] in love" with the African "woman in yellow" means, she decides that love cancels out the possibility of "rage" or "insult" (46). Instead of being "fraudulent," the love feels like an intense and insatiable hunger that is "always ready" to be sparked again by another appearance of the "canary-yellow dress" or "tar-baby fingers" (46). The "tar-baby fingers" signify the seductiveness and stickiness attributed to the "woman in yellow," the way that Jadine feels trapped by this woman's appearance. In *The Bluest Eye,* Claudia's feelings of "fraudulent love" for the white doll hide her latent feelings of "pristine sadism" and "fabricated hatred" (23). Jadine's feelings toward the "woman in yellow" must ultimately be understood as being just as complicated and multilayered. Instead of simply falling in love with this woman, Jadine finds her aesthetic assumptions shocked and disoriented.

Just as Jadine cannot "lay down" the spaciousness of her aesthetic experience of Son (158), she could not easily draw the "woman in yellow." Jadine imagines that the "woman in yellow" is "in-visible." Like philosophers of the aesthetic experience, Morrison makes us consider the "in-visible" as that which is imagined as the transcendent meaning of the real or the visible. The representation of the beauty of the woman in yellow is the most extreme example of the sham of "in-visibility" offered by Morrison.[9] When Jadine sees her, she sees a beauty that she cannot understand through dominant beauty standards. The physicality of this woman triggers feelings of inauthenticity in Jadine. Her image continues to haunt her, because she is a very dark-skinned woman whose beauty, unlike Jadine's, could never be attributed to an interracial look. If Jadine models a look sanctioned by a mainstream beauty industry, this woman has a look that, seemingly, could not be commercialized or even captured by a camera. According to Jadine's mistaken primitivism, her look cannot be mass produced, because she represents a "natural" beauty that is both physical and spiritual.

Jadine's eyes seem to have no buffer when they are overwhelmed by that authentic "woman's woman" (46), but the desire in her that is aroused by the sight of this woman is mediated by the ideology that has taught her to think this African woman possesses an "unphotographable beauty" (46). As a model who has had her face on the cover of a popular fashion magazine, Jadine is a photographable beauty according to the dominant ideological constructs of feminine beauty. Initially, if one is not thinking in depth about the mediated perception of Jadine, the "unphotographable beauty" of this woman can be understood simply as Jadine's sense of her unconventional, non-mainstream beauty. The reference to the "unphotographable beauty," however, draws attention to the fact that the lens of the modeling industry has not completely determined Jadine's way of seeing. When the "woman in yellow" "derail[s]" her (47), she is captured by a lens, a way of seeing, through which she does not normally look and one that is not part of her conscious aesthetic. Consequently, she experiences the "woman in yellow" as both beautiful and mysterious. Jadine feels that her gaze is linked to the gaze of "everybody else in the market" (46) when the African "woman in yellow" appears.

To understand how the "woman in yellow" appears to Jadine and "everybody else," it is useful to consider the conflicting feelings embedded in any desire for the exotic. These conflicting feelings are crystallized during Jean-Paul Goude's descriptions of his way of seeing Grace Jones, one of the models for his photography in *Jungle Fever.* In this collection of photographs and commentaries, he writes, "The strength of her image, then as now, is that it swings constantly from the near grotesque—from the organ grinder's monkey—to the great African beauty. You are constantly looking at her and wondering if she's beautiful or grotesque, or both and how can she be one if she is the other."[10] Jadine is an African American who is as susceptible to the exoticism embedded in the idea of the "great African beauty" as Goude is. As an African American model, Jadine feels that she meets the dominant standards of feminine beauty, but she herself is probably viewed as exotic by readers of the magazines that have included images of her. Nonetheless, unlike the "woman in yellow" Jadine does not have a skin color that can be likened to "tar" and have such a dazzling effect when it is seen against the color white. In *Jungle Fever* Goude describes the skin of Grace Jones as "blue-black" and explains that the color of her skin made her seem extremely photographable. The biggest difference between Goude's understanding of Grace Jones and Jadine's way of seeing the "woman in yellow" is the fact that he does believe that this "great African beauty" is photographable. Nonetheless, the lens through which he sees her as being so photogenic is not very different from the lens through which Jadine looks when she imagines that the "woman in yellow" is "unphotographable" (46).

It is implied that, in addition to her being larger than what Jadine considers a model size, the darkness of the skin of the "woman in yellow" contributes to Jadine's sense that she is "unphotographable." The notion that the dark skin of the "woman in yellow" cannot be captured by a camera and the "techniques for lightening skin" used by "professional photographers . . . when shooting black images" are rejected by Goude when he produces airbrushed images of Grace Jones as "a darker shade of blue-black-brown."[11] Jadine is "uncomfortable" with the way Margaret sometimes "stirred her into blackening up or universaling out" (64). One can imagine that she would interpret Goude's photographs as an example of the "blackening up" (64). The other option Margaret presents to her, "universaling out" (64), also disturbs her. The narrator explains this option as Margaret's "ferreting out what she believed were racial characteristics" (64), as if she is erasing any sign of difference between herself and Jadine. Jadine attempts to "resis[t]" both options, which feel like traps to her, and, when Margaret treats her in this manner, she remains "alert about things she did not wish to be alert about" (64).

The picture of the "woman in yellow" lingers in her mind, months after the incident has occurred, because it makes Jadine feel that she herself is "universaling out" (64): "The woman had made her feel lonely in a way. Lonely and inauthentic" (48). Normally Jadine does not subscribe to the idea of racial authenticity, but the visual appearance of the "woman in yellow" "stir[s] her into [wanting] to blacke[n] up" (64). When the "woman in yellow" is described as having tar-like fingers, it is apparent that she is Jadine's tar baby. Son can also be considered her tar baby. When they are living together as a couple in New York, he tells Jadine a folktale about how and why "tar babies" like her were created. He insists that Jadine was set up to be a visual trap: a feminine object that the white farmer has molded as that which Son, the black rabbit, should desire. He tells Jadine, "So he got this great idea about how to get him. How to, to trap . . . this rabbit. And you know what he did? He made him a tar baby. He made it, you hear me? He made it!" (270). Despite his intentions, the story does not totally explain the relationship between Jadine and Son. If Jadine is Son's tar baby, Son is captivated by an image that eludes him. "Tar" ultimately signifies fake authenticity, or artifice that disguises itself as the "real thing." In his storytelling about the creation of the tar baby, he deludes himself into thinking that he can simply put Jadine into a discourse he has already memorized. But his aesthetic experience of Jadine is something new and unfamiliar; she exceeds the framing in which he wants to place her.

When Jadine falls into the swamp, another tar baby story is enacted. After she saves herself from the swamp by holding on to a tree, she is covered with sticky "black stuff" (184). When Son and she try to wipe the substance off her before it dries, it is as if Jadine has gained a new layer of "tar-like skin," like the skin of the "woman in yellow." Removing the "black stuff" (184) from her is a painful process, and one wonders if her being covered by the "black stuff" symbolizes the "blackening up" that Margaret sometimes encourages, to Jadine's dismay. While rescuing herself from this "black stuff" (184), she feels that she is dancing with the tree that she climbs in order to escape the swamp, and she tells herself, "No point in looking down at the slime" (182). The "women hanging from the trees" have the opposite point of view; they look down at Jadine. The narrator explains:

> The women looked down from the rafters of the trees and stopped murmuring. They were delighted when first they saw her, thinking a runaway child had been restored to them. But upon looking closer they saw differently. This girl was fighting to get away from them. The women hanging from the trees were quiet now, but arrogant—mindful as they were of their value, their exceptional femaleness; knowing as they did that the first world of the world had been built with their sacred properties; . . . they wondered at the girl's desperate struggle down below to be free, to be something other than they were. (183)

The usage of the word "rafters" conveys the idea that the women have an actual home in the interlocking trees. The "women hanging from the trees" have an "exceptional femaleness" (183), whereas the tree with which Jadine dances to save herself is personified as male. The "women hanging from the trees" interpret Jadine's dance with the tree as a "desperate struggle down below to be free, to be something other than they were" (183). From their point of view, Jadine is "fighting," instead of dancing. It is implied that the "women hanging from the trees" do not fear the "black stuff" and that the "black stuff" is connected to their "sacred properties" (183). At the end of the novel, Therese advises Son to "[f]orget" Jadine, because "[s]he has forgotten her ancient properties" (305). The sense of the "sacred" and the "ancient" are quite different from the "comic book" picture that Jadine sees when she first approaches the trees surrounding the swamp: "the place looked like something by Bruce White or Fazetta—an elegant comic book illustration" (182). The sisterhood of the "women hanging from the trees" is comparable to the sense of "fraternity" Son needs. In this version of the tar baby tale, Morrison first makes the reader think that if Jadine had allowed herself to sink freely in the "black stuff" (184), she would have left her "comic book" world and gained a sense of the sacred. But then Morrison leads the reader to think more critically about "tar." The stickiness of the "tar" emerges as the insidiousness of the very idea that skin is the surface that overcomes the imagined binary between the soul and the body.

In Son's version of the tale, "tar" is the material of the white farmer's trap; Jadine is a "fake" black. Son displays feelings of both love and hate for Jadine, similar to Claudia's "fraudulent love" and "fabricated hatred" for the white doll. Jadine is scripted as the professional, integrationist, light-skinned black woman, and Son is the dark-skinned, nostalgic "country boy" who is uneducated and much more skeptical of white and black relations. Son begins to think that maybe he could simply substitute his love of Jadine for his love of the "pie ladies" in Eloe, until he sees Alma Estée in a red wig.

> So he had changed, given up fraternity, or believed he had, until he saw Alma Estée in a wig the color of dried blood. Her sweet face, her midnight skin mocked and destroyed by the pile of synthetic dried blood on her head. It was all mixed up. But he could have sorted it out if she had just stood there like a bougainvillea in a girdle, like a baby jaguar with lipstick on, like an avocado with earrings, and let him remove it. (299)

The color of the wig is described as the "color of dried blood," because, for Son, it signifies the violence of the antiblack racism underlying the dominant standards of feminine beauty. It also signifies the violence that he believes has been caused by the dominant white society: "Like an Indian seeing his profile diminished on a five-cent piece, he saw the things he imagined to be his, including his own reflection, mocked. Appropriated, marketed, and trivialized into decor. He could not give up the last thing left to him—fraternity" (168). He projects his sense of that which is authentically his, the "things he imagined to be his" (168), onto Alma. What he imagines as the wig's mocking of Alma feels like the mocking of "his own reflection" (168). Ironically, when he tries to remove the wig from Alma's head, he attempts to "[a]ppropriate," literally, the body of Alma. His intention is to liberate Alma, and yet he treats her body as an object that belongs to him.

His belief that African Americans are "[a]ppropiated, marketed, and trivialized into decor" (168) is even more intriguing if one considers Jadine's confession to Valerian that "Picasso is better than an Itumba mask" (74). The images that Son sees when he sees Alma in the wig, the "bougainvillea in a girdle," the "baby jaguar with lipstick on," and the "avocado with earrings," are almost textbook images of surrealism (299). René Magritte's surreal images include an image of a sky with a hole in it and a human body with a fish's head. Magritte's paintings cannot be processed through common sense; they confuse the viewer's sense of what is "real" and what is absurd. The common ground between the three surreal images that Son sees is the incompatibility of the pictured natural object and its artificial adornments, the girdle, the lipstick, and the earrings. In addition to the inspiration he received from African art, in the 1930s Picasso adopted the "double image" from the tenets of surrealism in order to capture how one object can metamorphose into another. Jadine appreciates the surreal, whereas Son is disturbed by it. The "double image" of Alma's "midnight skin" and the red wig horrifies Son, whereas Jadine, like a surrealist, wishes she could capture in one of her drawings the layering or doubling of the "black pearls of hair" and the red wig. Jadine wishes she could preserve the image in a drawing, whereas Son wishes he could destroy the picture by removing the wig. Jadine's ability to appreciate the picture of Alma and the wig is tied to her aesthetic assumptions rooted in the surreal, and Son's great discomfort with the picture is tied to his aesthetic assumptions that the red wig is a sign of white feminine beauty and of the self-hatred Alma has internalized because of antiblack racism. Their different racial beliefs lead to different aesthetic beliefs. Jadine's surrealist tendencies challenge her racial essentialism. The playfulness and disorderliness of the surreal juxtapositions and the surreal way of seeing the world are presented as an aesthetic solution to the rigidity of the racial essentialism that makes particular bodies correspond to particular abstractions.

Another reference to the surreal occurs when the narrator explains that during a conversation with Valerian, Margaret stops talking momentarily and simply stares at him with a dazed look, because "[l]ike a blank frame in a roll of film, she lost the picture that should have accompanied the word" (32). Valerian tells her that he has "ordered geese" for their Christmas dinner, and "[s]he stared at Valerian for suddenly she could not imagine it" (32). Margaret's vexation with the relation between words and pictures reminds one of the painting by René Magritte, entitled "Le trahison des images" (1929), the famous image of a pipe, underneath which are the words, "Ceci n'est pas une pipe." In reference to this image, W. J. T. Mitchell argues that "[i]t isn't simply that the words contradict the image, and vice versa, but that the very identities of words and images, the sayable and the seeable, begin to shimmer and shift in the composition, as if the image could speak and the words were on display."[12] When Margaret loses the "picture that should have accompanied the word," she begins to gesticulate: "She was moving her hands to show them how it looked" (32). At this point she is talking to both Valerian and Sidney, and the picture she tries to convey with her hands is "[r]oast turkey with the legs sticking up and a shiny brown top," as opposed to the geese that have already been "ordered" (32). Margaret's inability to visualize "geese" occurs because, while she was thinking about "turkey," her husband abruptly inserts the word "geese" into her thoughts. Morrison creates an exaggerated example of the way certain pictures cling to certain words. When Son sees the red wig, he feels as "dizzy" as Margaret feels when she loses her ability to connect words and pictures. Indeed, the incompatibility of the word "geese" and the picture Margaret had already created of turkey parallels the incompatibility created when the red wig is inserted into Son's mental picture of Alma. Both Margaret and Son live in a world in which there is often a one-to-one correspondence between sights and pictures and words and ideas. In Son's case, Morrison demonstrates how race and racism graft themselves upon this world of correspondence: Son has particular pictures of blackness that match particular ideas about blackness, and the picture of Alma with the red wig disturbs this order.

Another, earlier reference to the surreal, which helps one understand the significance of the other surreal images ("bougainvillea in a girdle," "a baby jaguar with lipstick on," and "an avocado with earrings" [299]), is Valerian's vision of Michael's face "smiling at him from the bowl of peaches" (144). When Margaret enters the dining room after finding Son in her closet, she is in such a state of shock that the only words she can say are "In my closet. In my closet" and "Black" (79). Before Margaret comes to the dining room and utters these words, Valerian "was already in complicity with an overripe peach" (144), because he imagines the surreal "double image" of the peach and the face of his son. Margaret's words become the verbal counterpart of the picture of Michael's face in the bowl of peaches. As Mitchell explains in his interpretation of the Magritte painting, "Le trahison des images," "it is as if the image [the picture of the face in the peach] could speak," whereas Margaret's words are more elliptical than expressive (Mitchell 68). Valerian understands the image as "both the winsome two-year-old under the sink and the thirty-year-old Socialist" (144). When a picture does appear that seemingly matches Margaret's words ("when the black man appeared" [144]), Valerian remains so comforted by the surrealness of the "double image" of Michael and the peach that he simply "invited the intruder to have a drink" (144).

Valerian's comfort with this surreal image opposes the anxiety Son feels when he sees Alma wearing the red wig. The multiple references to the surreal underscore that pictures can be difficult to "fix," a word used when Jadine struggles to "fix" the feelings that the woman in yellow triggers (48). Margaret has difficulty fixing pictures with words, and both Son and

Jadine strain to "fix" the particular visual images that overwhelm them. The red wig on Alma's head makes Son think her "midnight skin" is a sign of authenticity that he cannot relinquish (299). The sight of the red wig against Alma's midnight skin greatly saddens him, because he believes her skin is a literal picture of authenticity, home, and kinship. The red wig is a sign of artifice attached to the midnight skin, which Son believes is Alma's essence. Son desires to remove it from Alma's head, so that her midnight skin can continue to "speak" authenticity. Without the wig, Son would no longer see the surreal picture that disturbs him to such a great extent. Seemingly, instead of seeing a "bougainvillea in a girdle," a "baby jaguar with lipstick on," and an "avocado with earrings" (299), he would be able to see Alma as she "really was" (299).

The irony of Son's need to remove the wig and control the image of Alma is that Jadine supposedly has rid him of the need to imagine icons of authenticity, like his way of seeing the "pie ladies" and his nostalgic view of the "original dime" (299). When he reacts so vehemently to the sight of Alma wearing the wig, he realizes that he still believes in icons of authenticity. The text reads:

> He had it straight before: the pie ladies and the six-string banjo and then he was seduced, corrupted by cloisonné and raw silk the color of honey, and he was willing to change, to love the cloisonné, to abandon the pie ladies and the nickel nickelodeon and Eloe itself and Frisco too because she had given him back his original dime, the pretty one, the shiny one, the romantic ten-cent piece, and made him see it the way it was, the way it really was. (299)

Both before and after his conversion, when he romanticizes the signs of his past in Eloe and when he is seduced by the signs of Jadine, he believes he is seeing the world "the way it really was" (299). His romantic images of the coin, the pie ladies, and the banjo feel as rooted in the "actual" as Jadine's demystifications of them. Son cannot bear the surreal vision of Alma, because it blurs the lines of the actual and the imaginary and, consequently, disturbs his need to see the world "the way it really was" (299). By emphasizing that Son's understanding of the "real" is so liable to change and that his perception is so rooted in his understanding of the "real," Morrison suggests that unmediated perception, a perception that is not formed by particular ideologies, is impossible, and yet the illusion of this unmediated perception shapes Son's deepest feelings of love and fidelity.

The mediated perception, the ideology that makes him so emotionally invested in the appearance of Alma's hair, is most apparent when the reader remembers how Son looks at his own hair, while sneaking into Jadine's room in L'Arbe de la Croix. The text reads, "[He] stood before the mirror looking at his hair. It spread like layer upon layer of wings from his head, more alive than the sealskin. It made him doubt that hair was in fact dead cells. Black people's hair, in any case, was definitely alive . . . He knew perfectly well what it was that had frightened her, paralyzed her for a moment" (132). As he looks at his own hair, he arrives at a decision about the hair of "Black people." More specifically, the "alive[ness]" of his hair, and the hair of all "Black people," frightens Jadine, in his estimation, because she is alienated from "Black people." He romanticizes the hair he sees in the mirror to such an extent that he convinces himself that it really is more than just hair, more than "dead cells" (132). This romantic notion he has about the hair of "Black people" mediates or shapes his reaction to the appearance of Alma with the red wig. The wig covers what he believes is a sign of her "alive[ness]" and the "alive[ness]" of "Black people" (132). The figurative death enacted by the red wig, in Son's way of seeing, reminds one of Margaret's mother's way of seeing her daughter's red hair: "She was as puzzled as her husband but not as alarmed, although it did look funny at the nine-thirty mass: Margarette's head glowing like an ember among the coal-dark heads of her other children" (56). This passage implies that, when her daughter is not in public, Leonora is not as aware of the contrast between the "coal-dark heads" and "Margarette's head" (56), and that the red hair seems like an "ember" only when the family is in public and Leonora is looking through a "societal" lens. Similarly, Son's discomfort with the red wig is overdetermined by a societal lens, although he believes that there is an intrinsic contradiction and clash between the red wig and dark skin.

Son's perception is so heavily mediated by conflicting ways of seeing and conflicting ideologies that he is not fully conscious of what he actually sees and what he desires. He desires Jadine, and he desires everything that Eloe, his hometown, represents, which he believes he cannot have with Jadine. His desire is tied to what he imagines as the "real," and when his understanding of the "real" shifts, he feels that "[i]t was all mixed up" (299). He is not the only one whose perception is mediated, but he is the character through which Morrison most dramatically demonstrates the trauma of mediated perception. There are two moments in the text when the dream or fantasy of unmediated perception is most poignantly represented. One of these moments is when Valerian decides, "A dead hydrangea is as intricate and lovely as one in bloom. Bleak sky is as seductive as sunshine, miniature orange trees without blossom or fruit are not defective; they are that" (242). In effect, Valerian reasons at this point that one can be seduced simply by the "'is-ness' of things," and that when focusing on this "is-ness," one no longer makes value judgments in terms of what is "intricate," what is "lovely," or what is "defective" (242).

In this passage, Morrison stresses the idea that if there were no value judgments like the "lovely" and the "defective" to mediate aesthetic experiences, unmediated perception would be possible. The other narrative moment that highlights the possibility of unmediated perception occurs when Son aestheticizes Gideon's back.

> It was the black man he had seen off and on around the grounds. He stared at his back. Yardman, she called him. That was Yardman's back. He knew backs, studied them because backs told it all. Not eyes, not hands, not mouths either, but backs because they were *simply there,* all open, unprotected and unmanipulable as Yardman's was, stretched like a smokehouse cot where hobos could spend the night. A back where the pain of every canker, every pinched neck nerve, every toothache, every missed train home, empty mailbox, closed bus depot, do-not disturb and this-seat-taken sign since God made water came to rest. He watched the angle of the old man's spine and for no reason that he could think of tears stung his eyes. (139; italics added)

That which is "simply there, all open, unprotected and unmanipulable" epitomizes the idea of unmediated perception. Son is seduced by Yardman's (or Gideon's) back, because it creates a limitless desire in him. He cries because he is overwhelmed by the therapeutic powers of the back, which seems to be the place where all "pain . . . came to rest" (139). The soothing abilities of this back that is "simply there" symbolize the soothing abilities of unmediated perception. As this passage progresses, the unmediated perception of that which is "simply there" vanishes quickly and is replaced by images of white boys playing tennis "under their very own sun" (139). The narrator explains that the visions of the affluence and privilege of white people are "as familiar as the knuckle of his thumb" (139). His heart "careen[s]" into these visions of race and class hierarchy (139), while he is aiming for the raw beauty of that which is "simply there" (139).

Son's frustrated attempt to isolate his desires from his understanding of race, class, and gender is represented most dramatically in the following passage, in which he is in New York waiting for Jadine to meet him so they can begin their new life together, but in which he is unable to forget the way she acted when they first met and the way she supported Valerian during the ferocious Christmas dinner feud.

> Gatekeeper, advance bitch, house-bitch, welfare office torpedo, corporate cunt, tar baby side-of-the-road whore trap, who called a black man old enough to be her father "Yardman" and who couldn't give a shit who he himself was and only wanted his name to file away in her restrung brain so she could remember it when the cops came to fill out the report—five eleven, maybe six feet, black as coal with the breath and table manners of a rhino. But underneath her efficiency and know-it-all sass were wind chimes. Nine rectangles of crystal, rainbowed in the light. Fragile pieces of glass tinkling as long as the breeze was gentle. (220)

The litany of insulting stereotypes that emerge when he thinks about her "surface" demeanor makes one wonder if his hatred for particular aspects of Jadine is comparable to the "fabricated hatred" Claudia in *The Bluest Eye* feels for the white baby doll. One also wonders if his love for Jadine is as "fraudulent" as the love Claudia finds for the doll. This comparison between Claudia's mediated perception and that of Son seems most warranted when the narrator explains that "underneath [Jadine's] efficiency and know-it-all sass were wind chimes" (220). Claudia initially wants to "dismember" (20) the doll to find the secret underneath her exteriority, but instead of the entrancing sound of "wind chimes," Claudia discovers that the "secret" of the "Mama" sound the doll makes is a "disk with six holes," a "mere metal roundness" (21). Claudia demystifies the doll once she looks underneath its surface, whereas the fragility and gentleness of the wind chimes are just another cliché to which Son shifts after he abandons the pejorative stereotypes he attributes to Jadine.

Claudia "finger[s] the face [of the doll]" (21) as she wonders about the secret of its beauty. Son "finger[s]" the image of the white youth playing tennis and the magazine photographs of Jadine (116, 139). The significance of the repeated usage of this idea of "finger[ing]" is the fact that it is an attempt by both Claudia and Son to have a direct access to the objects of their mediated perception. When Jadine shows Son her photographs in the fashion magazine, Son cannot read the language, apparently French, in which the captions to the pictures are written. Like the times when Margaret "[l]ike a blank frame in a roll of film, . . . lost the picture that should have accompanied the word" (32), Son cannot read the words that accompany the pictures. When Jadine must translate the words for him, the reader is reminded of how mediated Son's perception is. When he touches the pictures with his finger, he may imagine that what he sees is "simply there," like Gideon's back (139), but he loses the direct, unmediated contact when he "lift[s] his finger from the picture to point at the caption beneath" and asks, "[W]hat does that say?" (116). The pictures themselves become the mediator of his perception when his eyes move from the photographs to Jadine's actual body:

> He lifted his head and looked at her. Her eyes were mink-colored just like in the pictures, and her lips were like the pictures too . . . The way they were when he used to slip into her room and wait hours, hardly breathing himself, for the predawn light to bring her face out of the shadows and show him her sleeping mouth, and he had thought hard during those times in order to manipulate her dreams, to insert his own dreams into her so she would not wake or stir or turn over on her stomach but would lie still and dream steadily the dreams he wanted her to have about yellow houses with white doors which women opened and shouted Come on in, you honey you! and the fat black ladies in white dresses minding the pie table in the basement of the church and white wet sheets flapping on a line, and the sound of a six-string guitar plucked after supper while children scooped walnuts up off the ground and handed them to her. (119)

The notion of the "insert[ion]" of dreams is peculiar, because it evokes the idea of hypnotism or brainwashing and is further evidence that Son cannot separate the ideological from the amorous. The picture of contrast in this passage, the "fat black ladies in white dresses" (119), unlike the other pictures of contrast discussed thus far, is not represented as producing a dramatic or overwhelming effect on the eye. These women are the residents of the "yellow houses with white doors which [they] opened [wide]" (6). In the magazine photographs, Son notices that Jadine's lips are always "wet and open" (116). The difference between these two different types of "open[ness]" reveals the sexual desire Jadine arouses in Son and the sense of security and home the "fat black ladies" represent (119). The libido remains dark-skinned, and quintessential femininity remains light-skinned (the whiter, the better). Son wants to "insert" the sensibility of these women into Jadine (119), so that he can have the "wet and open" lips and the "yellow houses with white doors" (119). Son's sense of the "open[ness]" of both Jadine and the "fat black ladies" can be compared to the description of the unmediated perception he imagines through Gideon's back as "simply there, all open" (139). Son wishes he had as direct a connection with Jadine and the "fat black ladies" (119) as his momentary connection with Gideon's back.

If Son could "insert" the dream of "yellow houses with white doors" into Jadine, his own "dream life" that was broken apart by her would be restored

(6, 119). The "wide surgical hunger" that "open[s] up" in Son when he eats the food on the boat (7), after having fallen in love with Jadine's voice, is comparable to the "hunger" that the "woman in yellow" causes Jadine to feel, which is also described as "open" (46). In both cases, the "openness" is ultimately rendered suspect by the mediated nature of their perception. In one of the arguments between Son and Jadine, the narrator describes their different worldviews and aesthetic assumptions in the following manner: "Each knew the world as it was meant or ought to be. One had a past, the other a future and each one bore the culture to save the race in his hands. Mama-spoiled black man, will you mature with me? Culture-bearing black woman, whose culture are you bearing?" (269). The "race" in Son's hand is the "fraternity" (299) so heavily connected to his feelings about Eloe, Florida, his hometown. The "race" in Jadine's hand, the group she represents, is most clear when she is on the plane going to Paris, thinking about the notion that a "grown woman did not need safety or its dreams" (290), and the narrator begins to explain the life of the "soldier ants" (290). Like the female soldier ants, Jadine ultimately decides that, instead of securing "safety" through others, she must be "the safety she longed for" (290). The idea that she no longer needs others to embody that "safety" reminds one of Valerian's ultimate understanding of the "world's beauty," in the sense that he and Jadine both decide that "you don't need someone to share it with [the world's beauty] or tell it to" (242).

Valerian survives his shock over what Margaret did to their son by focusing on the "world's beauty." After the loss of Jadine, Son's redemption is the guidance that Therese offers. After Therese escorts Son to the crossing, she warns him, in reference to Jadine, that "[t]here is nothing in her parts for you" (305), and tells him, "Don't see; feel" (304). This scene, at the very end of the novel, when he is with Therese at the crossing, is immediately preceded by his recollection, while talking to Gideon about Jadine, of the time when he was mesmerized by what was "simply there" in Gideon's back (139). Morrison suggests that Son will gain access to an unmediated perception and that he will experience a clear passage "when the mist lift[s] and the trees ste[p] back a bit as if to make the way easier for a certain kind of man" (306). This clear passage is what Pecola in *The Bluest Eye* cannot obtain when she feels trapped by the power of the visual: "Try as she might, she could never get her eyes to disappear . . . They were everything. Everything was there, them. All of those pictures, all of those faces" (45). The celebratory nature of the end of *Tar Baby* revolves around the fact that the "eyes" do "disappear." After the representations of how visualizations such as Alma's "midnight skin" anchor Son's sense of the aesthetic, Son is overwhelmed by his inability to see anything and his sudden connection with the legendary blind horsemen.

In one of her interviews, while emphasizing her general reliance on the visual as a means of propelling narrative forward, Morrison explains, "You could use a lot of rhetoric, but you don't need to do any of that if you simply see it. You see a person who is a simile, a metaphor, a painting."[13] When Jadine sees the "woman in yellow," when Son sees Alma wearing the red wig, and when Valerian first sees Margaret, they all see people as "a simile, a metaphor, a painting." At the end of the novel, unlike the representations of these visual experiences, Morrison does not allow the reader to "simply see," as if she tires of projecting "character" and "experience" from the "viewpoint" of the visual. It is significant that although the words "transcendent beauty" (46) are used explicitly in reference to the visuality of the "woman in yellow," the novel ends with a nonvisual image of Son's transcendence. As Son is seemingly "born again" as he learns to walk and then run, Therese's voice is described as being "near like skin" (306). If this image of her voice as "near like skin" is contrasted with the earlier description of the "transcendent beauty" of the "tar-like" skin of the "woman in yellow," it is apparent that the element of "tar" has been subtracted, the sticky substance of racial essentialism that traps Son in rigid notions of what is "black" and what is beautiful and makes Margaret see him upon their first meeting as "literally, literally a nigger in the woodpile," the direct rewriting of Faulkner's "nigger in a woodpile" reference in *Absalom, Absalom!* (83).[14]

Son's liberation from the "tar baby" is also signaled by Therese's emphasis on the choice that he has to either join the horsemen or to find Jadine. She tells Son, "This is the place. Where you can take a choice" (305), and "You can choose now. You can get free of her. They are waiting in the hills for you" (306). Earlier in the text, when Gideon tells Son, "Yallas don't come to being black natural-like. They have to choose it and most don't choose it" (155), Son's own "blackness" is treated as his biological destiny. When Son and not Jadine, one of the "yallas," must choose whether he will choose the horsemen or go to L'Arbe de la Croix, "blackness" is no longer figured as a "natural-like" embodiment (155), but rather a way of thinking. Morrison implies that Son's ability to "choose" blackness makes him less of a racial essentialist. The "natural-like" connection that Gideon proposes between the physical appearance of "blackness" and "being black" is what Jadine plans to "tangle with" in Paris (290); it is this sensibility that makes the "woman in yellow" appear to Jadine as an embodiment of "transcendent beauty" (46). Morrison, like Jadine, "tangles" with the notion that this African "woman in yellow" ultimately represents the locus of authentic black womanhood. Like Jadine, Morrison is both drawn to the surreal image of this "unphotographable beauty" and troubled by the sticky fetishism of "tar-like" skin at the heart of this counter-aesthetic.

As Morrison creates this tension between the aesthetic freedom of the surreal and the traps of racial fetishism, key questions emerge. Can the red wig against the "midnight skin" of Alma Estée, in *Tar Baby,* become an image of "Black is Beautiful"? Can we heal the imagined conflict between signs of "Black is Beautiful" and black drag? In the essay "Imitation and Gender Insubordination," Judith Butler presents drag as that which proves that gender itself is always drag, so that drag itself must not be understood as the "putting on of a gender that belongs properly to some other group."[15] As opposed to Butler's sense that "gender is a kind of imitation for which there is no original," Son, in *Tar Baby,* views Alma Estée's "midnight skin" as "authentic" and "original."[16] This imagined originality and purity is the precise reason why Son cannot fathom the red wig against the "midnight skin" of Alma Estée. In the 1993 afterword to *The Bluest Eye,* as Morrison situates the "Black is Beautiful" point of view as the impetus of this first novel, she explains that a "very dark" friend expressed her desire for blue eyes, and this confession compelled Morrison to know beauty for the "first time" and to contemplate its "shock" and "force."[17] She writes, "[T]hat moment was so racially infused (my revulsion at what my school friend wanted: very blue eyes in a very black skin; the harm she was doing to *my* concept of the beautiful), the struggle was for writing that was indisputably black" (211). The image of "very blue eyes in a very dark skin," like Alma's red wig against the "midnight skin," continues to signify racial self-hatred. When *Tar Baby* and *The Bluest Eye* are compared, part of Morrison's post–Black Arts movement vision becomes the recognition that, when black authenticity is no longer written on dark-skinned blackness and hybridity is no longer written on light-skinned blackness, it might be possible to reclaim "very blue eyes in a very dark skin" and a red wig against "midnight skin" as wonderfully surreal "Black is Beautiful" experiences.

five

Skin Color Geographies in *Paradise*

IN *Tar Baby,* Morrison unveils the insidious ways in which authenticity and hybridity are literally inscribed on skin as skin color becomes a surface with an incredible amount of depth, the depth of cultural authenticity and cultural hybridity. When dark-skinned blackness is invested with the power to signify black authenticity and the lighter shades of blackness continue to be imagined as physical manifestations of an altered state of original blackness, skin emerges as the fetishized edge that overcomes the binary of body and soul, surface and depth, only to reinforce the belief in the biology of race. As Morrison, in *Paradise* (1997), explores the surfaces with depth created by race, she connects the geography of the body to the geography of the black Southwest.

A letter written in 1891 by A. G. Belton to the American Colonization Society encapsulates the significance of the black Southwest towns founded in the 1880s and 90s. Belton writes, "We as a people are oppressed and disenfranchised we are still working hard and our rights taken from us times are hard and getting harder every year we as a people believe that Africa is the place but to get from under bondage we are thinking of Oklahoma as this is our nearest place of safety."[1] "Africa" is a metaphor without brakes in the African American imagination; it often signifies a prelapsarian state of wholeness, the mythical homeland often tied to images of "Africa" as one country, not the huge continent. Belton's letter raises similar questions about the image of the Southwest in the series of migrations that define African American cultures. In *Paradise,* as Toni Morrison remembers the black towns created in the Southwest at the end of the nineteenth century, she contemplates the fetishism of both racial authenticity and racial hybridity. As she reveals that the fetishism of both purity and mixture overdetermines racial fetishism, she imagines a trajectory from the body politics of the nineteenth-century black towns in the Southwest to the body politics of the 1960s and 70s Black Power movement. Remembering the historical reality of the black towns founded in the 1880s and 90s in the Southwest enables Morrison to unveil the insidious ways in which racial fetishism often revolves around a geography of bodies imagined as borderlines between what is authentic and pure and what is hybrid and exotic. The Southwest emerges as a liminal space representing the "open body," the black body rescued from both the fetishism of authenticity and the fetishism of hybridity.

The novel is the story of an "all-black town" named Ruby and the "Convent," which is a multiracial household of women who live on the outskirts of Ruby, Oklahoma. The reader is not told the particular racial identities of the women in the Convent, but the first line in the novel, "They shoot the white girl first" (3), signals that the Convent is not "all-black" like the town of Ruby. To be a fully respected citizen in Ruby, a person must be an "8-rock" (193), a term normally used in reference to coal to designate the depth of coal mines.[2] The founders of Ruby appropriate this term to mean "coal black[ness]" (160), "blue-black[ness]" (193), and "unadulterated" blackness (217). The coal that is "deep" in the mines is a parody of the idea that the "deep" human character and "transcendent beauty" of the woman in yellow in *Tar Baby* (1981) can be seen through her "tar-like" skin, her skin that is like distilled coal. The leaders in Ruby forget that "8-rock" is a metaphor, as they define human beings by their similarity to a thing, to coal. Through this literalization of a metaphor, Morrison signals the mistake of reducing human identity to skin color.

The "Disallowing" is the historical event that precipitates the construction of the "8-rock rule." In 1890, those who were to become the founders of Haven, the predecessor of Ruby, set out from Mississippi and Louisiana to "Negro towns already being built" in Oklahoma (13). Although the future founders of Haven heed the warning of the newspaper headlines telling settlers who want to join these towns to "Come Prepared or Not at All" (13), they are not allowed to join these "Negro towns" because they are darker than the people in these towns. Once they create their own town, they imagine that their "blue-black" skin is a "sign of racial purity" (194). The "Disallowing" propels them to begin to attribute meaning to the difference between darker-skinned and lighter-skinned "Negro" people. The narrator explains that when "the Disallowing" occurs, the "sign of racial purity they had taken for granted had become a stain" (194). They convert this "stain," or way of being seen, into an essence once they decide that their bloodlines must be "unadulterated and unadulteried" (217) if they are going to prosper.

In *Black Skin, White Masks,* Frantz Fanon argues that "[c]onsciousness of the body is solely a negating activity" when a black person watches the "white man's eyes" look at his or her body.[3] Fanon also asks, "What else could it be for me but an amputation, an excision, a hemorrhage that splattered my whole body with black blood?" (112). When the founders of Haven confront the gaze of the "[b]lue-eyed, gray-eyed yellowmen in good suits" (Morrison, *Paradise* 195), they experience their bodies as "stain[ed]" (Morrison 194), negated, and "splattered . . . with black blood" (Fanon 110, 122). Once they have their own town, the need to undo this "negating activity" leads them to imagine a "deep deep level" of existence and self-preservation in their "black blood" (Morrison 193). The "Disallowing" makes those who were shunned believe that a "new separation: light-skinned against black" is "of consequence, serious consequence to Negroes themselves" (194). The desire of the founding "Fathers" (194) of Haven and Ruby to protect that which was "disallowed," their "blue-black" skin (193), leads them to subscribe to the unspoken "blood rule" (195), the rule that "8-rocks" should marry and reproduce only with "8-rocks." The antagonism the "New Fathers of Ruby" (18) feel toward the Convent women is shaped greatly by their inherited memories of the "Disallowing." The narrator explains in the chapter entitled "Patricia" that "[e]verything anybody wanted to know about the citizens of Haven or Ruby lay in the ramifications of that one rebuff out of many" (189). The "Disallowing" is the basis of the eventual cohesiveness of Haven and Ruby: "Afterwards the people were no longer nine families and some more. They became a tight band of wayfarers bound by the enormity of what had happened to them" (189). When the narrator explains that in the raid on the Convent, the "target, after all, is detritus" (4), it is most apparent that the "New Fathers of Ruby" believe the Convent women, like the "fair-skinned colored men" (195), are a threat to the "8-rock"; as opposed to the solidity of rock, both are signs of fragmentation.

As if to underscore that both the Convent women and those who "disallowed" the future founders of Haven are "hated" in the same way, the idea of the "clarity" of hatred is used repeatedly in reference to both the Convent women and the "fair-skinned colored men" (195) of the "Disallowing." In the first chapter, one of the male raiders of the Convent feels that "[s]hooting the first woman (the white one) had clarified it like butter: the pure oil of hatred on top, its hardness stabilized below" (4). In the chapter entitled "Patricia," the "clarity of their [the founding fathers'] hatred" for the "fair-skinned colored men" is said to be more concrete than "their horror of whites" (189): "Their horror of whites was convulsive but abstract. They saved the clarity of their hatred for the men who had insulted them in ways too confounding for language: first by excluding them, then by offering them staples to exist in that very exclusion" (189). In the process of hating the "fair-skinned colored men" (195), the 8-rocks become convinced that they themselves embody an "unadulterated" blackness that must be protected from contamination (217).

The story of the death of the children of Deek and Soane (one of the leaders of Ruby and his wife) includes one of the most startling examples of the 8-rockers' belief in an "unadulterated" black body. Two sons of Deek and Soane are killed while fighting in the Vietnam War, and, when the dead bodies are sent to them, Deek remembers, from his own war experience, how body parts were put together after being blown apart. In the following passage, he wonders about the somatic integrity of the "blackness" of his dead sons:

> Easter and Scout were in integrated units and if Soane thought about it, she might consider herself lucky to know that whatever was missing, the parts were all of black men—which was a courtesy and a rule the medics tried hard to apply for fear of adding white thighs and feet to a black head. If Soane suspected what was likely—oh man . . . He did not want her even to imagine the single question he put to Roger—first with Scout then with Easter: Are all the parts black? Meaning, if not, get rid of the white pieces. Roger swore to their racial consistency. (112)

The idea of his sons' bodies being reconstructed with "white pieces" is horrifying to Deek not only because it reminds him of the violent nature of their deaths, but also because he believes in the "8-rock" rule, the somatic integrity of blackness. Morrison captures the ludicrousness of race by drawing attention to the ways in which the embodiment of race continues to matter even when bodies are no longer alive. When Deek asks Roger, the mortician, "Are all the parts black?" (112), he is imagining the racially mixed body that he and the other founders of Ruby and fellow inheritors of the pain of the "Disallowing" have been taught to despise.

Hybridity in the "All Black" Town

"Patricia" is the first chapter in which Morrison directly addresses the theme of "black" bodies that do not speak "unadulterated" blackness. Pat is the daughter of Delia, an "outsider" who marries into the Haven community (the predecessor to Ruby), and her lighter skin color, her hazel eyes, and light brown hair are treated by the 8-rocks as a literal inscription of the forces that could destroy the community of Haven and Ruby: "[It] [r]eminded them of why Haven existed, of why a new town had to take its place" (200). In a similar sense, Pat has "good wishes" for Ruby and also detests the town's privileging of the idea of "unadulterated" "blue-black[ness]" (217).

Pat is the self-appointed genealogist of the 8-rock legacy, the very legacy that excludes her because her father did not marry someone who is "pure black." She calls this genealogy her "history project" (187). Morrison makes the reader very conscious of Pat's own body as she describes the ways in which Pat composes her "history project." Indeed, Pat's own body movements and her sense of touch while composing the journal entries are given as much attention as the actual product she produces, the written statements themselves. For instance, at one point, Pat "ran her finger over their names [the names of the descendants of Zechariah Morgan]," and then "[s]coot[s] up the margin," and then as if she is sewing and not reading what she has already written, "another comment" is "threaded out from Zechariah's name" (191). Before Pat begins writing a new journal entry that she imagines is a way of talking directly to her deceased mother, she "wrote down her mother's name, drew a line under it, [and] enclosed it in a heart" (197). This drawn heart belies her feeling that she "alone had the required emotional distance" to interpret oral storytelling "freely but [. . .] insightfully" when there was no historical proof or historical documentation (188). Contrary to what she thinks, Pat is emotionally invested in the genealogical project, and writing the family histories is both a painful and a cathartic experience.

The pain of her body while writing parallels the heightened emotions the writing brings to the surface: "Pat stopped and rubbed the callus on her middle finger. Her elbow and shoulder ached from gripping the pen so hard" (201). The body aches she feels from the fury of her writing are examples of Paul Connerton's "incorporating practices" in the sense that, while Pat writes, there is what Connerton refers to as a "knowledge and a remembering in the hands and in the body" (95). While writing the log entry about her mother and father, she "remember[s] in the hands and in the body" the "inscribing practices" of the 8-rocks, the way in which their "blue-black" bodies are constructed as the literal inscriptions of the cultural strength and unity of Haven and Ruby. At one point she thinks about the residents as "blue-black giants" and thinks of her mother as the "first visible glitch" (196). While Pat creates the "family trees" of the Haven and Ruby families, she becomes "convinced that a new species of tree would be needed to go further, to record accurately the relationships" among the families (188). She thinks of the 8-rocks as "upside down trees", with "the trunks sticking in the air, the branches sloping down" (187). The idea of the "upside down" trees captures Misner's feeling that the 8-rocks "wanted duplicates," "rather than children" (161).

Through Pat, Morrison ultimately envisions the ways in which images of the "blue-black" can structure the deep desires of those who are interpellated as light-skinned blacks. Pat marries Billy Cato "partly (mostly?) because he had the midnight skin of the Catos and the Blackhorses" (198). And after she defends the 8-rocks against Reverend Misner's claims that they need to become more involved in affairs outside the town and that the school children need to learn that "Africa is [their] home" (210), she wonders, "[W]hy had she defended people and things and ideas with a passion she did not feel?" (214). After she burns the genealogical files and then washes her hands, she feels "clean" initially, until she thinks about the fact that there had been no deaths in Ruby and that the "recipe" for "immortality" that the 8-rocks had concocted seemed to be working so far (217). She reminds herself of Ruby's prosperity, the seeming "magic" of the "[u]nadulterated and unadulteried 8-rock blood" (217), and then regrets burning the "family trees": "'Dear God,' she murmured. 'Dear, dear God. I burned the papers'" (217). Immediately after the burning of her files, she watches her black tea water slowly becoming a clear color and thinks about the dilution of the "blue-black[ness]." The text reads: "She wiped her eyes and lifted the cup from its saucer. Tea leaves clustered in its well. More boiling water, a little steeping, and the black leaves would yield more. Even more. Ever more. Until. Well, now. What do you know? It was clear as water" (217). Even though Pat has been so hurt by the fetishizing of the darker skin tones, she cannot rejoice in this picture of the disappearance of "blackness." As she thinks about the 8-rocks' images of themselves as immortal, she has a "crooked smile" (217), as if she is both amused and pleased by their arrogance and strong will to survive. She regrets the burning of the genealogical files when she remembers everything that the 8-rocks endured since the "Disallowing" and feels that if they are indeed a "blessed" group of people, she has committed an act of blasphemy. The image of the black tea leaves becoming "clear as water" is similar to the final image in *Absalom, Absalom!* of the "bleach[ing] out" of Jim Bond. Faulkner's white characters, however, do not share Pat's feeling that this "bleach[ing] out" would be tragic.

At one point, in an argument with Reverend Misner, Pat tells him in reference to the 8-rocks: "'This is their home; mine too. Home is not a little thing'" (213). Reverend Misner responds, "But can't you imagine what it must feel like to have a true home? I don't mean heaven. I mean a real earthly home" (213). In "Home" (1997), Morrison explains that her "use of a house/home antagonism" arises from the fact that "so much of what seems to lie about in discourses on race concerns legitimacy, authenticity, community, belonging" (5). The wandering that precedes the founding of Haven and Ruby is one search for a home depicted in *Paradise*. The wandering of each of the young women who come to Consolata is another type of search for a home. Morrison explains in "Home" that her idea of a "true home" is "free and situated" and achieved by "convert[ing] a racist house into a race-specific yet nonracist home" (5). In "Patricia," she illuminates how the 8-rocks construct their bodies as "racist house[s]" (5).

The South American "Middlewoman"

In the next chapter, "Consolata," she strives to locate a "race-specific yet nonracist home" while representing the relationship between Consolata and Deacon (Deek). This effort is crystallized when their sexual affair ends and Consolata bends her knees in prayer and says, "'Dear Lord, I didn't want to eat him. I just wanted to go home'" (240). Consolata was "stolen" by the Catholic sisters, according to Penny and Clarissa (238), the only two remaining "native" girls in the final days of the school. The narrator explains that these Native American students "liked her because she was stolen, as they had been, and felt sorry for her too" (238). The American nuns "steal" Consolata when she is nine years old from the "shit-strewn paths of [a] city" that is presumably South American (223). She is taken to the Convent school and is both a servant in the household and one of the school's students. She must sneak from the Convent to meet Deek because the nuns would not approve of her sexual activity. Consolata thinks of Deek as the "living man" (225, 234), as opposed to the "living God" (225). When she meets Deek, she has been thoroughly indoctrinated by the nuns and she "worship[s]" Mary Magna (224). But Deek makes her "thirty years of surrender to the living God crac[k] like a pullet's egg" (225). The descriptions of how and why Deek has such an effect on her allow Morrison to develop fully the idea of a "race-specific yet nonracist home" ("Home" 5).

Deek and the others in Ruby remind Connie of the city in which the nuns found her. When Consolata is in her thirties and accompanies Mary to a pharmacy in Ruby, Consolata realizes that she "knew she knew" the people in the town, although she has never seen them before. Morrison writes:

> Something unbridled was going on under the scalding sun . . . As Consolata watched that reckless joy, she heard a faint but insistent Sha sha sha. Sha sha sha. Then a memory of just such skin and just such men, dancing with women in the streets to music beating like an infuriated heart, torsos still, hips making small circles above legs moving so rapidly it was fruitless to decipher how such ease was possible. These men here were not dancing, however; they were laughing, running, calling to each other and to women doubled over in glee. And although they were living here in a hamlet, not in a loud city full of glittering black people, Consolata knew she knew them. (226)

The body movements, the skin, the emotional expressions, and the sounds of the people of Ruby trigger the childhood memory of the city in which she lived until she was nine. The connection she makes between the people of Ruby and the people of the remembered place is based on the similar ways in which the people move. The connection is "race-specific" in the sense that she sees both the residents of Ruby and the people in her hometown as "black," but the connection is not "racist" because the movement of the people, the emotional expressions, and the sounds are the most significant basis of the connection, not the color of the skin. The "loud city full of glittering black people" (the childhood home of Consolata) and Ruby are superimposed in the mind of Consolata: the "all black town" named Ruby, Oklahoma, and the South American city become one.

The words "glittering black people" (226) can be interpreted as Morrison's way of downplaying the significance of the potential skin color differences between the people of Ruby and the people in the South American city where Consolata was born. While Consolata is feeling this connection between the two cultures, she sees Deek for the first time. When she sees him, she continues to hear "[s]ha sha sha. Sha sha sha," and the sight of his profile makes "the wing of a feathered thing, undead, flutte[r] in her stomach" (226). The social death that takes place when the American nuns indoctrinate Consolata and the Indian girls involves the erasure of some of their deepest cultural beliefs. This social death is represented as the nuns' intention "to help them despise everything that had once made their lives worthwhile and to offer them instead the privilege of knowing the one and only God and a chance, thereby, for redemption" (227). Deek enables Consolata to remember her "severed part" (*Jazz* 159), the culture from which she was uprooted. Indeed, she thinks of the "fire-ruined house" where they spend time together as "her mind's home" (*Paradise* 233).

In the description of Consolata's first sexual encounter with Deek, Morrison presents a harmonious relationship between the physical and the spiritual. As they drive in the dark, Consolata is said to be "sitting next to him who was darker than the darkness they split" (229). As they enter this "darkness," Consolata finds both a spiritual and a physical home. The text reads: "Consolata let the feathers unfold and come unstuck from the walls of a stone-cold womb. Out here where wind was not a help or threat to sunflowers, nor the moon a language of time, of weather, of sowing or harvesting, but a feature of the original world designed for the two of them" (229). The words "[o]ut here" signal that Deek has left the literal and figurative confines of Ruby, which is repeatedly defined in opposition to that which is "out there." The words "original world" echo Reverend Misner's understanding of the cross as the "original mark" and the "original sign" (145, 146). In this passage, the repeated image of feathers, such as "the wing of a feathered thing" (226) and "a feathered thing fighting for wingspread" (227), becomes clear. Deek's visual presence makes Connie hear an elusive sound of motion and flight (the "sha sha sha"). The darkness of Deek's skin color is experienced by Consolata as a "feature of the original world," and not as a racial "feature." The echo, the "sha sha sha," that Connie hears when she sees Deek is the abstract and "faint but insistent" basis of their bond (226). The abstract nature of this sound is an alternative to the concrete and racially essentialist basis of the bond between the 8-rocks: their pride in their "[b]lue-black" skin (193).

When the relationship with Deek ends, the "darkness" she and Deek "split" gains even more metaphysical dimensions as Consolata gradually begins to feel quite separate from the "visible world" (247). First, she gains "bat vision" when a "sunshot sear[s] her right eye" and "she beg[ins] to see best in the dark" (241). And then, instead of living in a "race-specific yet nonracist home" ("Home" 5), Consolata gradually moves into a world of "in sight" (247): "The dimmer the visible world, the more dazzling her 'in sight' became" (247). The "bat vision" (241), a subdued way of seeing in which shadows are easier to see than concrete forms, is replaced with "in sight" once she, as Lone phrases it, "step[s] in" to help Mary Magna and Scout Morgan (245, 247): "[t]he light that Consolata could not bear to approach her own eyes, she endured for the Reverend Mother when she became ill" (247). This "stepping in" is a clear reversal of the "thematic of witnessed dying [or witnessed pain]" which, as Phillip Novak argues, is acutely present in Morrison's range of novels, especially *Sula.*[4] Consolata's intervention is described as her "find[ing] the pinpoint of light" and "[m]anipulating it, widening it, strengthening it" (247). This "pinpoint of light" is a contrast to racial constructs of "light" skin. In *Black Skin, White Masks,* Fanon explains at a key moment that one seen as "black" can often feel that one's "whole body" is "spattered" with "black blood" (112). This idea that race is written upon the "whole" body is the antithesis of the "pinpoint of light" to which Consolata finds access. This "pinpoint of light" is what Consolata calls "seeing in" and "in sight" (247). This "in sight" temporarily blinds Mavis on her first day at the Convent when she sees Mary for the first time, because Mavis is just beginning her personal journey for "in sight." Once Mary Magna dies and Consolata begins to live fully in this state of the invisible, she longs for the "blind season" she experienced with Deek in which "she thought she was seeing for the first time because she was looking so hard" (248). She realizes that there are different types of "seeing in": that which entirely cancels out the "visible world" and that which becomes an alternative way of seeing the visible. Consolata experiences the latter when she and Deek are lovers. She loses him and it and then gradually gains the "pure sight" that makes her eyes "colorless" (248).

Ironically, this "pure sight" and colorlessness are shown to be inadequate when Consolata "imagine[s] how she must appear" (248): "[g]ray-haired, her eyes drained of what eyes were made for" (248). Then a vision of an unknown man comes to her, and her "in sight" is bombarded by his bright "color combinations" (104). Her first impression of this man is as follows:

> He wore a cowboy hat that hid his features, but Consolata couldn't have seen them anyway. Where he sat on the kitchen steps, framed by the door, a triangle of shadow obscured his face but not his clothes: a green vest over a white shirt, red suspenders hanging low on either side of his tan trousers, shiny black work shoes. (251)

The "visible world" becomes so "dim" to Consolata that normally she would see only the shape of the door frame and the "triangle of shadow" surrounding his face, but the colors of the man's clothing defeat the shadowiness of the unfulfilling, though transcendent, way of seeing that Consolata gains once her relationship with Deek ends. Consolata feels "half cursed, half blessed" by her "pure sight" (248). When she has the vision of the unknown man, she rediscovers the pleasure of the actual eyesight she had lost. The vision of this man with the "cowboy hat" (251), instead of the "wide flat hat" (226) Deek wears when she first sees him, offers a mirror image to Consolata. He has "tea-colored hair" and exceptionally green eyes, as she does (252). When he places himself "[n]ot six inches from her face" (252), she is given a close-up view of her own visual presence and is able to feel the oneness of self and other that she experienced while she and Deek were together. This man wears sunglasses, as Consolata does once she gains her "bat vision" (241), but he takes off his glasses to show Consolata that they share the same green eyes: "[h]is eyes, she saw, were as round and green as new apples" (252). A very similar image of shadowiness being overcome appears in *Jazz,* when Golden is momentarily able to see the actuality of the "wild" woman he abstracts to such a great extent: "[H]e looks into the shadow to find her face, and her deer eyes, too" (153). Consolata "find[s] her face" through the mirror image of the man in her vision and begins to heal after the loss of her kindred spirit, Deek.

The image of eyes that look like green "new apples" introduces the ongoing detailed descriptions of the food that Consolata prepares for herself and the women living with her. These descriptions of food are interspersed among the continuations of the individual stories of the Convent women. In each description of Connie's food preparation, Morrison draws attention to color, and as the passages progress, she begins to think about colors in the abstract, dissociated from race. At this point, the reader is led to think about the earlier moments in the novel when color is not racialized, such as the colors of the rock formation of which Gigi dreams and the "blinding white" color of Mary Magna when Mavis first sees her. The reader realizes that these earlier moments were preparations for the full-scale critique of racial meanings of color in "Consolata" and the remaining chapters.

The Revisionist Last Supper

The descriptions of food preparation culminate in the climactic dinner, reminiscent of the biblical "Last Supper," that Consolata serves the Convent women. The first description of Connie's food preparation describes the steps she takes before she can cook "two freshly killed hens" (252). The emphasis is on the way her hands maneuver the skin of the hens. The passage reads:

> She lifts the skin to reach under it, fingering as far as she can. Under the breast, she searches for a pocket close to the wing. Then, holding the breast in her left palm, the fingers of her right tunnel the back skin, gently pushing for the spine. Into all these places—where the skin has been loosened and the membrane separated from the flesh it once protected—she slides butter. Thick. Pale. Slippery. (253)

Before the hen can be roasted and browned, Consolata must insert the "pale" butter. The "loosen[ing]" of the skin of the hen and then the insertion of the pale material that will enable the hen to brown symbolizes a revisioning of the racial constructs of dark skin and pale skin. Instead of the two being defined against one another, in this image, the brownness of the roasted skin depends on the inserted "pale" material. The movements of Consolata's hands are "gently" violent as if Morrison wants to underscore that the revision of racial meanings of "skin" is rigorous work that must be done carefully.

After this food description, there is a lengthy passage continuing the narration of Pallas' story that begins in "Divine," and then the next food description is given.

> Consolata tilts the fowl and peers into their silver and rose cavities. She tosses in salt and scours it all around, then rubs the outer skin with a cinnamon and butter mixture. Onion is added to the bits of neck meat, hearts and giblets speckling the broth. As soon as the hens are roasted brown enough and tender she sets them aside so they can reclaim their liquids. (255)

This second passage contains more colors than the first because Morrison is thinking about the ways that color could be made independent of racial meanings. The beauty of the "silver and rose" has no connection whatsoever to race, and one would not expect to see such colors within such an ordinary object as a dead hen. The "cinnamon and butter mixture" "rub[bed]" on the "outer skin" of the hens evokes the colloquial saying in some African American linguistic communities that "it [blackness] doesn't rub off." Since the "cinnamon and butter" are "rub[bed]" on the skin (255), the reader is led to think about these colors as evanescent and glaze-like rather than being comparable to the "stain" of "racial purity" (194) that is the awful consequence of the "Disallowing" and the core of the "8-rock" sensibility.

The revision of racial meanings to make color independent of them is most heightened in the next description of food, which appears after a continuation of the story of Gigi begun in the chapter entitled "Grace." This continuation of Gigi's story ends with an image of her pent-up sadness: "even now, when she realized she had not approved of herself in a long, long time, her eyes were desert-skull dry" (257). Immediately after the melancholy tone of this statement, the most jubilant image yet of Consolata's food preparation appears: "Consolata is peeling and quartering small brown potatoes. She simmers them in water seasoned with pan juices, bay leaf and sage before arranging them in a skillet where they turn darkly gold. She sprinkles paprika and seeds of blackest pepper over them. 'Oh, yes,' she says. 'Oh, yes'" (257). The ecstasy and self-affirming nature of this moment for Consolata signals that through this food she will help Gigi locate "an unbridled, authentic self" (177). The gold and black color imagery represents Consolata's regaining of the "race-specific yet nonracist home" she shared with Deek ("Home" 5). In the next chapter, "Lone," Consolata is actually remembered by Deek as "a beautiful golden-skinned, outside woman with moss-green eyes" (279). The "seeds of blackest pepper" "sprinkle[d]" over the "darkly gold" potatoes are the aesthetic alternative to the "blue-black" "seeds" the 8-rocks aim to continue to "plant" in their family trees.

After the interspersed descriptions of the food preparation end, there is the scene of the climactic dinner in which the young women living in the Convent witness a physically altered Consolata suddenly ready to speak to the women collectively and assume the role of their teacher. During the preparation of the meal, Consolata gains knowledge about the sources of hunger that plague the women and herself. As they sit down to eat, she finally formally introduces herself to the women who have lived in her house for months and, in some cases, years. The text reads: "The table is set; the food placed. Consolata takes off her apron. With the aristocratic gaze of the blind she sweeps the women's faces and says, 'I call myself Consolata Sosa. If you want to be here you do what I say. Eat how I say. Sleep when I say. And I will teach you what you are hungry for'" (262). In contrast to the way in which Consolata's "uncontrollable" hunger makes her bite Deek's lip and make him fear that she "just [wanted] to lap the blood it shed" (279), that which she believes the Convent women "are hungry for" is "bloodless food" (265). The reader knows, based on the detailed descriptions of the food preparation, that Consolata does serve meat, but this meat is symbolically "bloodless." Perhaps Consolata does not see the blood as she cooks, because the blood is overshadowed by the intensity of the other colors: the "silver and rose" (255), the "darkly gold" (257), the "blackest" color (257), and the "cinnamon and butter" (255).

The link between hunger, bloodlessness, and color recalls particular descriptions in *Beloved* (1987) of Sethe's inability to appreciate color after the death of Beloved and the way in which Baby Suggs spent her last days "pondering color" (4). The image of Sethe becoming "as color conscious as a hen" (38–39), "after the 'Misery' (which is what [Stamp Paid] called her rough response to the Fugitive Bill)" (171), is rewritten when Consolata revels in the aesthetic quality of colors as she cooks the hens. The "Disallowing" shapes *Paradise* as much as the "Misery" shapes *Beloved.* Before Deek realizes that he has never stopped loving Consolata and attempts to save her from his brother's bullet, he rejects her and sees her as that which the 8-rocks must "disallow" because of the historical fact of the "Disallowing." The pain of the "Disallowing" makes the Haven and Ruby residents extremely "color conscious" and aware of the difference between lighter-skinned and darker-skinned blackness. When Consolata cooks the food, she becomes "color conscious" in a very different manner as she discovers the pleasure of a color that is both light and dark: the "darkly gold" (*Paradise* 257). The sustenance she finds in "color" is what Sethe remembers Baby Suggs needing as she approached death: Sethe remembers how "*starved* for color" Baby Suggs was during her last days (*Beloved* 38; italics mine).

Consolata is the "color conscious" cook whom Sethe is unable to be. Consolata wants to teach the Convent women to be as "hungry for" (*Paradise* 262) color as Baby Suggs was. The reader imagines that Baby Suggs, with her great hunger for color, "pondered" all the colors in the room and then yearned for more. Sethe feels that the "two orange squares [in the quilt]" articulate the other "dark and muted" colors in the quilt. These subdued colors are the presence of absence in her opinion, and by creating such a contrast, the orange makes this tangible sense of "absence shout" (*Beloved* 38). An absence that "shouts" is an apt description of the ghost of Beloved as well as of the way that ghosts of the past haunt each of the Convent women. When the Convent women are fundamentally "altered" (265) once they begin to understand the nature of their emotional hunger, the narrator explains that "if a friend came" to the Convent, the women would seem so different, and yet the observer would "at first b[e] unable to say exactly what was absent" (266). In contrast to the "shouting absence" of color in Baby Suggs' room, the narrator explains that this observer of the altered state of the Convent women would finally notice "how calmly themselves they seemed" and realize "what was missing: unlike some people in Ruby, the Convent women were no longer haunted" (266).

The move toward this nonromantic state of paradise begins in *Jazz.* At one point in *Jazz,* when Golden Grey imagines the possibility of his "no longer [being] haunted" by the father whom he never knew and the "blackness" he considers "unfathomable" (150), he decides, "I will locate it so that the severed part can remember the snatch, the slice of its disfigurement. Perhaps then the arm will no longer be a phantom, but will take its own shape, grow its own muscle and bone, and its blood will pump the loud singing that has found the purpose of its serenade. Amen" (159). The "phantom" or "severed part" that "grow[s] its own muscle and bone" (159) is comparable to the "alive[ness]" of the "open bod[ies]" (265) painted on the cellar floor. These alternative bodies "take [their] own shape" to such an extent that they seem more "alive" than the ones the women actually "wore" (265). Golden Grey and Consolata are literally orphans or "severed part[s]" (159), but all the Convent women are orphans in the psychological sense of not feeling a sense of belonging and searching for feelings of rootedness. Similarly, the founders of Haven were "orphaned" by those who committed the "Disallowing." Golden Grey, Consolata, the Convent women, and the 8-rocks are all "disfigured," but Morrison uses Consolata and the Convent women to imagine an example of a "severed part remember[ing] the snatch, the slice of its disfigurement" (159). Indeed, the narrator explains that the Convent women, "in spite of or because their bodies ache" (264), enter the "dreamer's tale," in which their body silhouettes on the cellar floor gain "muscle and bone" (159). Their aching bodies, or "severed part[s]" (159), literally "remember the snatch" when they lie on the floor of the cellar and Consolata paints "templates" of their bodies.

It is most apparent that they are "born again" when the revision of the opening of the Book of Genesis appears: "In the beginning the most important thing was the template" (263). In contrast to the biblical image of Eve being made from a part of Adam, the women's "templates" are the amorphous, abstract shapes Consolata paints around their bodies. As opposed to the insularity and closure in which the Ruby leaders believe, these templates are the epitome of "openness." The Convent women fill in these shapes. Instead of the taking apart that is figured in the biblical image of Adam's rib being removed, the templates allow the women to put many different signs together. The miscellaneous signs that are painted in the templates represent the particular losses the women have suffered, the "severed part[s]" that are reclaimed when the women begin the process of "no longer [being] haunted" and learn how to "re-member" painful "phantom[s]" (*Jazz* 159). For example, the "red peonies" are originally part of "the bleeding black boy scene" that haunts Gigi (*Paradise* 256). When they are painted in the "open body" of Gigi on the cellar floor (265), Morrison makes the reader think about both the wonder and risk of "art therapy." The wonder is that Gigi might gain a genuine empathy for the wounded young boy. The risk is that she simply aestheticizes and romanticizes the pain of the little boy's wounded body. The painted "peonies" are either a sign of Gigi's romanticization of pain or a sign of the deep connection Gigi shares with the wounded boy.

Cross-Racializing the Wound

In the two final chapters, "Lone" and "Save-Marie," it becomes apparent that Morrison wants the reader to think optimistically about the possibility of genuine cross-racial connections. Morrison further develops the idea of the "wounded body" becoming the "open body" and the idea that empathic cross-racial connection through pain is entirely possible. In "The Wound of History: Walcott's *Omeros* and the Postcolonial Poetics of Affliction," Jahan Ramazani argues that Walcott is deeply concerned with "cultural and racial hybridity" and that "[o]ne of Walcott's recurrent metaphors for cultural hybridity is the scar" (410). In the last two chapters of *Paradise,* it becomes abundantly clear that the images of violence done to bodies are being used to illuminate what Ramazani refers to as the "cross-racializing of the wound" (Ramazani 415).

In "Lone" when the massacre of the Convent women is described, this "cross-racializing of the wound" occurs when Deek is emotionally wounded by the wounding of Consolata, and his bond with his twin is severed. Morrison alters the "thematic of witnessed dying" by highlighting Deek's attempt to stop the death of Consolata, even though until the moment of his intervention he is one of the leaders of the violent raid on the Convent (Novak 186). The text reads:

> Deacon Morgan needs the sunglasses, but they are nestled in his shirt pocket. He looks at Consolata and sees in her eyes what has been drained from them and from himself as well. There is blood near her lips. It takes his breath away. He lifts his hand to halt his brother's and discovers who, between them, is the stronger man. The bullet enters her forehead. (289)

In the eyes of his brother, Consolata is the embodiment of the forces "out there" that have slowly infiltrated the boundaries of Ruby: "The women in the Convent were for him a flaunting parody of the nineteen Negro ladies of his and his brother's youthful memory and perfect understanding" (279). Morrison reveals that this "perfect understanding" is quite flawed in that it depends on the premise that "8-rock" black bodies are literal inscriptions of the cultural beauty and strength of Ruby and Haven. When Deek "sees in [Consolata's] eyes what has been drained from them and from himself as well" (289), he can no longer read her body, as his brother does, as a literal inscription of that which should remain "out there" so that it will not threaten that which is inside Ruby. He sees his own loss through her loss, or more accurately, he re-members his own loss through the re-membering of her loss. Deek sees the presence of Consolata's loss; that which "has been drained" (289) reappears in her eyes. His own loss and the possibility of his recovery are placed alongside her own loss and the possibility of her recovery. The "blood near her lips" is the blood of one of the wounded women. And yet the reader is reminded of Deek's own blood that is on her lips after she bites him. If this blood is understood as both the blood of the Convent woman and the reappearance of the blood of Deek, then the blood ultimately symbolizes the deep connection Deek shares with the Convent women once he witnesses the wounding of Consolata.

Ramazani argues that there "are the undeniable risks of Walcott's free riding of the wound trope across moral and historical divisions, but his [Walcott's] wager is that they are risks worth taking" (415). Similarly, when Morrison places the pain of Consolata's physical wound alongside the emotional wound of Deek, she takes the risk of mystifying the pain and violence inflicted on Consolata. To avoid this risk, she emphasizes how deeply Deek is affected by the sight of her being shot. Deek is fundamentally "altered" (265) by the murder of Consolata, and his consciousness expands past the confines of Ruby and the 8-rock sensibility after being unable to save her from his twin brother's bullet. Perhaps the most emphatic examples of how Deek's insular 8-rock sensibility changes after Consolata's death are the descriptions of how he begins to feel "exotic" (300) and how he speaks fondly of a wide range of beloved, faraway places in a manner so strikingly similar to the way in which Consolata tells the Convent women about her beloved childhood memories in her native country.

A juxtaposition of the two following passages from "Consolata" and "Save Marie," the final chapter in the novel, reveals the way in which Deek and Consolata ultimately share such a similar sense of the "beautiful": one that can heal the "moral and historical divisions" (415) between the leader of a patriarchal "all-black town" ironically named after a woman and the "certainly not white" "Reverend Mother" (223, 265) of a multiracial convent with a "blessed malelessness" (177). In the first passage, the narrator explains what Consolata told the Convent women, and in the second one, the narrator explains what Deek told Reverend Misner.

> [S]he told them of a place where white sidewalks met the sea and fish the color of plums swam alongside children. She spoke of fruit that tasted the way sapphires look and boys using rubies for dice. Of scented cathedrals made of gold where gods and goddesses sat in the pews with the congregation. Of carnations tall as trees. Dwarfs with diamonds for teeth. Snakes aroused by poetry and bells. Then she told them of a woman named Piedade, who sang but never said a word. (264)

> He spoke of a wall in Ravenna, Italy, white in the late afternoon sun with wine colored shadows pressing its edge. Of two children on a beach offering him a shell formed like an S—how open their faces, how loud the bells. Of salt water burning his face on a troop ship. Of colored girls in slacks waving from the door of a canning factory. Then he told of his grandfather who walked barefoot for two hundred miles rather than dance. (301)

The openness of the faces Deek remembers recalls the "open bod[ies]" the Convent women discover with Consolata's guidance (265). The "loud . . . bells" in Deek's memory recall the "loud dreaming" that begins immediately after Consolata tells the Convent women about her memories of her native land (264). Consolata remembers the merging of the boundaries between the sidewalk and the sea, the "gods and goddesses" and the congregation, the small stature of dwarfs and the magnificence of diamonds. Deek's memory of "wine colored shadows" articulating the "edge" of a "white wall" also signals the undoing of boundaries.

His memory of how the "wine colored shadows" "pres[s]" the "edge" of this wall can be contrasted to the way in which the words and the "painted fist" inscribed on the "Oven" cause it to be treated as a "wall" (101), instead of being treated as a body (in the references to its mouth and lip). At one point when feeling outraged over the debate over the words on the "Oven," Steward cannot imagine how the younger generation would "wan[t] to alter words of beaten iron" (99). Instead of being beaten into a wall, the "wine colored shadows" gently "pres[s]" the wall Deek remembers seeing in Italy. The evanescence of the "wine colored shadows" is Deek and Consolata's alternative to the enclosed "all-black town" of Ruby (5). Furthermore, the "wine-colored shadows" are examples of synaesthesia, as is the "fruit [Connie remembers] that tasted the way sapphires look" (264).

Morrison suggests that these memories of Deek and Consolata are examples of literal food and aesthetic sustenance, whereas once the "Oven" becomes a "wall," it becomes a source of division, not a source of nourishment.

There are ultimately many ways of reading the words on the "wall of the Oven" (101): "Beware the Furrow of His Brow" (86, 93); "Be the Furrow of His Brow" (87); "We *are* the power . . ." (93); "Furrow of His Brow" (93); and "Be the Furrow of *Her* Brow" (159). When Steward shoots a bullet into Consolata's forehead, the statement "Be the Furrow of *Her* Brow" (159) gains a heightened significance. The wounded "[f]urrow of her [Consolata's] brow" does not symbolize an angry God, as the "furrow of his Brow" does, but rather the damage done to Connie's sacred body. The "Oven" is viewed as a "sacred body" by the Haven and Ruby residents before it figuratively loses its "mouth" and "lip" and is rendered an inarticulate "wall" (101). When Soane and Lone care for Connie after she has been fatally wounded, they close her eyes, but her wound appears as another "eye" that is "wet and lidless" (291). This "third" eye that cannot be closed represents the inviolateness and sacredness of the "open body" Consolata and the other woman discover together (291, 265). In *What Else But Love?* Philip Weinstein argues in reference to Sethe in *Beloved* that Morrison "understands the body as sacred despite the damage done to it" (77). In the last chapter of *Paradise,* "Save-Marie," the sacredness of the damaged body is demonstrated through Deek's ways of seeing "outside of [the] loss" (301) he feels after the violence inflicted on Consolata. "[O]utside of that loss" (301), he discovers a sacred beauty in his wife, Soane.

Before the massacre in the Convent, he feels that his wife, Soane, "was as beautiful as it was possible for a good woman to be; she kept a good home and did good works everywhere" (112). After Consolata's death, he stops separating physical beauty from moral goodness or spirituality. Indeed, he wishes he could tell his wife: "[S]he was grand, more beautiful than he believed a woman could be; that her untamable hair framed a face of planes so sharp he wanted to touch; that after she spoke, the smile that followed made the sun look like a fool" (301). When Deek finally attributes a transcendent beauty and sacredness to the body of Soane, he is both connecting her to his way of seeing Consolata and separating her: seeing her "outside of that loss" (301). Rather than emphasizing the physical differences between Soane and the "golden-skinned" woman (279), or suggesting that Deek's love for Consolata demonstrates his internalization of antiblack racism, Morrison celebrates the way in which Soane and Consolata become superimposed in Deek's new way of seeing.

Morrison's focus on that which Weinstein identifies as the "sacred" nature of the "damaged" body is more heightened in *Paradise* than in any of her other novels. Misner's contemplation of the Christian "cross" as both "ordinary and sublime" (146) underscores the centrality of this thematic of the sacred though damaged body. Another explicit reference to the sacred though damaged body is the image of the cross that Seneca makes during one of her acts of self-mutilation: "Seneca did another street. An intersection, in fact, for it crossed the one she'd done a moment ago" (262). Seneca damages her body and also marks it with a sacred sign. Her self-mutilation is her impossible attempt to transcend her body.

The most horrifying aspect of her self-mutilation is that she imagines her body as "out there," the name Morrison uses throughout the novel to refer to the world beyond Ruby and the characters' experiences of rigid boundaries between self and other. In the last chapters of the novel, Morrison presents "out here" as the experience characters have when they overcome the feeling that there are rigid and traumatic boundaries between self and other. At a key moment in "Lone," the second reference is suddenly made to "out here" (270), the first reference appearing when Consolata and Deek are having the affair and Consolata feels that she is "out here" in the "original world" with him (229). As Lone drives back to Ruby after going to the Convent to warn the women of the danger she heard the "8-rock" men plotting against them, she thinks about the "road between Ruby and the Convent" (270) as a specifically female road of passage, a road on which women walked and men drove. As she drives on this road, she feels connected to the women whom she remembers or imagines walking this road: the women who become a part of the Convent after traveling through Ruby and those who come to the Convent for assistance during troubled times. The fact that Lone feels connected to these female pedestrians even as she occupies the male position of driving through the road is another example, like Deek's ultimate connection with Consolata, of the overcoming of otherness that occurs in the last two chapters of the novel.

This road is another site of the "new color combinations" (104) celebrated throughout the novel as an alternative to the way of seeing embodied in the "8-rock rule" of the "all-black town" (5): "[o]ut here in a red and gold land cut through now and then with a black rock or a swatch of green" (270). These colors, red, gold, black, and green, are the colors of the flag of Ghana, the first black African colony to receive its independence (in 1957) and the colors of Pan-Africanism (the "red is the blood, the yellow is the sun, the black is the skin, the green is the land").[5] Under British rule, the area that is now Ghana was called the "Gold Coast." Ruby, the "all-black town," is mentally colonized by the lingering effects of the "Disallowing" on its leaders. Deek gains mental independence from this colonization through the "golden-skinned woman" (279). Instead of offering Deek a literal homeland, as Ghana was embraced by Pan-Africanists, Consolata helps the Convent women and him realize that they are "hungry for" a spiritual home (262).

In "Save-Marie," the last chapter of the novel, the Pan-African colors (red, black, green, and gold) are rewritten as brown, white, green, red, and "plum black" (305) and used once again to signify the need to move from racialized skin color to a reclamation of the sheer range and abstract quality of color itself. Reverend Misner and Anna Flood "doub[t] the convenient mass disappearance of the victims" of the massacre and go to the Convent "to look for themselves" (303). They discover that the bodies and any sign of the violence have disappeared, but instead of finding signs that the dead bodies were hidden or destroyed, they find signs that the Convent women transcended their suffering, instead of simply dying. The colors brown, white, green, red, and "plum black" (305) frame this scene:

> It was when he returned, as they stood near the chair, her hands balancing brown eggs and white cloth, his fingers looking doubled with long pepper pods—green, red and plum black—that they saw it. Or sensed it, rather, for there was nothing to see. A door, she said later. "No, a window," he said, laughing. "That's the difference between us. You see a door; I see a window."
>
> Anna laughed too. They expanded on the subject: What did a door mean? what a window? focusing on the sign rather than the event; excited by the invitation rather than the party. (305)

The addition of the "brown" and the "white" to the Pan-African colors and the subtraction of the "gold" or "yellow" can be interpreted as a rewriting of the image of the "woman in yellow" in *Tar Baby.* The whiteness of the eggs carried by the "woman in yellow" accentuates her "tar-black fingers" (46). Anna, on the other hand, "balanc[es] brown eggs and [a] white cloth" (305). The brown color against the white is not as sharp a contrast as the white against the black. The "plum black" as opposed to the "tar black" also signals that Morrison is undoing the starkness of the contrast between whiteness and blackness and presenting the "transcendent beauty" of this range of colors, instead of the "transcendent beauty" of the "tar-black[ness]" (47) of the "woman in yellow." In *Tar Baby* the "woman in yellow" holds the "three chalk-white eggs in the air" (47), "aloft between earlobe and shoulder" (45), whereas the brown eggs are described as "warm umber in [Anna's] hands" (305). The texture of Anna's eggs is aestheticized, in addition to the aestheticization of the colors, unlike the eggs of the "woman in yellow," which are "untouchable" and as suspended in an unfamiliar aura as the body of the woman who carries them (45). The "woman in yellow" "float[s]" through the automatic door of the Paris supermarket (46). A very different type of passageway is described immediately after the colorful picture of Anna and Reverend Misner holding the eggs and the peppers: the "door" to the "other side" that Anna "sense[s]" and the "window" to the "other side" that Reverend Misner "sense[s]" (305).

Consolata and the Convent women become a part of this "other side" after the massacre. Instead of finding the dead bodies of the women, Anna and the Reverend "sens[e]" their escape to the "other side" (305). The narrative explanation that Anna and Reverend Misner fall prey to thinking about the "sign" of this "other side," rather than the "event," the "party" itself (305), illuminates the narrative assertion in "Divine" that the "cross [Reverend Misner] held was abstract; the absent body was real" (146). The "window" and the "door" to the "other side" are not the concrete manifestations of the "other side," for "there was nothing to see" (305). Anna and Reverend Misner discover the realness of the "other side," the fact that the "absent" bodies of Consolata and the Convent women have not been obliterated but are in "another realm" (301). Morrison emphasizes the realness of this other "realm" and "event," because she finally aims to overshadow the trauma of the construction of race and gender with "the unambivalent bliss of going home to be at home—the ease of coming back to love begun" (305, 318). She intends for this home, this "other side" that Consolata and the Convent women enter after the massacre, to be understood as both "ordinary and sublime" (146) or paradise on earth.

In the final image of the text, the "ordinary and sublime" frame the picture of Piedade and Consolata "down here in Paradise" (318): the "sea trash gleams," the "[d]iscarded bottle caps sparkle near a broken sandal," a "small dead radio plays the quiet surf," and Consolata's "emerald eyes adore the black face" of Piedade (318). Consolata has early childhood memories of Piedade, who was a "singing woman who never spoke" (285). With this last picture of Consolata's "emerald eyes" and Piedade's "black face," Morrison returns to the image, presented in *The Bluest Eye* (1970), of "very blue eyes in a very black skin" (211). Instead of signifying racial self-hatred, however, the final image in *Paradise* is one of love. The "black face" is "framed" by the background of the ocean, instead of being "framed" by the paradigm of race. The concreteness of the faces of both women dissolves into the abstract quality of colors. Indeed, the face of the woman with "emerald eyes" is not described as one concrete color, but rather a site in which "[a]ll the colors of seashells—wheat, roses, pearl—fuse" (318). Before this final image, there are "resurrection" scenes in which Gigi, Mavis, Pallas, and Seneca have encounters with people who were a part of their pre-Convent life. In her "resurrection" scene, Pallas is described as "beatific" (311). It is implied that after the Convent raid, Gigi, Mavis, Pallas, and Seneca become angels living on earth. It is also implied that Consolata is the only one who actually dies during the Convent raid and enters the realm of "paradise." The reader is led to finally understand Consolata as a Christ figure whose body at the end of the novel is both "absent" and "real" (146), like the Christ figure that Reverend Misner envisions when he contemplates the meaning of the cross. As a revisionist Christ figure, the "gospel" that Consolata teaches the reader is that the body can be reclaimed as "open" and not marked, and color can be reclaimed as entirely abstract and not a racial phenomenon.

In *Paradise,* Morrison proves the truth of Barbara Christian's recognition that theory takes place in literature as she transmutes the contemporary discussion of the binary, sex versus gender, into a focus on race versus culture. The 8-rock leaders in *Paradise* believe that blackness is a natural, visual mark, whereas the central character, Consolata (Connie), ultimately emerges as a supernatural healer who experiences blackness as a fantastically elusive, nonracial, but unmistakably cultural, connection. She demonstrates that, given the incredible naturalization of race, supernatural tactics may be necessary. The Southwest ultimately becomes the supernatural space, the "wild west," in which Morrison wrestles to separate cultural hybridity from the fetishism of racially hybrid bodies.

six

The Critique of Dilution Anxiety in *Sent for You Yesterday*

JUST as Morrison, through the 8-rock metaphor, captures the roots, depth, and authenticity tied to the dark-skinned phallus of the Ruby patriarchs, the rendering of skin color as a phallic organ is at the heart of John Edgar Wideman's *Sent for You Yesterday* (1981). This post–Black Arts movement novel unhinges dilution anxiety, fear of loss of "authentic blackness," and the often unconscious transformation of skin color into a phallic organ. Wideman makes the black male albino a sign of the castrated black man. His representation of albinism as castration is very similar to the images of albinism in Afrocentric texts explaining the biological benefits of melanin. In *Melanin: The Chemical Key to Black Greatness* (1988), an Afrocentric response to scientific racism, albinism is described in the following manner: "The albino (white man) had numerous body defects due to the lack of the genetic material to produce EUMELANIN."[1] Wideman explores images of the albino in black gazes and confronts the anxiety that the black albino might produce when people unconsciously associate strength and health with dark-skinned blackness. Looking through Brother as if he is a mirror, the other characters discover their own fear of loss of authentic blackness. Wideman makes "see through skin" the prime ongoing description of Brother; this central character is the "diluted" body that makes people look at the lack that terrifies them. As Wideman depicts the dilution anxiety that shapes other characters' reactions to Brother's albinism, he foregrounds images of the black phallus as he explores the unconscious ways in which fetishized skin color becomes a phallic organ.

Wideman's central focus on black masculinity is now beginning to receive critical attention. While situating Wideman's work in black postmodernism, Madhu Dubey, in *Signs and Cities: Black Literary Postmodernism* (2003), brilliantly confronts the contradictions that shape his representations of male voyeurism. Rolland Murray's *Our Living Manhood: Literature, Black Power, and Masculine Ideology* (2006) includes an analysis of the connections between Wideman's depictions of black masculinity and his emergence as a writer during the 1960s Black Power movement. Wideman, in a 1994 interview with Ishmael Reed, explains his sense of the unrecognized productivity of the Black Power movement. He states, "Black Power is a very complex concept. [. . .] From Black Power doesn't automatically follow anti-Semitism, racism, etc. [. . .] Black Power is not the demon."[2] *Sent for You Yesterday,* one of Wideman's post–Black Power texts, is now being read by critics as a direct response to the Black Power movement. My focus on the dilution anxiety triggered by Brother's albinism seeks to place *Sent for You Yesterday* as a quintessential post–Black Power/Black Arts movement novel in which Wideman reclaims the kinship term "Brother" as used during the Black Power/Black Arts era and explores the anxieties underlying the celebrations of the black phallus at the core of the Black Power/Black Arts movement. In the process of depicting the anxieties surrounding black men's relation to the phallus (cultural power), Wideman often includes two-dimensional images of black and white women even as he seeks to render black maleness in its full complexity. In *Sent for You Yesterday,* his ultimate critique of dilution anxiety (fear of loss of authentic blackness) does not include a critique of the lack tied, through the male gaze, to women's bodies. Wideman's depiction of women, in *Sent for You Yesterday,* is a means to an end, the ultimate celebration of the albino Brother as the "Soul Brother" who will live forever in the memories of others and who can never be castrated even though he lacks the Black Power "kryptonite" (the dark skin fetishized during the Black Power movement).[3]

Brother, the main character, is a "black" albino whose albinism is experienced by other African American characters as grotesque and inert. After describing the discomfort that racial essentialists feel when confronted by Brother's albino skin color, Wideman wrestles to liberate Brother from the trauma of racial embodiment and place him in an eschatological or otherworldly realm. Wideman creates mixtures of the eschatological and the scatological as he demonstrates the ways in which the body can be experienced as inanimate and the ways in which the body can be experienced as a site of motion and music (a "dream of some other place" [26]). John French, for example, imagines that silence would "break" his body apart and make it feel amputated. Wideman writes, "When Albert stopped playing you could look down at your toes and see that black pit start to open. See your crusty toes dug in at the edge of nothing. You could snap your fingers once and seven years be over. You could keep snapping till the skin breaks and the bones break and ain't even a raw bloody stump left to wiggle" (69). Once this passage is connected to the phallic desire of Albert in the scene with the "fine woman" who is "[s]o white she could be black" (72), the "raw bloody stump" John imagines as a consequence of the end of the music signals that no one really has the phallus and that the possibility of its loss spurs the fetishizing of the object of desire.

The descriptions of Albert's phallic desire and the "fine woman" who is the object of this desire appear after the descriptions of how John imagines that he would feel castrated without the sound of Albert's "fine piano music" (70). The "fine piano music" finally represents the eternal life gained once Albert dies, and it is remembered by the imagination of others and by the hands of Brother. The "fine woman" finally represents the circumstances that killed Albert; Albert's involvement with the "fine woman" is the reason he is killed. As part of their sexual "play," as she "twirls [the towel] till it's taut and pops it over the foot of the bed" (73), the unnamed lover tells Albert, "I ought to break your neck. I ought to whip you back out in the street" (73). The previously "limp" towel becoming "taut" symbolizes the fear of castration underlying male illusions of having the phallus. In addition to being "so white she could be black" (72), the woman is so "perfect" (72) she could transform herself into a phallic male, instead of a "castrated" woman.

Wideman continues to ponder sexual and racial experiences of lack and the masking of lack in the narrative about the relationship between Lucy and Carl. Lucy Tate, when a young teenager, remembers Albert through "a piece of his head" or "skull" (104) that remained in the living room of the Tates after he was murdered. Lucy shows this piece of skull to Carl French, her teenage lover, during their first sexual encounter. Lucy tells Carl, "I could tell you something about being grown. And show you something too" (101). And when Carl responds, "Show me" (101), Lucy exhibits three signs of what happened when Albert was murdered. The first sign is the rocking chair in which Mrs. Tate was sitting when the shooting happened, the bullet holes in the piano are the second sign, and the third sign is the piece of Albert's skull Lucy has safeguarded in the "top drawer of the dresser in the far corner of her bedroom" (103). Carl does not believe that this object is what Lucy says it is. When she shows it, he is expecting her to show her body to him, but instead she shows the object, then misrepresents it, in Carl's opinion, as "Albert Wilkes' skull" (104). Carl feels that she is "[t]esting his manhood" (105). As he tries to interpret the object, he considers a range of signifiers: "A pearl. A baby tooth. A chip of ivory. A piece of seashell. A rare, white pebble from the grimy hillside where the trains run" (104). After thinking about this range of possible signifiers, he decides that the object is "just a seashell sliver" (105).[4] While he and Lucy are sitting on her bed, Lucy places the object between them, and once Carl gathers the courage to pick up the object and give it back to Lucy, they become physically intimate.

Initially the object is a substitute for her body, when she shows it instead of undressing herself as Carl expects. The object is also a love potion in the sense that it propels their first coitus. Since Lucy is the one who produces the object and places it between them, it does seem that the object is also a substitute for the phallus, especially when she tells Carl, "This the biggest piece I found. Clean just like you see. No blood. No hair. White and clean" (105). Carl remains incredulous, as if he refuses to let her control the phallic object. Wideman writes: "Carl stares down at the seashell. He would taste it if he had the nerve. Run his tongue over it and taste the salt. He knew better than to believe what she said. Albert Wilkes a black man like him. Bones had skin. You'd see the brown of Albert Wilkes if it was really him laying there" (105). The idea that "[b]ones had skin" is a vivid example of that which Frantz Fanon referred to as the "internalization [interiorisation]—or better, the epidermalization [epidermisation]—of this inferiority."[5] Carl refuses to believe that the "white" object could be the remains of Albert Wilkes, "a black man like him" (105). His desire to "taste" the object strengthens the idea that the object is a substitute, phallic object: "if he had the nerve," Carl would place this phallic object in his mouth and "[r]un his tongue over it" (105).

As he attempts to "conquer" Lucy's body, he remains as bewildered as he is when staring at the piece of Albert's skull. The smoothness and abundance of Lucy's skin overcompensates for the lack of the "brown" skin he expects to be a part of Albert's skull: "Little Lucy so smooth, so much naked Lucy skin he doesn't know where to begin, where to stop" (106). In this image her skin is a landscape to be conquered, and as the passage progresses, he imagines his sexual organ as a "train flying like a giant black bullet" (107), an image which recalls the "scare game" (18) that Carl and Brother play when they are young boys. In the moment of orgasm, Carl imagines that, instead of his sexual organ being the "giant black" bullet-like train, the train is a force that "smashes into him and shrinks to the size of a BB and roars out again full size through the end of his joint spewing black smoke onto Lucy's belly" (107). In the "scare game," Carl and Brother would stand at the train tracks, watch the approaching trains, and then attempt to wait until the last possible moment before running across the tracks. The loser of the game is the person who becomes "scare[d]" and runs across the tracks first. Before Doot explains the game, he imagines Carl thinking about "an ocean rushing to the end of the world" (18), an image which confirms that the train symbolizes another world, and life after death. When Carl imagines a train "smash[ing] into him" during the moment of orgasm, instead of the train "tracks . . . tak[ing] him somewhere else" (27), he dies on the tracks and does not make it to "some other place" (26).

Immediately before Lucy and Carl become physically intimate, Lucy weeps over the murder of Albert Wilkes. When Carl imagines his sexual organ as a bullet-like train, it is clear that the lovemaking between himself and Lucy is an odd reenactment of the death of Wilkes. Wilkes dies as he plays the piano and Carl feels that he is dying when he has the orgasm. Lucy's body is the aim and object of Carl's lovemaking, whereas Lucy's object or aim during the lovemaking is to hear the "sweet, sweet good music" (102). She tells Carl before they become physically intimate, "Sometimes I think I'd be willing to die if I could play one time as fine and sweet as Albert Wilkes played that afternoon" (102). Albert Wilkes is shot because he "played" with the body of the unnamed white woman; racial and sexual politics cause him to die in the middle of the piano performance he is giving for Lucy and Brother. Through the piece of the skull, Lucy imagines that she can separate Albert from the realm of masculinity and make him a sign of that which Carl's lovemaking cannot penetrate. This idea is conveyed when Lucy sends Brother, "that first morning after" (111), to deliver the following message: "That she hadn't given. She had showed him something. She showed it to him, but it was still hers, like that piece of Albert Wilkes in the handkerchief in her drawer" (111). Lucy has learned that, through the lens of the dominant ideology of heterosexual relations, she has, indeed, lost "something" (111) in this first sexual encounter. She inveighs against this notion of loss by insisting that she "showed" Carl "something" and that, unlike "something" given, "something" shown remains in one's possession.

Unlike Lucy's sense that she lost nothing in their first sexual encounter, Carl loses control of his bodily functions, to such an extent that he wonders at the moment of orgasm if he has urinated or ejaculated: "But it's not black and not smoking. A little sticky whitish puddle and scattered driplets, cool to the touch as he finally tests one with the tip of a finger. Not black, not smoking and thank God, not pee" (107). Carl thinks that if the object were a piece of Albert's skull, it would have to be "brown," because "[b]ones have skin" (105). And he expects his semen to be "black" (107), because he imagines that his sexual organ looks like a "giant black bullet" (107). It is significant that he conceives of his libido as "black" (107), and not "sun-brown" (37), like his mother's way of seeing his own skin and that of "her and the girls" (37), or "[p]ale like all the Frenches" (123), which is how the middle-aged Lucy views Carl. Carl associates the color "black" with virility and potency, an association that is a foreshadowing of Samantha's relationship with Brother. Although Carl imagines his libido as "black," immediately prior to the second sexual encounter between Lucy and Carl, which happens years after the first, he mentally undresses Lucy's "sun-darkened" body to find the "lighter" parts: "The skin lighter and softer in those places under her clothes she had let him see, let him touch once" (113). The phallus that Lucy supposedly lacks is figured as her lack of the male sexual organ and her lack of the "black libido" Carl attributes to himself. When Carl realizes that he has not ejaculated "black smoke" (107), but rather "a little sticky whitish puddle" (107), Carl's own lack is no longer masked. In contrast to the "train flying like a giant black bullet" (107), the littleness of this "whitish puddle" reminds the reader that "[f]or a moment at least, [Lucy] has what he 'lacks.'"[6]

When Carl feels that he is being hit by the "train" of his own desire and feels the possibility of his own lack, he imagines Brother "grinning" and "laughing" (107), in a manner very similar to the way in which he later remembers "Albert Wilkes's skull grinning up from the bed" (113). At the very beginning of this second chapter, it is explained that Brother, at the age of twenty-one, suddenly begins to play the piano with the same phenomenal style as Albert Wilkes, without any training. Brother and Albert are both connected to the music, which is presented as a contrast to the representations of the physical beauty John French, Albert Wilkes, and Carl French attribute to Freeda, the unnamed white woman, and Lucy, respectively. In "A Musical Theory of Sound and Motion," Eduard Hanslick, while differentiating between speech and music, decides that "in music the sound is an object, i.e., it appears to us as an end in itself."[7] As explained in the analysis of each voyeur scene or lovemaking scene, when the respective male characters fetishize the physical appearance of the respective women, they experience the bodies of the women as objects of "beauty" that are not ends in themselves, but rather a means of the males believing that they do, indeed, have the phallus. When Lucy remembers Wilkes through the piece of skull, she separates him from phallic desire and places him, along with Brother, in her realm of desire for the "sweet, sweet good music" (102), which Hanslick reminds us makes sound itself into "an object" that is "an end in itself" (Hanslick 602).

Music's ability to cancel out the embodiment (the stasis) of race is developed in the representation of the relationship between Brother and Samantha. When Brother first meets Samantha, she is humming a song and dancing, and she nonverbally "beckon[s] him into her dance" (131). So that she will not fear Brother's albinism, Samantha rereads a medical dictionary definition of melanin, in terms of its "sound and dance" (135), in an effort to purge the words of the antiblack racism she believes is embedded in them. In this section of "The Courting of Lucy Tate," Lucy visits Samantha at Mayview, a hospital for the mentally disturbed, to which Samantha is committed after her son, Junebug, dies. As the story of Samantha, Brother, and Junebug is told, the narrative voice shifts between Samantha and the omniscient narrator, who is apparently Lucy talking to Doot, who remains "inside the weave of voices" (93).

In the early stages of Samantha's relationship with Brother, after they have become sexually involved, Samantha remains frightened of his albinism. She wonders whether the condition is contagious and wonders what exactly causes it. Samantha's libido is figured as "black" and her sexual involvement with someone as "white" as Brother unnerves her, initially. When the "blackness" of her libido is conveyed, Wideman repeats the eschatological image of the Ark, the image of a refuge in which one waits until the end of one world and the beginning of another. The "Ark," however, now becomes Samantha's image of her own body, as well as her image of the home in which she raises ten children. The third-person narrator and Samantha's narrative voice repeatedly refer to the "Ark." One of the first references to the "Ark" is:

> Samantha slept only with the blackest men. Men black as she was because in her Ark she wanted pure African children. Then Brother at her door and in her bed that afternoon. Sure enough nigger nose and nigger lips, even nigger silence when he was finished and rolled his bones off her belly, but always that unsettling lack of color, like snow in July, and even though it felt good, part of her held back, part of her was aware it wasn't supposed to be this way.

> She could see through his skin. No organs inside, just a reddish kind of mist, a fog instead of heart and liver and lungs. She was afraid his white sweat would stain her body. (134)

The reference to the "unsettling lack of color" (134) recalls Doot's description, toward the beginning of the novel, of Brother's "strange color, or lack of color, that whiteness" (17). The men Samantha normally dates seem to possess the phallus, in her eyes, by virtue of being the "blackest men" (134). She herself also possesses what others consider the "blackest" skin. Carl tells Doot, "When I hear of beautiful African queens, Samantha comes to mind. She's the image. Black and comely . . . Ninety-nine and forty-four one hundredths percent black . . . Ivory snow black" (123). Wilkes' unnamed lover is "[s]o white she could be black" (72), and Carl reckons that Samantha is so black she could be "ivory snow" (123). In both cases, the interchangeability of the stark whiteness and the stark blackness demonstrates how constructs of race and constructs of physical beauty spectacularize and exaggerate visual difference.

When Samantha imagines that Brother lacks an external organ, skin color, as well as "organs inside" (134), she exaggerates his lack of melanin and shapes him into the epitome of otherness, with his "white sweat" and lack of "heart and liver and lungs" (134). The idea of "white sweat" reminds one of Carl's feeling that "[b]ones have skin" (105), in the sense that Samantha imagines that Brother's color or "lack of color" must be evident in every part and every excretion of his body, and Carl imagines that even the bones of Wilkes must be "brown" (105). In her study of Lacan, Elizabeth Grosz reminds us that, in a psychoanalytic sense, as a woman negotiates her relation to the phallus, she may experience "the whole of [her] body" as a phallic organ, when she engages in narcissism, or she might experience "parts of her body" as phallic, when in the throes of hysteria.[8] Samantha, when a younger woman, is represented as falling prey to narcissism, and, as an older woman, she is portrayed as a hysterical patient in a mental hospital. Her narcissism is most apparent when she "inspect[s]" her body in a mirror, after she has sexual intercourse with Brother: "As soon as he left she inspected every square inch of her glossy, black skin in the piece of mirror hung on the bathroom door" (134). The usage of the word "glossy" in reference to Samantha's "black skin" signals that Samantha attributes a heightened sense of presence to it. The multiple meanings of the word "glossy" (shiny, superficial, and a photographic print) confirm that the mirror into which Samantha looks is not just the literal mirror hanging on the door, but also the mirror of racial and beauty constructs. When she "inspect[s]" her own body, she objectifies her own body and exhibits it to herself, as she looks for any signs that Brother's "white sweat" "stain[ed]" it (134). Wideman directly introduces the notion of her "blackest" skin becoming a substitute phallic organ when he presents the image of Samantha "inspect[ing] every square inch" of the "glossy" skin, as if the distance and amount of her "black skin" is a huge overcompensation for the lack tied to Brother's albino skin as well as the lack that antiblack racism attributes to blackness.

After Samantha performs her self-examination in the mirror, she goes to the "Carnegie Public Library" with her children to look up the word "melanin" and figure out what exactly Brother's "unsettling lack of color" means (134). The scientific language of the medical reference books reminds Samantha of the education she received at Fisk University, an education that she did not complete and one that she views as miseducation and antiblack. She associates the "spectacled, lemon-colored lady" (135) working at the library reference desk with those teachers at Fisk who thought that "crossing t's and dotting i's had something to do with becoming a human being and blackness was the chaos you had to learn to whip into shape in order to be a person who counted" (135). After Samantha reads the definition of melanin, she realizes that while reading she had lapsed back into "the tone of voice she thought she had forgotten" (135), the voice of those who she believes attempted to miseducate her and teach her to hate "blackness." The first sentence in the definition is "Melanin is the brown to black pigment that colors the skin, hair and eyes" (134). When Samantha reads these words, the word "colors" invokes the idea of staining, and suddenly instead of focusing on whether or not Brother's "white sweat" can stain, she is reminded that "scientific" theories of race treated her blackness as a disorder, and the "scientists" may have been as unnerved by the sight of her skin as she is by Brother's albinism. Samantha most likely began by looking up the word "albino" and then saw a cross-reference stating "see melanin." When she goes to the library, she intends to investigate Brother's condition, but as she reads about melanin, she feels her "glossy black skin" (134) is being "peeled back" (136).

Before going to the library, Samantha tells Brother that she intends to "make a perfect black body" for the "sleeping shelves around the wall" in her "Ark" (132). In the next chapter, "Brother," the political ideology that shapes her concept of a "perfect black body" is stated most explicitly when Brother remembers her telling him, "*Brother, I can't stop. While I got life I got to give life. They're killing us faster now . . . It's a crying shame how they do us. So I can't stop. When we cross over, I want a million, million black feet to run up the bank and a million, million black voices shout hallelulah in the promised land*" (165; italics in original). Samantha believes that a genocide of African Americans is happening and convinces herself that, by having "perfect" or "pure African children" (134), she can fight against it. Her focus on the "blackest men" (134) as suitable fathers of her children demonstrates that she associates lighter complexions with what she perceives as the genocide of African Americans. Like Son in *Tar Baby,* Samantha believes in the somatic integrity of "blackness," the idea that "blackness" should look a certain way and that its certain look should be protected and preserved. Instead of solely detesting the forces that she believes are causing the genocide, "white" is a "color she hate[s]" (131). When Brother first appears, she views him as a "white blackman" (131), but she is not immediately repelled because she believes his facial features are "stamped" by "nigger, the blackest, purest kind" (131) and she believes he can hear "music only . . . in her head" (131). Their musical bond *and* the concrete "stamp[ing]" (131) of her visual fixation parallels her thoughts about the "promised land" *and* the notion that even in the "promised land" race will continue to have meaning (165). Samantha is tormented, because she believes in this eschatological place (the "promised land") and also has a deep-seated belief in the visual "stamp[s]" of race (131).

When she rereads and rewrites the dictionary definition of melanin, focusing on the "sound and dance" of the words (135) instead of the scientific meanings, the conflict between her eschatological vision and her racial essentialism is highlighted. Samantha produces an alternative to the scientific definition, which begins with the words "melanin is" (134). Instead of defining "melanin," she "defines" blackness by enumerating what "blackness" has done and will do. The text reads:

> She read the words again, this time listening to their sound and dance and understood that melanocytes, the bearers of blackness, descended from royalty, from kings whose neural crest contained ostrich plumes, a lion's roar, the bright colors of jungle flowers. Even before birth, before the fetus was three months old, the wanderlust of blackness sent melanocytes migrating through the mysterious terrain of the body. Blackness seeking a resting place, a home in the transparent baby. Blackness journeying to exotic places with strange-sounding names. Settling beside railroad tracks, at crossroads, the epidermal-dermal junction . . . Blackness would come to rest in the eyes; blackness a way of seeing and being seen. Blackness crouched in the shadow of the uveal tract would be a way of being unseen . . . Blackness something to do with long journeys, and eyes, and being at the vibrating edge of things. (135)

In the medical reference book definition, "cells" are said to "migrate to their resting places in the skin at the epidermal-dermal junction" (134). Samantha, while listening to the "sound and dance" of the words "epidermal-dermal junction" (135), decides that they sound like a train stop and that "blackness" must temporarily settle there in the process of its evolution. In the original definition, Samantha reads, "These cells migrate to their resting places . . . in the eyes" (134–35), and when she rereads it and rewrites it in her mind, "blackness" is a "way of seeing and being seen" and a "way of being unseen" (135), an object-like essence and an aesthetic experience.

In her revision, "blackness" is also a sign of the eschatological, the spiritual realm one finds after "long journeys" and "at the vibrating edge of things" (135). In the original definition, the "neural crest" is mentioned as the place where the "melanocytes are derived embryologically" (134), but in Samantha's "sound and dance" (135) it is a magical ornament the ancient "kings" of "blackness" wore, one that "contained" sound, such as that of a "lion's roar" (135), as easily as it "contained" the form of "ostrich plumes" and the "colors of jungle flowers" (135). The original definition explains that pigment cells travel to the leptomeninges, a part of the central nervous system, and in the continuation of the passage cited above, Samantha likens the "sound and dance" of the word "leptomeninges" to a "striped, tiger-colored planet broadcasting jazz into the vast silence of the Milky Way" (135). The playfulness and complete detachment from the paradigm of race within this last image suggests that music temporarily takes her out of the realm of essentialism. As if to remind the reader, however, that Samantha remains tormented by the paradigm of race and is not able to separate "blackness" from the constructs of race, Wideman ends this passage with Samantha thinking to herself that the entire rereading and rewriting of the medical definition is "[w]hat she had known all along" (136). If this statement is true, Samantha does not purge herself, through the rereading and rewriting, of her essentialist understanding of "the blackest, purest kind" of "features" (131) and the "perfect black body" (132). Rather, she reveals that aesthetic and eschatological experiences of "blackness" can be grafted on the essentialist view of "blackness."

The emphasis on the constant movement of "blackness," the "wanderlust" (135), and the fact that Samantha can reread and revise only when she is under the influence of "sound and dance" can be appreciated more fully when it is compared to the aesthetic privileging of motion in Wideman's later novel *Reuben* (1987). In this novel, a contemporary character named Reuben is obsessed with the nineteenth-century photographer, Eadweard

Muybridge, whose aesthetic agenda was to interrogate the nuances of the relationship between motion and stillness as he attempted "to capture motion in still photographs."[9] Reuben is fascinated by Muybridge's 1887 photographic text, which Wideman renames "Animal Motion," instead of "Animal Locomotion." In this text, Muybridge captures the moment when all four legs of a running horse are simultaneously off the ground. In this image, the horse looks like it is flying instead of running.

> Reuben has imaginary conversations with Muybridge and, at one point, hears him say:
>
> For centuries words had reigned. And words engender stillness; they chill intellect and body. I preached motion, explosion of boundaries, exploration of the acts that precede language, give language its excuse for being. After all, dance was the first speech, wasn't it? . . . I was anatomizing motion to unveil its mysteries and discovered motion is irreducible. (63)

When Samantha rewrites the medical dictionary by focusing on the "sound and dance" of the textbook words, she also "preach[es] motion" and inveighs against the "words [that] engender stillness" (63). In an imaginary conversation between Reuben and Muybridge, Muybridge confesses that his photography does reduce motion and "anatomiz[e] it" (63), even though his goal was to produce the effect of motion through a succession of photographic stills. Samantha feels that the medical definition has "anatomiz[ed]" the "wanderlust of blackness" (135), and in her revision, she tries to reclaim the motion. Ultimately, however, as her litany of the actions of "blackness" progresses, the reader realizes that Muybridge's confession is true: "motion is irreducible" (63).

The character, Reuben, while contemplating whether or not "motion was life" (47), decides that: "Extraction was the problem. Releasing the genie from the jar, cutting these strips of photos into separate frames, multiplying them infinitely, stacking them and flipping through them fast enough so they ripple into motion, life" (47). This passage refers to a series of photographs taken by Muybridge, entitled "woman kneeling for jar" (47). Reuben is entranced by the twelve photographs, recording the nude woman "walking, then bending," then "kneel[ing] daintily, her bare bottom a heavy petaled flower" (46). The "genie [on] the jar" is the "elusive secret of motion the photographer sought" (47). It is "[l]ocked inside" an inanimate object, the jar, just as what Samantha feels is the "wanderlust of blackness" is "locked inside" what she views as inanimate objects of science, "melanocytes," "melanin," "neural crest," and so forth. In her revision of the medical definition, Samantha takes these photograph-like, object-like words and attempts to "multipl[y] them infinitely" (47). The limits of her efforts are similar to the limits of Reuben's and Muybridge's attempts to convert inert objectifications of the female body into a lifelike movie. It is apparent, when Samantha "inspect[s]" herself in the mirror (134), that she has learned to objectify her own body and her own "blackness," and this objectification of the body, like Reuben's and Muybridge's objectification of the nude woman's body, is antithetical to the endless motion of which she dreams, that which she understands as the "wanderlust of blackness" (135).

The connection between Samantha's dilution anxiety and her sense of death is most apparent when she appears "splotchy" (188) once she is aging, as if her death will occur once the "glossy, black skin" is entirely discolored. As Wideman explicitly connects her "glossy, black skin" to the black phallus (when she "inspects every inch" of it), Samantha's fear of death is linked to her fear of the ongoing genocide of African Americans. Because of his albinism, Brother, even while alive, looks like death to Samantha. When Lucy comes to the asylum to tell her that Brother has died, she responds: "I know he's dead. Knew before you and anybody else. Course he's dead. Been a ghost since I been knowing him. Ain't never been nothing but a ghost" (128). The words "nothing but a ghost" suggest that Brother always seemed more like an image than an actual person. When Samantha expresses this feeling to Lucy, she is understating her sense of loss over Brother's death in order to avoid her pain over his death and the death of Junebug. Nonetheless, Brother's albinism did make his body seem almost unreal to Samantha, and she does imagine him, during their physical intimacy, as "the ghostly white fog" (136). To the extent that Brother is more of an image to her than an actual person, and a "white blackman" (131, 132), she treats him as an embodiment of that which she refers to as "blackness . . . a way of being unseen" (135) in her revision of the medical definition of melanin. She herself is treated explicitly as an "image" when Carl tells Doot, "When I hear of beautiful African queens, Samantha comes to mind. She's the image" (123). But there is a fundamental difference between the transparent relationship Carl imagines between Samantha's "coal black[ness]" and "African queens" (123), the way in which he believes that Samantha is the stable referent of "African queens," and the representations of Brother as a ghost or the presence of absence.

Brother's psychological struggle to escape his bodily trap and be unseen is narrated through a sequence of his dreams, culminating in the description of his thoughts before his suicide. He realizes that being an embodied image of transparence is not a means of being genuinely "unseen." He wants to "unsee" himself as a "see-through" body, as a presence of absence. For Brother to be reconstructed as the absence or abstraction of presence and not the presence of absence, Wideman introduces in this chapter the idea that Brother "could be whatever he wanted to be": "Believe what you need to believe, but brother was special like that. Not some spook or hoodoo, but a man who could be whatever he wanted to be" (199). In the first chapters of the novel, the representations of Brother are the descriptions of how others see him. In this final chapter, Brother's own experiences of his body are described.

When the "Brother" section begins, Brother dreams that he is in a "black pit" entangled in a "mass of bodies," but nonetheless alone (159). The narrator explains that Brother begins to have this "train dream" (159) when he is twenty-one and that he "knew the dream could kill him, knew it could take him again and again until its work was finished" (159). This "train dream" can be compared to the "scare game" Brother and Carl play when they are young boys. In the "scare game," the train feels like a form of salvation, and Brother always wins. Sometimes, Carl is too scared to run across the tracks; he waits too long, attempting to win the game, and then cannot bear to run at all. When Carl loses the game in this fashion, he sees Brother on the other side, "not dead like he ought to be, but wagging his bald head and signifying with his whole self" (18). On the other side of the tracks, Brother is alive and "whole," although Carl reasons he "ought to be dead." This game prefigures the suicide of Brother that is described toward the end of the novel. Carl can see Brother's "whole self" only when Brother is in the space where death "ought to be" (18). Brother can be seen as "whole" only when he loses his body. Wideman emphasizes that Brother's body appears fragmented because other characters literally experience skin color as a type of container and actually view Brother as having no skin.

When Carl plays the "scare game," he is scared of leaving his family, but he "dream[s] of running away" (19) and "los[ing] himself" (26). He envies what he perceives as Brother's lack of roots and evanescence and associates him with that which cannot be named. He associates the train tracks with "somewhere else" and "those faraway streets . . . that have no names" (27). And he conceives of Brother as "No name. No color. No nothing if you think about it" (27). Carl's qualification, "if you think about it," is significant, because it is similar to his assertion that "[t]he streets were Homewood but they were not real till he thought them" (26). As a child, he imagines that he creates the streets of Homewood every day by mentally conjuring them. Doot emphasizes that, unlike Carl's mastery of the streets of Homewood, Brother exceeds Carl's mental thoughts. Brother's nameless "nothing[ness]" is like Carl's image of the nameless other world down the train tracks: "Somewhere shimmering like the steel rails just before they curve out of sight. Sky drops to meet gravel and steel at that shimmering point. The world is as thin as tissue paper there. You could poke your finger through it" (27). In this image the hardness of the "steel rails" is a sharp contrast to the sheer texture of the "tissue paper" (27). At the meeting point, "that shimmering point" (27), between the harsh concreteness of "gravel and steel" and the excessiveness of the sky, Carl imagines a world of evanescence in which he places Brother. The "scare game" makes Carl romanticize disembodiment. The game symbolizes the possibility of salvation at the "end of the world" (18), a time when people will be able to "ru[n] away" (19) and lose their bodies that are as harsh and concrete as the "steel rails" (27).[10]

In "The Courting of Lucy Tate," Doot asks Carl and Lucy, "But didn't Brother kill himself?" and Lucy responds: "Found Brother dead on the tracks. Wasn't no blood so he was dead before the train hit him. It was something else or somebody else killed him, killed him just like they killing everything worth a good goddamn in Homewood" (120). Lucy's reconsideration of Brother's suicide as a murder, the idea that "something else or somebody else" kills him "before the train hit him" (120), conveys the idea that rather than intentionally harming himself, Brother lies on the train tracks to escape the perpetual form of death that he was living. In the last chapter, Brother's muteness, except for the scat-singing, is represented as being caused by the psychological grip that the "train dream" has on him and the pain he feels when Junebug burns to death. The description of his trauma in the "train dream" leads Wideman to a full critique of dilution anxiety, the fear of loss of authentic blackness.

The third-person narrator explains that "the taste of soot clogged his mouth and it was too late to say anything more now" (172). After he has made a "wood box" casket for Junebug, one that is represented as being an alternative to Samantha's "Ark" (170), he sings a song of redemption to his dead child:

> Sang to him to save his life. Because he was just a baby. Because he didn't know a thing about leaving or coming back again. So I had to tell him what I knew. Where I had been . . . I sang to him about crossing oceans. Always being on one side of the water and the sun sets in the west while it's rising in the east on the other side . . . And the sky's not full of stars but one bright

> star we only see pieces of because the darkness is a raggedy curtain pulled across it till we know better. (170–71)

Similar to the way in which Samantha rereads and revises the medical definition of melanin, Brother revises his "train dream" in this song for Junebug. He attempts to tell Junebug the horror of the "train dream" but discovers that "different words came out" (172), words that convey a much more comforting understanding of the relation between death and life than that of the recurring "train dream." In the description of the "train dream," Wideman repeats the image of the "black pit," which, as previously explained, is originally John French's frightening picture of "what happened sometimes when a song was over" (69), the "the silence after things end" (69). In his "train dream," Brother feels that this "black pit" has opened and he is trapped in it. Perhaps the most frightening aspect of this dream is the fact that Brother struggles in vain to "disentangle what belonged to him from the mass of bodies struggling in the black pit" (159). When he sings to Junebug, he does not tell Junebug about this "black pit" (159), this image of hell, which John French imagines as the realm of "nothing" (69), but rather Brother sings about a heavenly realm which is represented as the simultaneity of the sun setting and rising, as a state of resurrection or "coming back again" (170), and as the full view of all the "pieces" of the "one bright star" (171).

As opposed to Samantha's mystification of blackness when she attempts to revise the medical definition (a scene which begins with her need to make sure that Brother's "unsettling lack of color" will not stain her "glossy black skin" [134]), Brother understands that race itself is a "raggedy curtain." He demystifies Samantha's images. When Samantha is revising the medical definition, she is with the children whom Carl later tells Doot are "[a]ll . . . black and beautiful like Sam . . . [e]xcept Junebug" (123). As Brother sings to the child who seemingly lacks Samantha's "black beauty," his tutelage that the darkness at the end of a day is just a "raggedy curtain" can be extended to also mean that the skin color that Junebug's mother mystifies is also just a "raggedy curtain" (171), a cover or mask, and not an essence. In this passage, Wideman celebrates the demystification of skin-as-essence. Nonetheless, he does replace one mystification of the body with another: the Christian body (the body as a mere covering of the soul) replaces skin-as-essence.

The similar tone in Samantha's revision of the medical definition and the song Brother creates for his son, instead of telling him about the "train dream," becomes evident in the continuation of Brother's song. Brother explains:

> But then I told him the secret. That there was more. More fire and pain and singing. That I had been through it all before. That nothing stopped. That I had crossed the ocean in a minute. That I had drowned in rivers and dangled like rotten fruit from trees. That my unmourned bones were ground to dust and the dust salted and plowed. That I had been chained and branded like an animal . . . That I had even lost my color and lost my tongue but all of that too was only a minute. (171)

Samantha's litany of what "blackness" does parallels Brother's litany of what African Americans have endured. It is significant that he uses "I," instead of "we," because it underscores that he is a survivor and an eyewitness and not a part of the "mass of bodies struggling in the black pit" (159). Similar to Samantha's attempt to capture the motion of "blackness," Brother's list would seemingly never end if it were to fully capture the idea that "nothing stopped" (171) and "[t]hat he had been through it *all* before" (171; italics mine). When he explains that he "had even lost [his] color" (171), the reader thinks about Samantha's fear that her "glossy, black skin" may have been "stain[ed]" by Brother's albinism and Lucy's feeling that once Samantha is in Mayview, the mental health hospital, "her skin [is] splotchy and split like it's ready to bust open" (188). Lucy describes Samantha's mental illness as "[b]lack fingers letting go one by one like threads popping when you rip a seam (183). When Samantha "los[es] the last of the little grip she had" (183), she can no longer pretend that her "glossy, black skin" is a substitute phallic organ, and she is forced to confront the lack that was covered by her obsessive attachment to it. Samantha's fears that the supposed lightening of African Americans is connected to the genocide of African Americans are refuted by Brother's insistence that, even though he "lost [his] color," he did not disappear but continued his steady movement and continued to live his many lives.

Brother's emphasis on his suffering and resurrection, in his song to Junebug, evokes the biblical imaging of Christ. This evocation is strengthened when he is presented as a healer. When Lucy finds the drawings he made, with wings on human bodies, she imagines that as Brother made the sketches, people were being healed and raised from the dead. The text reads: "She could see Brother's hand, pale as the paper, moving across each sheet. Like the magic hands of the old-time healers. See him laying on his white hands and see through them to the old Homewood streets, the people coming to life at his touch" (194–95). As he draws, his "lack of color" is camouflaged as the color of his hands blends with the color of the paper. Lucy finds Brother's drawings once he is dead and begins to remember Brother as a healer. While he is alive, Brother is not recognized as a community healer. In fact, he often feels that he is a visual sign of obscenity, with "his bare white hanging out," like "nakedness" that needs a "cover" (174). Before Brother finds his "wings," his desire to have his "lack" covered is so strong that at one point he imagines that his tan jacket could become his skin. At this point, instead of being able to "rip a seam" (183) and "le[t] go" of "that envelope of skin" (183), or the need to believe that his subjectivity is not "split" (188), he dreams that he could enclose his "whole self" (18) in an inanimate object, the tan jacket.

On the "particular moonless night" (173) when Brother imagines that his tan jacket could offer him psychological security, he feels that this evening is "double dark," and he wishes that he "could lose himself in the skin of his tan jacket" (173). As he walks through the streets of Homewood, he sees crowds of people going to a religious revival located outside in a tent. When he first notices the movement of the people toward the "bright tent" (174), he feels that he is watching their religious journey from "the darkness of his own shadowy form which he felt enclosing him like a black eggshell" (174) and "from that little patch of nowhere stinking of pee and carpeted with broken wine bottles" (174). He initially desires to go to the revival, but he worries that his body will be seen and that violence with be inflicted on him, since the "bare white [is] hanging out like a streetlamp begging the kids to stone it" (174). Ultimately, Brother doubts the genuineness of the revival, and the moving people seem like "[r]aggedy boatloads of Homewood people sailing for the Promised Land" (176). Like the "mass of bodies" in the "train dream" (159), the bodies of the moving people seem entangled in a way that Brother cannot understand. He imagines that their "feet all came together in blackness not even [his] eyes could see" (176). This image of linked feet suggests that they are moving slowly toward the "Promised Land" and they may actually appear to be inert.

When Brother wishes he could go to the revival, he expects to see movement, to witness the ecstasy or religious trance of the participants. He imagines that the tan jacket could be his alternative "salvation tent" (175). In the jacket he imagines himself laughing so heartily that "his whole body [is] jumping and twisting and turned inside out" (173), just as he imagines the people at the revival will "[s]hout Hallelujah and shake dance in the aisles" (174). In the first chapter, Brother's face appears to Doot to be an inverted face, a "blank skull" with a "blubbery octopus mouth" (16). When Brother revels in the idea of his body being "turned inside out" (173), the inversion of the body no longer signifies the grotesque, but rather his dreams of disembodiment. The tan jacket is a material object that he imagines could offer him a means to be disembodied. As he "sank deeper and deeper into the neck of his tan jacket" (173), he feels that he has gained "another face" (173), one that "star[es]" back at the world" (173), unlike the pure corporeality continually attributed to his albino face, and most vividly enacted in the descriptions of his reaction to Samantha's explanation of Junebug's death: "His face turned to stone while he listened. Like a giant chalky stone and somebody had chipped eyes and nose and mouth in it and give it a name but it still ain't alive" (140). To escape from these feelings that he is as much an object as chiseled stone, on this one "double dark" evening (173), he imagines that the tan jacket could cover him until he was "nothing but an eye" (174), a form of consciousness freed from the body.

After he indulges in the fantasizing about the jacket, Brother finally laments the fact that the jacket is just a jacket and not the means of his salvation and escape from his feelings of pure corporeality. His disenchantment with the tan jacket is represented as being connected to his disenchantment with the people walking to the revival. He decides that neither the "salvation tent" nor the tan jacket can provide the coverage he needs to escape the oppressiveness of his skin, that which he experiences as "the bare white" and "the nakedness" (174). At this moment, which is clearly before he gains his wings and is ready to sing the song of redemption to Junebug, his thoughts about committing suicide are triggered not by his sense that life continues when one dies, but rather by his frustration with the idea of souls being trapped in bodies: "The dry hot stale wind of thousands of trifling souls, old souls stuffed in drawers" (177). The full significance of this reference to "souls stuffed in drawers" can be appreciated only if it is interpreted as a critique of Lucy's need to keep the piece of Albert Wilkes' skull in the "skinny top drawer of the dresser" (103) and a critique of the fetishism of female bodies in the scenes in which Freeda, Albert's unnamed lover, and Lucy are undressed by the male voyeurs. In the specific context of the passage, when Brother is thinking about the misguided movements of those going to the revival, he is thinking about the box-like qualities of coffins and graves in the Allegheny Cemetery (177). The specific context, however, only partially enables one to understand why the coffins are compared to "drawers" (177).

When Lucy keeps the piece of Albert's skull in her bedroom drawer, she feels that she is safeguarding much more than a piece of bone. Indeed, she tells Carl, "Shot poor Albert Wilkes to pieces that day. And I saved me one" (103). When Brother laments the idea that "old souls are stuffed in drawers" (177), he is indirectly critiquing Lucy's notion that an actual piece of Albert, a sign of his spirit, could ever be safeguarded in the narrow confines of an inanimate object, such as her "skinny top drawer" (103). Lucy believes that to remember Albert and his "sweet, sweet good music" (102), she needs to keep the piece of skull. When Brother wonders why people think coffins can contain "souls" (177), he imagines the graves in the Allegheny Cemetery "opening" and a "wind flood floating them through the streets" (177). Since at this point in Brother's trajectory he has not yet found his "wings" and his more optimistic view of the eschatological, he imagines that once the "old souls" are freed from the graves, they are then crushed by the feet of pedestrians like himself. In the description of the "souls" being freed and then crushed by feet, the juxtaposition of the scatological and the eschatological is emphasized with the image of "somebody's dry bones, somebody's body busted open and dry as a broken wine bottle" (177). Once the "souls" are crushed, they are no longer described as "souls," but as "dry bones" and "somebody's body" (177), as if Brother decides that there is no such thing as a "soul," and when a body is no longer alive, a person is simply reduced to nothing.

At this point when Brother is thinking so pessimistically about what happens after death, he thinks about suicide, and the image is not an entirely peaceful surrender to another form of life, which is how his actual suicide is represented, once he has gained his "wings" and is thinking much more optimistically about what happens after death. After imagining himself crushing the freed "souls," which were really just "dry bones," he considers: ". . . lying down right there in the middle of the pavement. Not another step forward or backward ever. Just let all the strength run out his body and crumple here on the pavement and listen while the sidewalks die and the bricks tumble down and the sky cracks, and rain dry as talcum powder buries everything" (177). In this passage his death is passive, but not so peaceful. After he lies down, the violent end of the world occurs, and the violence is then hidden or "burie[d]" by the rain, which masks the odor of death and destruction with its deceptive "talcum powder" scent (177). The reference to the talcum powder invokes the idea that even though in this image Brother's dead body is not "stuffed" (177) in a drawer-like casket, it is "stuffed" in a drawer-like world in which rain seems more like talcum powder than condensed water. Throughout the first two chapters, Wideman's repeated references to the biblical image of Noah's Ark propel one to think about this image of the rain as a sign of Brother's disbelief, at this point, in God's promise to Noah that he will not destroy the world again and that the rainbow will be a token of this covenant.

In one of the descriptions of his final understanding immediately prior to his suicide, the word "drawers" is used again, and this time, the other meaning of the word is evoked, that of underwear. The text reads:

> Brother never could see all the way across to the other side. Something always in the way. The broad rows of tracks themselves. . . . But seeing down the tracks was easier than seeing across. Than smashing your eyes against that wall running alongside the steel rails.
>
> But Brother can see past the wall tonight. Through it, around it, over it and under it. He'd been under that skirt. Seen the drawers and what's under the drawers and what's under what's under the drawers. He'd seen it all . . . Play the scare game one more time. Teach Junebug wasn't nothing to be afraid of. Teach them all. (181)

In this passage the significance of the recurrent images of the idea of lack and the masking or covering of lack becomes clearer. Instead of participating in the setup of phallic desire, as John French, Albert Wilkes, Carl French, and Samantha do, in which someone must *have* the phallus and someone else must *be* the phallus and overcompensate for the lack of the phallic organ, Brother experiences lack and absence and has learned not to fear them. This idea is conveyed through his debunking of the sexual and racial fetish, the notion that he has "been under that skirt" and is no longer seduced by fetish objects, whether the fetishized object is the skirt, the drawers, "what's under the drawers," or "what's under what's under the drawers" (181).

This debunking can be interpreted as a critique of the racial and sexual fetishism represented throughout the novel: Samantha's fetishism of Brother's albinism, John's fetishism of the feminine beauty he attributes to his wife during his voyeurism, Albert's fetishism of the whiteness and feminine beauty he attributes to his lover during his voyeurism, and Carl's fetishism of Lucy during their physical intimacy. The night of the revival, when Brother feels the "dry hot stale wind of thousands of trifling souls, old souls stuffed in drawers" (177), he is despondent, because even though he knows that the drawer-like graves cannot hold "souls" and the "salvation tent" cannot hold "souls," he is still seduced by the possibility that his own tan jacket could become his "drawer," that an inanimate object could rid him of his feelings of being "bare" and "naked," and of a form of lack. When he feels that he has "[s]een the drawers and what's under the drawers and what's under what's under the drawers" (181), he is no longer enticed by the idea of being "stuffed" in a drawer, because his sense of being in "that little patch of nowhere stinking of pee and carpeted with broken wine bottles" (174) is replaced with his sense of having "see[n] all the way across to the other side" (181). Brother's ability to see "the other side" and to feel that life continues when one dies is directly connected in this passage to his ability to debunk the sexual fetish. The fact that he is debunking the sexual fetish and the racial fetish becomes clearer when the reader recalls Doot's fear, expressed at the beginning of the first chapter, that if he looked directly at the albino skin of Brother, he would "see through him, under his skin, because there was no color to stop [his] eyes, no color which said there's a black man or white man in front of [him]" (15). The "color" that Doot feels must "stop [his] eyes" is an example of the "wall" Brother "can see past" once he has "seen it all" (181). Doot is afraid to see "under [Brother's] skin" (15), but Brother revels in being able to see "under" the racial fetish of skin color and the sexual fetish.

Brother feels that to "[t]each them all" (181) about "the other side" in which "souls" are not "stuffed in drawers" (177), he must kill himself. His suicide becomes the means through which he transcends the grotesqueness attributed to his albinism. The overall frame of the entire novel, Doot's storytelling, happens after Brother has killed himself. Doot, Carl, and Lucy feel that Brother is resurrected when he is remembered through stories and music, an idea which is most clearly conveyed when he reappears at the end of the novel in the doorway of Lucy's residence (208). As previously stated, Lucy tells Doot that Brother was killed by "something else or somebody else" before he killed himself (120). His suicide is represented so favorably that it does seem that he lies on the train tracks to escape the death-in-life he has been enduring. In one representation of the suicide, he is seduced by the "icy metal" of the train tracks, which is described as if he experiences it as a substitute phallic organ. The narrator explains, "He rubs the hard back of the rail. Strokes it one last time gingerly like it's sharp as the edge of a straight razor. Nothing to be fraid of. It all starts up again" (182). The eroticism of this passage is overstated; it does seem that Brother experiences physical intimacy with the "hard back of the rail," and an indisputable picture of masochism emerges when he "strokes" the "sharp[ness]" of this razor-like rail (182). It is implied that his reasons for wanting to die, the messages he wants to deliver, do not match his own actual experience when he commits the act. In a sense, the train rails themselves become the pair of "drawers" that seduce him, even when he believes he is escaping the realm of seduction and phallic desire.

The train, on the one hand, is a symbol of the eschatological, a symbol of "the other side" (181), which Brother can "see" before he kills himself and where he believes he will be when he dies. Yet the train is also referred to in two particular representations of the sexual fetish, during the eroticizing of Brother's suicide and in the description of Carl's orgasmic moment when he is physically intimate with Lucy. In the latter scene, Carl, as previously discussed, imagines that a train is rapidly approaching, like a "giant black bullet [aimed] at his back" (107). As the orgasm occurs, he feels that he is once again playing the "scare game" that he and Brother played as children. If this scene is compared to Brother's being seduced by the "hard" (182) and razor-like rail when he commits suicide, one wonders if the moment when Brother commits suicide should be interpreted as an orgasmic moment. The erotic aura of the description of the suicide suggests that Brother may experience the simultaneity of death and sexual pleasure that Carl only imagines during his physical intimacy with Lucy. If Brother has an orgasmic moment with the "hard back of the rail" (182), then the image emerges of Brother being the receptacle of the rail's penetration, a penetration which is seemingly self-inflicted, as he "rubs" and "strokes" the "hard" and "sharp" object (182). In the description of the sexual intercourse between Brother and Samantha, Brother is not represented as simply the male penetrator, and Samantha is not simply the female receptacle. Samantha moves vigorously as Brother ejaculates, and the narrator wonders if her "spasms" are "sent to welcome or kill what he spilled in her womb" (134). Furthermore, the concavity of Brother and Samantha's assertive movement is described: "As he caved in on her breasts she grabbed his skinny backside" (134).

The concavity of Brother is repeated with a fundamental difference when Brother, in one of his wishful contemplations of being disembodied, imagines that "his body [is] going limp" (178) and his "chest caves and his navel is folding into his backbone" (178). In the full context of this passage, he is remembering "when he felt like a balloon, when he held the string in his hand and a balloon with his funny face bobbed closer and closer to the sun" (178). His actual face is particularly prone to damage by the sun's rays because of his albinism. The image of his own body deflating like the balloon might and his "chest cav[ing]" (178) seems to be his vision of what being able to approach the sun would feel like. Instead of "cav[ing] in" on someone else's body, as he does when he "caved in on [Lucy's] breasts" (134), when he imagines his body "going limp" (178), the "cav[ing] in" does not enable him to feel "settled" and at rest, but rather makes him "star[t] to rise" (178), as "the lightness and giddiness of a height he'd never dreamed overtakes him" (178). Before this rising action is experienced, his body feels so deflated that he likens it to "nothing but a string, a string attached to the flat kite he's become" (178). The kite image is significant, as an alternative to the balloon, because it does not have a "funny face painted on it" (179) and seems to represent a state closer to complete disembodiment, when he will fly and glide through the air without any strings attached.

In an earlier passage, when Brother watches this balloon "floating miles up in the sky" (172), he wonders "what it would feel like to cut the string . . . and watch the balloon jet away" (172), and although the kite does have a string, the "lightness and giddiness" of the kite is the closest approximation given for what the cut string would feel like. The string of the balloon is "anchored to the busted sidewalk of Finance street" (172), whereas during the kite experience, his body seems to become the string itself as he imagines himself rising. Instead of caving in on Samantha's breasts, in the kite image Brother's body caves in on itself and changes shapes until it is so light the wind is able to lift it. When the part of Brother not anchored to the busted sidewalk is envisioned as "the sun-dimpled bubble of his bald head floating miles up in the sky" (172), it becomes most clear that Wideman is contrasting the concavity or depth imagined during experiences of physical intimacy with the concavity and depth of the eschatological. The image of the "sun-dimpled bubble" is a rewriting of Brother lying concavely over Samantha, after he has gained an orgasm through the supposed concavity of her vagina. The image of the concavity of a "sun-dimpled bubble" is also a contrast to the image of Brother's wishing that he could hide in his jacket, as he "hunched deeper, pulling his shoulders up around his eyes" (176).

After the extended description of the transcendence Brother feels when he imagines himself as a kite, the reader is told that, during this entire imaginary experience, he was actually in the process of urinating outdoors. Instead of actually cutting the string, and becoming disembodied, he was in the process of attending to one of the more base bodily functions. After the extended description of "the lightness and giddiness of a height he'd never dreamed" (178), the narrator curtly explains that "he tucks his joint back inside his pants and zips up his fly" (179). Like the string of the balloon, his "joint" keeps him "anchored" and unable to achieve the disembodiment of which he dreams. His inability to actually cut the string parallels his inability to rid himself of his feelings of entrapment in pure corporeality, an inanimate, object-like body. When he "tucks his joint back inside his pants" (179), it does seem that, compared to the "lightness and giddiness" he feels when he imagines that he is the kite, he feels quite contained and "zip[ped]" up" (179), as if he were a "sou[l] stuffed in drawers" (177).

The explicit reference to Brother's "joint" (179) makes the reader think about an earlier image in the text when Brother imagines that, if the string of the balloon with his "funny face painted on it" were cut, it might "finally fall back to earth" and become the "dirty rubber" that "some little kid" would "pick . . . out of the gutter" and "stretch . . . and poke . . . and maybe put his mouth on" (172). When Brother fears that if the string were cut, the balloon may "fall back to earth" and become "dirty rubber" (172), the psychoanalytic idea that phallic organs are really covers and masks of lack and absence is reinstated once again. Instead of the phallus being reduced to the penis in this image, the phallus is reduced to the "dirty rubber" (172), which emphasizes how imaginary the equation between the penis and the phallus is. Brother fears that, if the "pale balloon" (172) does return to "earth" as "dirty rubber" (172), "some little kid" might "blow it up again" (172). When the male sexual organ is "blow[n] . . . up" as a phallic organ, it overcompensates for feelings of lack. When Samantha looks in the mirror at "every square inch of her glossy, black skin" (134), her way of seeing her skin color overcompensates for her knowledge that antiblack racists construe her skin color as lack. When Brother feels that his entire body has been blown up and wishes that he could become limp and "flat" as a kite, his idealization of disembodiment overcompensates for his feeling of entrapment in pure corporeality, to such an extent that he decides to kill himself.

The image of the "dirty rubber" falling back to "earth" (172) suggests that Brother's own resurrection and reappearance, at the end of the novel, may not be as ideal a moment as it seems. The sexual fetishism of the train rails also suggests that the suicide may not actually lead to the experience of disembodiment he envisions through the kite image. In "Cultural Narratives Passed On: African American Mourning Stories," Karla Holloway asserts that "[d]isembodiment is an odd and challenging space from which to express desire."[11] To a great extent, other characters make Brother's disembodiment the "odd and challenging space" of his glory; his death enables them to beautify him.[12] When Brother kills himself, he enacts or performs the deathlike images others have attributed to him, such as Freeda's loathing of him when he seems "dead in that bag of white skin" (36).

The image of Brother as the presence of absence is most developed when he dreams that he is in a train returning to Homewood, and the ghostliness attributed to him because of his albinism is connected to the ghostliness of the imagined resurrection of the "long dead Albert Wilkes"

(160). Initially, in this dream, Brother is looking through a train window at the face of Albert, which is "there always but parts of it come and go" (160). Brother can only see parts of this "see through" or transparent face that merges with the constantly shifting background created by the train's movement. As he looks at this face, or through this face, he is perplexed because he thinks that he himself has become Albert, but the face outside the train appears to be a ghostly, fragmented face of Albert. As the dream progresses, he imagines that he is in the Tates' residence, watching Albert play the piano. As Albert plays, he looks through Brother's face just as Brother imagines that he himself is Albert. The image of their two gazes both looking through each other evokes a sense of compounded or double absence: Wilkes is "[t]rying to see something" (162), instead of seeing the presence of absence. As ghosts, both he and Brother cannot be seen for what they are. This idea is captured when Brother decides that "[m]aybe he is the window glass" (162). Glass, one can argue, can never be seen for what it is; one always sees through it. As the presence of absence, the face of Brother is "caught somewhere in the middle" (162), in the territory between presence and absence, between appearances and referents.

In this dream, as he becomes frustrated with these visions of the presence of absence, he feels that "he's waiting for a time, maybe night-time, when he'll be able to see it all and clearly" (161). This notion of "see[ing] it all and clearly" (161) is best understood as the ability to understand everything concretely, as if abstractions do not exist.[13] The dream initially terrifies Brother, like the other recurring train dream. Brother imagines that his face appears to Albert as a "flag changing shape" (162). This description is intriguing, because as a flag or banner of ghostliness or the presence of absence, its "changing shape" is belied by the fact that it is a banner, a predetermined sign. No matter how much the wind blows it, it remains stuck to the pole that determines its meaning. This pole is the ideology that Carl describes as "color to stop my eyes, . . . color which said there's a black man or white man in front of you" (15), the ideology that constructs Brother as an appearance that seemingly does not "stop [Doot's] eyes" (15).

The fabrication of the idea that albinism is the presence of absence as well as the beautification of this idea is rendered most vividly when Samantha remembers how her other "black and beautiful" children reacted when they saw Junebug for the first time (123).

> Junebug is a warm lump against her shoulder. A part of herself drained of color, strangely aglow. Her children don't understand yet. Perhaps they can't see him. Perhaps they look through his transparent skin and see only the pil-

> low on which she's propped his head. She lowers her gaze to his pale, wrinkled skin, his pink eyes, then stares across him to their dark faces. (138)

The words "pale, wrinkled skin" (138) represent the appearance of Junebug when Samantha considers "blackness a way of . . . being seen" (135), as a nonabstracted presence. Samantha aestheticizes this "pale, wrinkled skin" so that it becomes "transparent skin" and "a part of herself strangely aglow" (138). But when she "lowers her gaze" and cannot look through "his pale, wrinkled skin," the reader is reminded of the fabricated nature of the "transparent skin" (138), his "way of being unseen" (135). Samantha converts the presence of the "pale, wrinkled skin" into a presence of absence, the "transparent skin" (138).

When Samantha "stares across" Junebug, it is as if she is looking at the train tracks as Brother does and realizing that "seeing down the tracks was always easier than seeing across" (181). The inability of the "dark faces," her other children, to see Junebug's beauty is akin to "that wall running alongside the steel rails," the one which Brother "smash[es] [his] eyes against" until he learns to see the eschatological. In *Reuben,* Wideman captures the way in which the spiritual can seem intensely present in the realm of the worldly and the corporeal, when the protagonist contemplates the idea that "[h]eaven presses down on us" (134). In this same novel, Wideman also refers to the "envelope of body wrapping the idea" of a person (106). When Samantha aestheticizes the "envelope of body wrapping" Junebug, she imagines that it is a sign of "[h]eaven press[ing] down" (134), the spiritual presence of absence. The catharsis Samantha feels after revising the medical definition, when "she had no fear" and "enjoyed the strangeness" (136), is the catharsis Brother wants to offer "them all," when he rewrites the train dream as Junebug's song. In Samantha's revision of the medical definition of melanin, she celebrates the notion of "blackness" "[s]ettling beside railroad tracks, at crossroads, the epidermal-dermal junction" (135), because she feels the settlement in the skin layers is only one stage in the constant movement of "blackness." Because this "settling" does not happen in the "epidermal-dermal" region of Brother, he has what Samantha initially understands as an "unsettling lack of color" (134). In order to lose her fear of Brother, Samantha extracts the idea of him as the "unseen" from the "envelope of body wrapping" it (106).

The idea of the unseen being extracted from the "envelope of body wrapping" Brother is similar to Reuben's dreams of actually recovering the "woman's form transposed into the jar's clay" (47). As Reuben becomes obsessed with the photograph of the "woman kneeling for jar [*sic*]" (47), he worries about having feelings of necrophilia. He desires the "long dead" (160) woman in a way that he could never desire a living woman. When the disembodiment of Brother is celebrated, it is implied that his beauty can be experienced only when he is dead. The potential for the aestheticizing of disembodiment to lead to necrophilia is underscored in the description of how Lucy safeguards Albert's skull. Lucy connects the skull to Albert's music, as if she hopes to extract the music from the inanimateness of the skull. She mourns the death of Albert, even as she remembers the agreeableness of the scene of his death, when he played the "sweetest song a dead man ever played for his own funeral" (102). The song that Brother sings to Junebug is another "sweet" song delivered by a man preparing to kill himself. Brother wants Junebug to remember his song in the manner that Lucy, when a middle-aged woman, remembers Albert Wilkes' "funeral" song. The murder of Albert occurs when Lucy is a youth. Years later Lucy can still hear the song, as she sits in the rocking chair that was "wounded" by the bullets of the policemen who killed Albert.

In the description of what the song sounds like to the middle-aged Lucy, Wideman presents an alternative to the images of the ghostly presence of absence. This scene presents a nonvisual figure of authenticity. Instead of the beauty of the "unseen," Wideman describes the beauty of the unheard, "the thousand things it took to make the note whole":

> Play. She commands Albert Wilkes again. Play. She hums his song. A song so full of Albert Wilkes the pieces of him falling around her, drifting lazy and soft like huge, wet snowflakes and she can see the shape of each one. Falling like snow or rain or the names in the stories Carl tells Doot.
>
> Albert Wilkes's song so familiar because everything she's ever heard is in it, all the songs and voices she's ever heard, but everything is new and fresh because his music joined things, blended them so you follow one note and then it splits and shimmers and spills the thousand things it took to make the note whole, the silences within the note, the voices and songs. (189)

The atmosphere of death is seemingly entirely erased from the "new and fresh" song Lucy hears when she is middle-aged (189). The overwhelming "full[ness]" of the song, the "song so full of Albert Wilkes," belies the "pieces of him falling around her" (189). The "pieces" do not sound like "pieces." Considering the novel's images of the metonymic function of skin color in the paradigm of race, Lucy's way of hearing this song provides a less visually oriented way of thinking about fragmentation and wholeness. For example, in the description of Lucy's youthful perspective of Albert's music and his death, the lingering sign of Albert's blood on the piano keys is depicted as "a purplish stain on the ivory like the pigment showing through at the roots of dark people's fingernails" (101). In this image, when blood and melanin are compared and significance is attributed to the color of the skin underneath fingernails, Wideman captures the way in which the paradigm of race treats skin color as if it is a part signifying the whole of the body, both externally and internally. The linkage of blood and melanin reminds us that the words "black blood" have been culturally ingrained as a way of referring to "black" ancestry. Albert's music, his blood, and the "pigment showing through [. . .] fingernails" all begin to merge when Lucy, as a teenager, remembers the murder she witnessed as a youth (101). When she hears Albert's song, many years later, the visual "holes in the piano" and the "blood on the keys" are displaced by the beauty she attributes to the movement of the "pieces" within the "whole" note (101, 189). When these "pieces" within the "whole" note are imagined as "[f]alling like snow or rain or the names in the stories Carl tells Doot" (189), it is most clear that Wideman is elevating both the sound of Albert's music and the language of Doot's storytelling as a means of presenting that which Judith Butler conceives as the "loss of the loss," the overcoming of the dilution anxiety that makes Brother's albino skin a sign of the lost black phallus. The descriptions of what the middle-aged Lucy hears in Albert's song are a celebratory alternative to the skin-color fetishism that renders Brother the presence of absence.

From Sent for You Yesterday *to* Philadelphia Fire *and* Two Cities

Whereas *Sent for You Yesterday* is a strong critique of the visual demand for blackness, Wideman's later novel, *Philadelphia Fire* (1990), is a full exploration of the spatial and temporal confusions of blackness. As Wideman meditates on the tragedy that occurred to the Afrocentric organization MOVE, he unveils the time warp attached to the MOVE members murdered in the 1985 bombing on 6221 Osage Avenue. Timbo tells Cudjoe, "They were embarrassing, man. Embarrassing. Trying to turn back the clock. Didn't want no kind of city, no kind of government. Wanted to love like people live in the woods. Now how's that sound? A Garden of Eden up in West Philly. Mayor breaking his butt to haul the city into the twentieth-first century and them fools on Osage want their block to the jungle."[14] In the late 1980s, young black American urban culture included the "nation clock," a red, black, and green clock on a thick rope worn around the neck, with the 4 C batteries "not included," a clock with an 8- or 9-inch diameter with bright lights, like a headlight, as the young black men navigated the urban landscape. This clock was one urban enactment of the chant, "What time is it? Nation time!" In *Philadelphia Fire* and *Two Cities* (1998) Wideman discovers "thick time" as he meditates on the MOVE leader, John Africa. In order to respond to the MOVE bombing, Cudjoe, the narrative persona of Wideman, decides that he must be "many places at once" (*Philadelphia Fire* 23). The Afrocentrism of the MOVE organization is also rendered as "many places at once." The surname of the MOVE members, Africa, becomes a sign of "thick time," not the shameful primitive, but a sign of what Achille Mbembe refers to as a "sign of several temporalities" and the "time of entanglement."[15] Wideman rescues Afrocentrism from the grip of celebratory discussions of melanin and ancient African kingdoms and makes his Afrocentric inquiry a study of how the sheer movement of blackness is often aestheticized in enactments of black pride.

Wideman wonders, in *Philadelphia Fire,* about the significance of the MOVE members literally claiming "Africa" when they make "Africa" their surname. In *Philadelphia Fire,* by virtue of meditating on splitting and loss, Wideman ultimately represents Afrocentrism as being as elusive and dislocated as the cultural hybridity that shapes the sensibility of Cudjoe, the key narrative voice. One of Wideman's greatest achievements, in *Philadelphia Fire,* may indeed be the attempt to locate the novel itself in the gap between a tribute to the Afrocentric group, MOVE, and a tribute to the necessity of cultural hybridity. In one of Wideman's later novels, *Two Cities* (1998), he continues to develop a new aesthetic revolving around a new sense of temporality ("thick time'). This thick time is Wideman's replacement for the "thick skin" created by the science of race and countered, but not displaced, by the "Black is Beautiful" movement. In this thick time, the paradigm of the black mirror stage (interpellation itself) is replaced with the trope of photography, a type of experimental photography in which new ways of capturing space and time are imagined. In *Two Cities,* as Wideman connects his own process of writing to Martin Mallory's process of creating photography, he contemplates new models for understanding time, space, and "Africa" in the African American imagination. The maps of the skulls made by nineteenth-century racist phrenologists is evoked, in *Two Cities,* when Wideman describes the recognition of the photographer Martin Mallory that the "map is [his] head" overdetermines his need to "map" John Africa, the black urban primitive. Wideman muses, "Maybe he doesn't have to lose his friend after all. Maybe these pauses a chance for

John Africa to slide beside him again, real as the memory [. . .] The map in your head, your hands, the million pictures your eyes snap to guide your feet and ears and lungs are blurred."[16] As Wideman interrogates but refuses to classify or dissect the black urban primitive, he imagines that "time and space are thicker" than they appear in the "thin time" of racial narratives of progress.

Wideman rewrites primitivist images of Africa as "blank darkness" by imagining John Africa as "thickness." The words "time and space are thicker" evoke the depth of blackness that John Africa represents. Wideman does not simply indulge in a celebration of the meaning of "Africa" in the African American imagination. As he thinks about what it means for the MOVE members to make "Africa" their surname, he places the crisis of representation at the center of the novel. The process of creating photography becomes his prime metaphor for the crisis of representing blackness. At the beginning of *Two Cities* the image of the dark room is used as both a photography reference and a reference to the body of John Africa. The image of John Africa as the blurred face in the dark room that reflects like a mirror underscores that the photographer Martin Mallory makes this MOVE leader a medium for the production of images that do not appear, that are always in the process of appearing or "developing," a compelling description of post-Soul blackness.

In order to fully appreciate his meditation on photography in *Two Cities,* we must remember the use of Muybridge in *Reuben* (1987) and compare the meditation on capturing motion through photography, in *Reuben,* to the meditation on layering images through photography, in *Two Cities.*[17] Reuben, in his conversations with Muybridge, realizes that the attempt to capture motion through photography is flawed because motion is "the sum of all the tiny inchings forward but something greater, irreducible."[18] In contrast, Martin Mallory's aesthetic agenda as a photographer, in *Two Cities,* is rendered laudable, the attempt to make photography comparable to a collage. Wideman moves from the focus on Muybridge and the "anatomizing of motion," in *Reuben,* to a focus, in *Two Cities,* on the collages of Bearden and the sculpture of Giacometti (*Reuben* 63). Through Martin Mallory's conversations with Giacometti and Bearden, Wideman contemplates the interplay of time and space that structures the longevity of images of the black primitive. Wideman ultimately suggests that a certain type of photography that is more like sculpture and collage than normative photography is the key model of the type of lens that would redeem the historical crisis of representing blackness. Bearden explained his discovery of "time sense" in pictures in the following manner: "I finally think I'm beginning to understand what makes a picture move—what time sense in a picture means—leading plane by plane—step by step in a series of counter-points."[19] As Wideman thinks about the "time sense" that Martin Mallory contemplates as he attempts to make the MOVE bombing visible, he imagines Martin Mallory exposing the film again and again as he "took pictures on top of pictures" (211). This fuller description of this photographic technique is: 'Well, he said he fixed his camera so he could he take a dozen, a hundred without turning the film. Said every picture was there on the film and one day he would or somebody would figure out a way so everything he was photographing could be printed for people to see" (211). Mallory produces images that cannot be developed, negatives that can be understood only if one learns how to visually interpret "thick time." This "thick time" "looked like somebody had scratched all over [the negatives] with silvery ink. An inside-out world, glowing like the bones of Kwami's X-rayed chest that night in the emergency ward" (140). Mallory's aesthetic represents the "inside-out world" in which "time and space are thicker."

Wideman describes Mallory's photographic witnessing in the following manner: "and everyone found inside dead so who knew, who could tell the truth [. . .] [he] sees their invisible presence in the vacant space he shoots over and over, shooting and not allowing the film to advance" (175). This subversive arrested motion produces the layered images that combat the arrested development images of MOVE as the dangerous Afrocentric primitive. Wideman desperately takes "pictures on top of pictures" as he, like Mallory, imagines that he is the perpetual witness of the bombing that rewinds and plays without the assistance of Cudjoe's tape recorder. As opposed to Cudjoe's tape recorder, in *Philadelphia Fire,* that alienates Margaret Jones as it "captures" her voice, Wideman, in *Two Cities,* makes the camera an image of Paul Connerton's incorporating practices, that which Connerton, in *How Societies Remember,* presents as a "knowledge and a remembering in the hands and in the body," an apt description of the reclamation, by Wideman, of an embodied blackness that does not reiterate racial essentialism.[20] As Wideman moves from *Sent for You Yesterday* to *Philadelphia Fire* and *Two Cities,* he continues to present blackness as an embodied movement, an experience of space and time that is not a condensation of space and time.

epilogue

Post-Dilution Anxiety

IN the post–Black Arts movement landscape, the critique of fetishism of shades of blackness is transforming into vehement critiques of the very notions of authentic blackness and hybrid blackness. As Wideman and Morrison foreground the role of the phallus in skin-color fetishism, their post–Black Arts movement visions include pointed critiques of the dilution anxieties and fantasies that shaped the Black Arts and Black Power movements. Wideman and Morrison's post–Black Arts movement novels advocate a reclamation of the sheer beauty of the excess in the range of skin color that has been coded "black." Their post-dilution visions converge when they both attempt to capture the allure of different shades of blackness without falling prey to the sometimes direct, sometimes subtle script of light-skinned blackness as the castrated black phallus and dark-skinned blackness as the abundant black phallus. In a 1997 interview, Wideman confesses, in a manner striking comparable to Morrison's admissions in the 1993 afterword of *The Bluest Eye,* that his interest in representing the body politics of shades of blackness cannot be separated from his interest in the "Black is Beautiful" sensibility. He writes, "Color has mystery, allure. So I want to take that back, I want to privilege color—what's special about it. This has a lot to do with identity, with pride, with Black is Beautiful. We do *see* it so it does change things and make things quite attractive. I don't want to give that up. At the same time, color is a badge and used against us. [. . .] I'm interested in its aesthetic dimension aside from the social evaluations of dark being bad and light being good."[1] In Morrison's and Wideman's post–Black Arts movement visions in *Paradise* and *Sent for You Yesterday,* the "allure" of representing the beauty of shades of blackness becomes the allure of their complicated desire to keep a "Black is Beautiful" ethos even as they critique skin color fixations.

Skin as a container, a site of inscription, and a surface with depth is rewritten through Wideman's move to "see through" skin and Morrison's move to an art therapy that marks templates of the body as opposed to actual bodies. When Morrison ends *Paradise* with the image of dark skin and emerald eyes, the blue eyes no longer signal desire for whiteness, and the dark skin is no longer a sign of the 8-rock fear of loss of authentic blackness. As Morrison and Wideman critique the investments in light-skinned blackness as a literal inscription of cultural hybridity and dark-skinned blackness as a literal inscription of cultural authenticity, they show that the fetishism of skin color has naturalized the conflation of race and culture. Dark-skinned blackness becomes a sign of authentic black culture in the "Black is Beautiful" sensibility of the Black Power and Black Arts movements. In *Tar Baby,* Morrison depicts light-skinned blackness as becoming a sign of hybrid culture when Jadine's cosmopolitanism is viewed by other characters as inseparable from her "yalla" skin. In *Paradise,* Morrison rescues cultural fusion from the potential fetishism of Consolata's golden skin when she celebrates the local cosmopolitanism that makes the "sha sha sha" the sound of a cultural home that is somehow both a stable ground and a way of traveling. In their ultimate critiques of skin-color fetishism, Morrison and Wideman expose skin color (shades of blackness) as the raw edge between race and culture as they reveal the wounds that occur when *experiences* of cultural authenticity and hybridity are reduced to visual marks of race.

In current gender studies, Judith Butler has paved the way to complicating any quick and easy separation of sex and gender. Butler argues that, rather than understanding "sex" as the biological and gender as the social construct, we must understand that "sex" is just as much a construct as gender. In a similar sense, the seeming difference between race and culture has been upset in Walter Benn Michaels' analysis in *Our America: Nativism, Modernism, and Pluralism* (1995). Michaels argues that the "modern concept of culture is not, in other words, a critique of racism; it is a form of racism" (129). As he confronts the insidiousness of race, he insists that attempts to separate culture from race are pure wishful thinking.[2] In *Paradise,* Morrison employs the supernatural as she courageously embraces the challenge of separating culture from race. As Morrison and Wideman depict skin-color fetishism, they seize the challenge of beginning to think about an African American cultural specificity that is *not* racial authenticity and a cultural fusion that is *not* racial hybridity.

My focus on the fetishism of shades of blackness leads to many questions tied to the comparison of the categories race/culture and sex/gender. In gender studies, "sex" is now the contested term, as it is no longer simply the biological. The fetishism of shades of blackness elides the difference between "race" and "culture" as the ideas of authenticity and hybridity are written on the dark and light skin. When Morrison and Wideman move to the vision of post-dilution anxiety *and* post-dilution desire, they attempt to reclaim culture as separate from race. When this race/culture tension is juxtaposed with the sex/gender tension, the longstanding images of effeminate, light-skinned blackness and virile, dark-skinned blackness demonstrate that race gives gender difference a heightened type of visibility. Even if we may not fully agree with Homi Bhabha's sense that sex is the hidden fetish (a "secret") and race the "most visible of fetishes," the constructs of effeminate light skin and virile dark skin do underscore that race literally "colors" the castration anxiety at the core of constructs of female lack and male abundance.[3] When dark-skinned blackness is fetishized, as a type of black fetishism of blackness, there is a huge overcompensation for the lack tied, in antiblack racism, to blackness. Dilution anxiety, the deep investment in an authentic blackness, fuels this type of fetishism. Morrison and Wideman, in *Paradise* and *Sent for You Yesterday,* hail a post-dilution anxiety sensibility, a conscious move away from the rarely spoken but insidious connections between images of darkening and lightening black bodies and images of phallic penetration and castration.

The post-dilution sensibility is a core part of the current post-Soul gestures that remain too open to be called a *movement.* In the field of contemporary African American visual culture, the very words "post-Soul" and "post-black" are now being used to signal new, contemporary ways of thinking about African American and black diasporic identities. The term "post-black" was coined by the curator Thelma Golden, in the catalog written for the 2001 exhibit "Freestyle." In this catalog, Golden explains: "A few years ago, my friend, the artist Glenn Ligon, and I began using the term 'post-black.' [. . .] 'Post-black' was shorthand for post–black art, which was shorthand for a discourse that could fill volumes . . . Glenn was better at identifying the traces and instances of it than I was, but the moment he said it, I knew exactly what he meant".[4] The "post" in "post-Soul" becomes the move from "Black is Beautiful" back to Langston Hughes' proclamation in "The Negro Artist and the Racial Mountain" (1926) that "[w]e know we are beautiful. And ugly too. The tom-tom cries and the tom-tom laughs."[5] The recursivity of the moves from the internalization of the antiblack gaze to the collective reclamation of black self-love to a more individual and three-dimensional style that can be both beautiful and ugly cannot be pinned down as a linear move from the Harlem Renaissance to the Black Arts movement to the post-Soul (post-black) movement.

Glenn Ligon (the artist who, with the curator Thelma Golden, galvanizes the term "post-black") reshapes Gertrude Stein's images of "negro sunshine" in an installation art entitled *Warm Broad Glow* (2005). With this direct response to "Melanctha," including an electrical light displaying the words "Negro Sunshine" as if it is a storefront sign (figure 11), Ligon shows that white modernist images of "negro sunshine" were always glaring fabrications. It is significant that Ligon engages Stein's modernist work in this post-black production. In "Light it Up, or How Glenn Ligon Got Over," Richard Meyer argues that, by reminding viewers of the heavy past of antiblack racism, Ligon makes *Warm Broad Glow* a critique of some of the facile, romantic "post-black" gestures. The images of the yellow modern and the black primitive in "Melanctha" is the racialized timeline of new, light-skinned blackness and the old, dark-skinned blackness that Ligon wants to upset.

The 1960s and 70s aesthetic warfare privileged visual signs of blackness (hair, skin, and clothing). These visual signs gained depth in this "Black is Beautiful" body knowledge. The tension between the body as surface or depth is at the core of the phenomenology of blackness in the novels that are now often called "post-Soul." In *Sent for You Yesterday,* post-Soul is the shift from the black mirror stage (Wideman's striking depiction of a racialized mirror stage that both evokes and rewrites Lacan's mirror stage) to blackness as the "Soul" that is produced (the "wanderlust") when "blackened" subjects, constantly objectified by race, reclaim blackness as a cosmic journey, comparable to Sun Ra's space travel.[6] This redefinition of blackness emerges forcefully in the key scene, when the "coal-black beautiful woman" named Samantha, after literally looking in a mirror, rushes to the library, where she reads and then re-reads (revises) a dictionary definition of "melanin" in order to imagine that the discourse of race transmutes into pure jazz and space travel, a new cosmology of blackness. Wideman, in *Sent for You Yesterday,* like Morrison in *Paradise,* celebrates the move beyond the racial mirror stage. When he critiques the naturalized creation narratives of race, his deconstructive furor becomes most ferocious. The alternative creation narrative emerges when he describes the death of the

Figure 11. *Glenn Ligon,* Warm Broad Glow *(2005). Neon, paint; 36 x 192 inches, 91.4 x 487.7 cm. A.P. 1/2; Ed. of 7 (Courtesy Regen Projects, Los Angeles)*

albino, Brother, when he stops moving and the constant re-creation of Brother when his lumpy dough (the objectified albino body) becomes a subject only when it is not inert. The resurrection of blackness is figured as the move past dilution anxiety to the recognition that blackness "never stops" (171).

This constantly shifting blackness is also vividly portrayed, in *Paradise,* in the images of the diasporic blackness that is as elusive and as specific as the sound ("sha sha sha") that makes Consolata remember the "glittering black people" in her South American hometown (226). In *Paradise,* the icons of the black power fist and the red, black, yellow, and green Pan-African colors change shapes as they circulate and become tied to "new color combinations" (104). The subversive power of this embodied movement, as an alternative to skin-color fetishism, continues to delineate the post–Black Arts movement ethos. In Colson Whitehead's recent novel *Apex Hides the Hurt* (2006), the focus on the perpetual motion of a historically all-black town renamed "Struggle" is posited as the ultimate alternative to the main character's obsession with new, multicultural flesh-colored bandages that replace the Band-Aid that is named "flesh-colored," even though it matches only white skin tones. The main character is a nomenclature consultant in the advertising industry who has an uncanny ability to create the perfect names for a range of products. One of his most resonant names is "Apex," the name he gives to the multicultural flesh-colored bandages. The multicultural flesh-colored bandage is represented, in a pivotal passage, as a "camouflag[ing] [of] wounds."[7] This idea of the "camouflaging of wounds" resonates as a larger way of understanding the reasons light-skinned and dark-skinned blackness are fetishized. The wound of race is effaced through the attribution of depth (whether beauty, cultural authenticity, or cultural hybridity) to skin color.

The nomenclature consultant decides that the invisible bandage would never have the same marketing success as the flesh-colored Band-Aid since "we sought ourselves" (90). Whitehead uses the tension between invisible bandages and multicultural flesh-colored bandages to set up a meditation on the role of skin color in our continued investment in race. He writes:

> Even he had to admire the wonder of it all. The great rainbow of our skins. It was a terrain so far uncharted. Pith helmets necessary. The fashioners of clear adhesive strips almost recognized this but didn't take the idea far enough. The world of the clear strip was raceless; it did not take into account that we sought ourselves, like sought like, that a white square of white cotton wadding attached to transparent tape dispelled the very illusion they attempted to create. Criminy—an alien square of white on the skin, well that was outside the pale of even the albinoest albino. The deep psychic wounds of history and the more recent gashes ripped by the present, all of these could be covered by this wonderful, unnamed multicultural adhesive bandage. (90)

The references to the "albinoest albino" and the "deep psychic wounds" show that, like Wideman's work in *Sent for You Yesterday,* Whitehead, in this passage, is processing the *coloring* of the wounds of race. The fetishism of shades of blackness stems from different wounds. The fetishism of light-skinned blackness is often the wound of racial self-hatred, and the fetishism of dark-skinned blackness is often the wound of dilution anxiety.

In a 1997 interview, Wideman explains this duality of the wound in the following manner: "My grandmother was what we call 'color struck,' and that meant that she didn't like dark people—she didn't think they were good looking. She was really taken by light, 'bright' people. She herself could pass for any race. So there's that. Then there's also the *sign* of blackness as brotherhood, as community, as soul brother. Founding a political movement on the notion that black is beautiful" (*Conversations* 202). When Brother reclaims the albino Brother as the epitome of the "soul brother," he wrestles to separate the Black Power/Black Arts "sign" of blackness from skin color. When we remember Baraka's image of "two male tits and navel and the penis [as] a big face," it is clear that the Black Arts movement "sign" of blackness was the black phallus.[8] When this phallus is rendered, during the Black Arts movement, as a dark-skinned original that represents Africa, roots, and origin, light-skinned blackness emerges as a sign of the castration of the race, hence Gwendolyn Brooks' use of the very words "diluted Negroes" in "The Life of Lincoln West" as she depicts a "very" dark-skinned child being interpellated as the "real thing" (*Blacks* 487).

The castration of African American men is playfully rewritten in *Apex Hides the Hurt.* As Whitehead depicts the toe injury of the unnamed nomenclature consultant, he playfully makes an injured toe into the wounded body part. The great emphasis on this injured body part becomes very tied to the assignment the nomenclature has been given (to decide the official name of the town that used to be all-black and has now become a town of middle-class, interracial prosperity). The town is now named "Winthrop," but one of founding black fathers wanted it to be named "Freedom." The nomenclature consultant finally decides that he will resurrect a long-lost name that the other founding black father wanted—the name "Struggle." The novel ends with a connection between this name and the consultant's ongoing bodily injury (the hurt toe). This injury is described as the "site of his most famous injury" (190). Through the lens of post-slavery trauma, the "most famous injury" tied to black male bodies is castration. Whitehead moves to the injured toe as he, like Jacques Lacan, demonstrates that the "phallus is a signifier," not any particular body part. Whitehead gives concrete form to Lacan's understanding of the phallus as the elusive name for the master signifier when the narrator poses the question, "What is the word [. . .] for that elusive thing? It was on the tip of his tongue. What is the name for that which is always beyond our grasp? What do you call *that which escapes?*" (183). Whitehead links the power and limits of naming and the power and limits of the multicultural flesh-colored bandage. The very title of the novel, *Apex Hides the Hurt,* evokes the healing and hiding of the skin wounds caused by race. Finally Whitehead makes it unclear whether the main character has actually suffered the toe injury or he has a phantom pain that leads to the doctor's sense that the limp is psychosomatic. The ambiguity surrounding this alternative castrated body part enables Whitehead to denaturalize the idea of castrated black male bodies.

Whitehead's focus on the interplay of wounds and names, as he zooms in on the advertising business and contemporary consumer culture, is the vital work that can deconstruct contemporary images such as the advertisement in figure 12. The light-and-dark interplay in this advertisement cannot be separated from the interplay between words and the space with no words. In *Apex Hides the Hurt,* Whitehead includes a scene in which the unnamed protagonist realizes that, when he names the multicultural flesh-colored bandages, he has, in effect, "named a mirror" (109). As people match their skin tone and the colors of the various flesh-colored bandages, the product (the multicultural bandage) functions as yet another racial mirror, yet another naturalization of race. The advertisement in figure 12 reveals the larger significance of Morrison's and Wideman's post-dilution anxiety explorations of skin-color fetishism. The man's face is the mirror that is literally named within this marketing venture. The words are:

> 100%
> SATISFACTION GUARANTEED
> GUARANTEED TO DEFY STEREOTYPES,
> DOUBLE-TEAMS, GRAVITY AND WINTERS
> THAT WOULD MAKE A POLAR BEAR CRY
> GUARANTEED TO GO HARD
> FROM
> SHOOTAROUND 'TIL THE LAST WHISTLE ECHOES
> GUARANTEED TO BRUISE EARDRUMS
> SHATTER GLASS, SET OFF
> CAR ALARMS AND
> NEVER GET INVITED
> TO KARAOKE

The words "GUARANTEED TO GO HARD" and "100% SATISFACTION GUARANTEED" reduce the man's face (his subjectivity) to his sexual abilities. The advertisement clearly presents the black athlete as the black phallus. It also epitomizes the tension between Lacan's sense that the "phallus is a signifier" and Fanon's insistence that the "Negro is the genital" (*Black Skin, White Masks* 180). As the light brightens parts of the man's face, the words become legible. The violence of the language renders the man a super-masculine object, a castrated threat, not the actual threat implied in the words "guaranteed to defy stereotypes." The words, the signifiers, superimposed on the man's face are the societal phallus that makes the man into the "genital." Lacan argues that language castrates everyone, as it makes all of us exist within lack and deferred desire. This advertisement shows how the violence of racial discourse beautifies the castration of black subjects. The lightened parts of the face highlight the darkness around the eyes. Through the Black Arts lens, the ferocity of the gaze would signal rage against the dilution of his dark-skinned blackness (against the light that is castrating him and writing on his body in this manner). Through the

Figure 12. *2006 advertisement*

lens of the post-dilution anxiety vision of Morrison and Wideman, and its extension in the work of younger novelists such as Colson Whitehead, the ferocity of the man's gaze in this advertisement is a call to smudge the words in order to begin rewriting the scripts of "old," dark-skinned blackness versus "new," light-skinned blackness, virile, dark-skinned blackness versus feminized, light-skinned blackness, and authentic, dark-skinned blackness versus diluted, light-skinned blackness.

notes

introduction

1. Jonathan Kaufman, "Obama's Bid Turns Focus on Class Split among Blacks," *Wall Street Journal,* January 22, 2008.

2. In *Civilization and its Discontents* (1930), Freud writes, "I once discussed the phenomenon that it is precisely communities with adjoining territories, and related to each other in other ways as well, who are engaged in constant feuds and in ridiculing each other—like the Spaniards and Portuguese, for instance, the North Germans and South Germans, the English and Scotch, and so on. I gave this phenomenon the name of 'the narcissism of minor differences,' a name which does not do much to explain it. We can now see that it is a convenient and relatively harmless satisfaction of the inclination to aggression, by means of which cohesion between the members of the community is made easier" (72). This final focus on the cohesion created by this narcissism of minor differences is a fascinating lens through which to analyze colorism. The privileging and shunning of lighter and darker shades of blackness, within colorism, may simply reinforce the imagined cohesiveness of biological blackness that the one-drop rule created.

3. This emergent work on colorism and literature includes Jacquelyn McLendon's work on the politics of skin color in Jessie Fauset and Nella Larsen's fiction (1995) and Caroline Streeter's more recent analysis of the fetishism of shades of blackness in Gayl Jones' *Corregidora* and *Daughters of the Dust.*

4. See *The Color Complex: The Politics of Skin Color among African Americans* (1993), written by Kathy Russell, Midge Wilson, and Ronald Hall (New York: Doubleday, 1993). Margaret Hunter's *Race, Gender, and the Politics of Skin Tone* (2005) is the most recent book-length study of colorism. Hunter compares the colorism in African American and Mexican American communities. In *Shifting: The Double Lives of Black Women in America* (2003), Charisse Jones and Kumea Shorter-Gooden argue, "Colorism is perhaps the most potent manifestation of the lily complex" (the "lily complex" is their term for the desire to be white). They consider "colorism's typical pattern, with

dark skin being seen as bad, ugly, and evil, and light skin as good, pure, and beautiful" as well as the reverse, the "reaction formation" that makes people who have "bought into the lily complex, who have internalized the notion that dark skin, kinky hair, and African features are ugly," victimize people who are "too light" (196). In the article "Skin Color and the Perception of Attractiveness Among African Americans: Does Gender Make a Difference" (2002), Mark E. Hill provides case studies of the gendered aspect of colorism, the greater significance that skin color plays in the lives in African American women. Kathe Sandler's film *A Question of Color* (1982) is a groundbreaking documentary addressing colorism.

5. In the following passage, from the essay "Notes on Trauma and Community," the sociologist Kai Erikson uncovers what it really means to consider trauma as collective: "'Trauma' becomes a concept social scientists as well as clinicians can work with. I want to use my broadened vocabulary, in fact, to suggest that one can speak of traumatized communities as something distinct from assemblies of traumatized persons. Sometimes the tissues of community can be damaged in much the same way as the tissues of mind and body, as I shall suggest shortly, but even when that does not happen, traumatic wounds inflicted on individuals can combine to create a mood, an ethos—a group culture, almost—that is different from (and more than) the sum of the private wounds that make it up. Trauma, that is, has a social dimension" (Cathy Caruth, ed., *Trauma: Explorations in Memory* [Baltimore and London: Johns Hopkins University Press, 1995], 18). The sociologist and social worker Joy Leary has added the focus on slavery to posttraumatic stress. In her nationwide lectures, her goal is to fight against what she views as a national amnesia concerning slavery.

6. Kalpana Seshadri-Crooks, *Desiring Whiteness: A Lacanian Analysis of Race* (London and New York: Routledge, 2000), 3–4.

7. Lacan's own theory of the phallus can be interpreted as a sham of transcendence. The phallus does not transcend the male sexual organ.

8. F. James Davis, *Who is Black? One Nation's Definition* (University Park: The Pennsylvania State University Press, 1991), 33–34.

9. Audrey Elisa Kerr, "The Paper Bag Principle: Of the Myth and the Motion of Colorism," *Journal of American Folklore* 118.469 (2005): 272.

10. Dudley Randall, ed., *The Black Poets* (New York: Bantam Books, 1970), 297–98.

11. Brooks initially conceptualized "The Life of Lincoln West" as a novel. The short story, published in 1963, was later published as a poem in 1970. The short story and the poem are identical except for the use of the stanza format in the poem.

12. Gwendolyn Brooks, *Blacks* (Chicago: Third World Press, 1987), 487.

13. Bhabha writes, "First, the fetish of colonial discourse—what Fanon calls the epidermal schema—is not, like the sexual fetish, a secret. Skin, as the key signifier of cultural and racial difference in the stereotype, is the most visible of fetishes, recognized as 'common knowledge' in a range of cultural, political, and historical discourses, and plays a public part in the racial drama that is enacted every day in colonial societies" (78). Homi Bhabha, "The Other Question: Stereotype, Discrimination, and the Discourse of Colonialism," in *The Location of Culture* (London and New York: Routledge, 1994), 78.

14. Sigmund Freud, *Civilization and Its Discontents,* trans. James Strachey (New York and London: W. W. Norton, 1961), 72.

15. W. E. B. Du Bois, *The Souls of Black Folk* (New York: Signet Classics, 1995

[1903]), 45.

16. Jean Toomer, *The Wayward and the Seeking: A Collection of Writings by Jean Toomer,* ed. Darwin Turner (Washington, DC: Howard University Press, 1980), 123.

17. Jean Toomer, *Cane,* ed. Darwin Turner (New York: W. W. Norton, 1988 [1923]), 151.

18. This current study of black masculinity has gained wings with texts such as *Hung; Black Male; The Envy of the World; Hoop Roots;* and *Traps: African American Men on Gender and Sexuality.*

19. Frances Cress Welsing, *The Isis Papers: The Keys to the Colors* (Chicago: Third World Press, 1991), 96. The overt engagement with psychoanalysis in Welsing's Afrocentric account reveals the relevance of psychoanalytic theories of fetishism to studies of black body politics. Since *The Isis Papers* is published by Third World Press, founded by Haki Madhubuti, one of the central figures in the Black Arts movement, this Afrocentric text can easily be viewed as a concrete legacy of the Black Arts movement.

20. Susan Bordo, *The Male Body* (New York: Farrar, Straus and Giroux, 1999), 101.

21. William Faulkner, *Absalom, Absalom!* (New York: Vintage Books, 1990 [1936]), 302.

22. Ibid.

23. Wallace Thurman, *The Blacker the Berry* (New York: Collier Books, 1970).

24. William H. Grier and Price M. Cobbs, *Black Rage* (New York: Basic Books, 1968), 49, 59.

25. Cruse uses the very word "emasculated" as he presents the impotency of the Harlem Renaissance. He writes, "A cultural renaissance that engenders barriers to the emergence of the creative writer is a contradiction in terms, an emasculated movement" (37). Harold Cruse, *The Crisis of the Negro Intellectual* (New York: Quill, 1984 [1967]).

26. Dudley Randall, *After the Killing* (Chicago: Third World Press, 1973), 7.

27. M. M. Bakhtin, *The Dialogic Imagination,* ed. Michael Holquist (Austin: University of Texas Press, 1981), 84.

28. Anne McClintock, *Imperial Leather* (New York and London: Routledge, 1995), 38.

29. Pierre Nora theorizes about the "site of memory" in "Between Memory and History: Les Lieux de Memoire," trans. Marc Roudebush, in *History & Memory in African American Culture,* ed. Genevieve Fabre and Robert O'Meally. New York and Oxford: Oxford University Press, 1994.

chapter one

1. Siobhan Somerville's *Queering the Color Line* (2000) provides a foundational analysis of the larger queering of race embedded in many American modernist texts.

2. Deborah Mix, "Tender Revisions: Harryette Mullen's *Trimmings* and *S*PeRM**K*T*" *American Literature* 77:1 (March 2005).

3. Daniel Scott, "Harlem Shadows: Re-Evaluating Wallace Thurman's *The Blacker the Berry,*" *Melus* 29 (2004).

4. Fanon writes, "The Negro is the genital. Is this the whole story? Unfortunately not. The Negro is something else. Here again we find the Jew. He and I may be separated

by the sexual question, but we have one point in common. Both of us stand for Evil. The black man more so, for the good reason that he is black. Is not whiteness in symbols always ascribed in French to Justice, Truth, Virginity?" (108), in Frantz Fanon, *Black Skin, White Masks,* trans. Charles Markmann (New York: Grove Press, 1967 [1952]). In *Freud, Race, and Gender,* Sander Gilman explains, "Thus the clitoris was seen as a 'truncated penis.' Within the turn-of-the-century understanding of sexual homology, this truncated penis was seen as an analogy not to the body of the idealized male, with his large, intact penis, but to the circumcised ('truncated') penis of the Jewish male. This is reflected in the popular *fin de siècle* Viennese view of the relationship between the body of the male Jew and the body of the woman. The clitoris was known in the Viennese slang of the time simply as the 'Jew' (*Jud*). The phrase for female masturbation was 'playing with the Jew'" (38–39). Sander L. Gilman, *Freud, Race, and Gender* (Princeton: Princeton University Press, 1993).

5. The images of the black primitive in *Three Lives* are a blackening of the white lesbianism in *Q.E.D.,* as Stein rewrites the lesbian love triangle in *Q.E.D.* as the African American heterosexual and homoerotic love triangle in "Melanctha," the second story in *Three Lives.* The lesbian love story is transmuted into the queer desire in "Melanctha" that cannot be easily categorized as heterosexual or lesbian.

6. During the Harlem Renaissance, or New Negro movement, poets were very aware of the common conflation, in modernist celebrations of the primitive, of the words "negro" and "primitive." In *The Ideologies of African American Literature* (2001), Robert Washington presents black primitivism as African American participation in the modernist lens, which viewed African Americans as exotic primitives and "Africa" as the "purest embodiment of emotional and sexual freedom," raw emotion, and untainted culture outside of the "waste land" (32). "Heritage," one of the poems included in *The New Negro* (1925), is a riveting meditation on the meaning of the primitive in the African American imagination. As Countee Cullen muses on the stereotypes of the primitive that are anchored in stereotypes of "Africa," and the meaning of "Africa" in the African American imagination, he asks, "What is Africa to me?" (250). Like *Three Lives,* "Heritage" can be interpreted as a projection of homoerotic angst onto the primitivist screen. Cullen may have written the poem to Harold Jackman. Homoerotic desire may lead Cullen to this meditation on the primitive. If so, like *Three Lives,* "Heritage" reveals the way in which primitivism is often spurred by an embrace of what is imagined as taboo sexuality.

7. In *Gertrude Stein and Richard Wright: The Poetics and Politics of Modernism* (1998), Lynn Weiss refers to the "autobiographical Adele" (82). Although Stein's thwarted relationship with May Bookstaver makes it so easy to read Adele as a depiction of Stein herself, when we compare *Three Lives* and *Q.E.D.,* the persona that emerges as Stein herself is a conglomerate of Melanctha, Jefferson Campbell, and Adele.

8. I borrow the words "corporeal enactment" from Judith Butler's *Bodies That Matter.*

9. Eldridge Cleaver, *Soul on Ice* (New York: Delta, 1991 [1968]).

10. Audre Lorde, "Uses of the Erotic: The Erotic as Power," in *Sister Outsider: Essays and Speeches* (Freedom, CA: Crossing Press, 1984), 53–59.

11. Thurman's goal is the exposure of the sheer trauma that colorism creates, whereas Stein, as Daylanne English argues, adopts a clinical tone. English persuasively argues that this clinical tone is related to Stein's drawing on her experiences as a med-

ical student at Johns Hopkins, where she "first discovered Negroes." Thurman includes passages in *The Blacker the Berry* that critique people's ability to talk about colorism without concentrating on the material effects of it in the lived experiences of actual subjects reduced to bodies.

12. David Eng, *Racial Castration: Managing Masculinity in Asian America* (Durham and London: Duke University Press, 2001).

13. The love triangles in "Melanctha" present a cubism that also defies the binaries. Melanctha is the third term that transcends the binaries.

14. As opposed to the imagined peculiarity of Melanctha's catering to Rose, Rose's maternal support of Melanctha is naturalized by the dark-skinned black mammy stereotype: "Melanctha badly needed to have Rose always there to save her. Melanctha wanted badly to cling to her and Rose had always been so solid for her" (231).

chapter two

1. The role of this racialized castration anxiety in *Absalom, Absalom!* is one of the few topics that have not been exhaustively analyzed in Faulknerian criticism. Critics as different in orientation as Hortense Spillers and Philip Weinstein have laid a strong foundation for this burgeoning avenue.

2. Charles Peavy, *Go Slow Now: Faulkner and the Race Question* (Eugene: University of Oregon Books, 1971), 33.

3. Ibid.

4. James Baldwin, *Nobody Knows My Name* (New York: Vintage Books, 1954), 126.

5. "Letter to the North" was originally published as "Letter to a Northern Editor."

6. Anne Goodwyn Jones writes, "I began to suspect that Faulkner was representing and critiquing another ideology, related to and supporting that of the unified subject but different from it in crucial ways. This ideology had to do with gender, but not with the more familiar notions of the possession and/or loss of the phallus; it had to do with what men do with the phallus, with masculine performance. In brief, this ideology linked (male) power with male sexuality—phallus and penis—in a single overdetermined act: the act of entering an 'other.' I called it the ideology of penetration, and looked for research that might confirm or reject my hypothesis: that Faulkner's dismembered bodies worked as a critique of the ideology of penetration." Anne Goodwyn Jones, "Desire and Dismemberment: Faulkner and the Ideology of Penetration," in *Faulkner & Ideology,* ed. Donald Kartiganer and Ann Abadie (Jackson: University Press of Mississippi, 1995), 130.

7. In the preface to *The Mansion,* Faulkner writes, "Since 'living' is motion, and motion is change and alteration [. . .] therefore the only alternative to 'motion' is un-motion, stasis, death." William Faulkner, *The Mansion* (New York: Vintage Books, 1959), 44.

8. Joseph Blotner, ed., *Selected Letters of William Faulkner* (New York: Random House, 1977), 185.

9. Ibid.

10. The word "creature" is used at an early moment in the text, in one of Rosa's narrations, to signify the state of all Southern humanity "since 1861." Rosa tells Quentin, "I

don't plead youth, since what creature in the South since 1861, man woman nigger or mule, had had the time or opportunity not only to have been young but to have heard what being young was like from those who had" (12). When she adds "nigger or mule," one is forced to think about the different meanings of the word "creature." When the word is used in reference to "niggers," it does not mean a "living being," but rather a "beast" or "subhuman."

11. Laura Mulvey, *Fetishism and Curiosity* (Bloomington and Indianapolis: Indiana University Press, 1996), 5.

12. *Colored,* 2002, mixed media assemblage with hand mirror, 14.5 in. by 30 in. by 1.5 in.

13. Lumedia Facial Brightener is distributed by Bremenn Labs. It is sold at stores such as Saks Fifth Avenue and Bloomingdale's.

14. Lynn Haney, *Naked at the Feast: A Biography of Josephine Baker* (New York: Dobb Mead, 1981), 88.

15. The cultural production of blackness within modernist primitivism occurred simultaneously with the competing and mutually constitutive discourses of racial uplift, the New Negro ideology, and black cosmopolitanism. The idealization of black cosmopolitanism resounds when Josephine Baker remembers her first trip to Paris: "My life passed in review before me. I saw Bernard Street and my raggedy playmates. . . . When the Statue of Liberty disappeared over the horizon, I knew I was free." Lynn Haney, *Naked at the Feast: A Biography of Josephine Baker* (New York: Dobb Mead, 1981), 47. We must, however, compare this idealization of Paris to Baker's recognition of the racialized primitivism in Paris.

16. Jack Flam and Miriam Deutch, *Primitivism and Twentieth Century Art* (Berkeley: University of California Press, 2003), 416.

17. Wilhelm Worringer, "Im Kampf um die moderne Kunst: Die Antwort auf den Protest Deutscher Kunstler," in *German Expressionism: Primitivism and Modernity,* trans. Jill Lloyd (New Haven: Yale University Press, 1991), 57.

18. Hale Woodruff, ca. 1972. Quoted by Romare Bearden and Harry Henderson. *A History of African-American Artists from 1792 to the Present* (New York: Pantheon Books, 1993), 201.

19. William Johnson was one of the central Harlem Renaissance painters. In 1930, while thinking about African American artists' relation to African art, he expressed this notion of the inseparability of blackness and primitiveness. This passage is cited in Sieglinde Lemke, *Primitivist Modernism: Black Culture and the Origins of Transatlantic Modernism* (Oxford: Oxford University Press, 1998). The passage written by Stein appears in *Three Lives* (New York: Vintage, 1909), 86. The passage written by Faulkner appears in *Absalom, Absalom!* (New York: Vintage, 1986 [1936]), 92.

20. Marianna Torgovnick, *Gone Primitive: Savage Intellects, Modern Lives* (Chicago and London: The University of Chicago Press, 1990), 11.

chapter three

1. Tommy Lott, "Du Bois's Anthropological Notion of Race," in *Race,* ed. Robert Bernasconi (Oxford: Blackwell, 2000), 68.

2. In *The White Image in the Black Mind,* Mia Bey demonstrates that Martin Del-

aney was central to this tradition of engaging with the "racist science." In his 1879 text, *Prinicipia of Ethnology: The Origin of the Races and Color with an Archaeological Compendium of Ethiopian and Egyptian Civilization from Years of Careful Examination and Enquiry,* Delaney elevates the "black race" in a manner very similar to contemporary Afrocentric texts. Delaney atempts to explain "scientifically" why the temperaments of the "black, yellow, and white" races are "positive, medium, and negative." Mia Bey, *The White Image in the Black Mind* (New York and Oxford: Oxford University Press, 2000), 96.

3. LeRoi Jones, *Black Art* (Newark, NJ: Jihad Productions, 1966), 2.

4. Ibid., 652.

5. In 1967 Faith Ringgold started her exploration of "black light." Spectrum Gallery had a "Black Light" exhibit of Ringgold's work in 1969. Ringgold explains, "In 1967 I had begun to explore the idea of a new palette, a way of expressing on canvas the new 'black is beautiful' sense of ourselves. The way we see color is influenced by the colors that surround us. Our own color for instance is indelibly etched in our mind and, unless someone tells us otherwise it influences overall sense of color. As an artist and woman of color I had become particularly interested in this idea. I had noticed that black artists tended to use a darker palette. White and Light colors are used sparingly and relegated to contrasting color in African-American, South African and East African Art. In Western art, however, white and light influence the entire palette, thereby creating a predominance of infinite, pastel colors and light and shade or chiaroscuro" (162). Dan Cameron, Richard Powell, Michelle Wallace, eds., *Dancing at the Louvre: Faith Ringgold's French Collection and Other Story Quilts* (Berkeley: University of California Press, 1998).

6. H. Rap Brown, *Die Nigger Die!* (Chicago: Lawrence Hill Books, 1969), 5.

7. In *Sent for You Yesterday,* John Edgar Wideman imagines a character Samantha discovering a non-essentialist understanding of "black is beautiful" when she discovers that blackness is a "way of seeing and being seen," both a way of thinking and a bodily enactment (135). John Edgar Wideman, *Sent for You Yesterday* (London: Flamingo, 1981), 135.

8. Ahmed Alhamisi and Harun Kofi Wangara, eds., *Black Arts: An Anthology of Black Creations* (Detroit: Black Arts Publications, 1969), 19–20.

9. This 1967 issue of *Ebony* includes a cover story on natural black hair. The cover image is framed by the words "Natural Hair—New Symbol of Race Pride." Davis Llorens, "Natural Hair—New Symbol of Race Pride," *Ebony* 23:2 (December 1967): 139–44.

10. Larry Neal, "Any Day Now: Black Art and Black Liberation," *Ebony* 24:10 (August 1969): 58.

11. Toni Cade Bambara, ed., *The Black Woman: An Anthology* (New York: Penguin, 1970), 18.

12. In *Report from Part One* (1972), Gwendolyn Brooks remembers how Black Arts movement devotees chastised *Ebony* magazine for its inclusion of bleaching cream advertisements and light-skinned models.

13. LeRoi Jones and Larry Neal, eds., *Black Fire: An Anthology of Afro-American Writing* (New York: William Morrow, 1968), 226.

14. A. B. Spellman, "Big Bushy Afros," *International Review of African American Art* 15:1 (1998): 53.

15. Gwendolyn Brooks, *Report from Part One* (Detroit: Broadside Press, 1972), 167.

16. Haki R. Madhubuti, *GroundWork: New and Selected Poems of Don L. Lee/Haki R. Madhubuti* (Chicago: Third World Press, 1996), 17.

17. William J. Harris, ed., *The LeRoi Jones/Amiri Baraka Reader,* ed. Amiri Baraka (New York: Thunder's Mouth Press, 1991), 218.

18. Terry Eagleton, "Ideology and Its Vicissitudes in Western Marxism," in *Mapping Ideology,* ed. Slavoj Žižek (London and New York: Verso, 1994), 216.

19. Maulana Ron Karenga, *The Quotable Karenga* (Los Angeles: US Organization, 1967), 3.

20. In a 1969 interview, Brooks refers to Don Lee's *Don't Cry, Scream* (1968) as an example of the poetry that convinced her that "the whole concept of what 'good poetry' is is changing today, thank goodness. I think it's a very healthy thing" (RFPO 149).

21. In a 2000 conversation with the author, poet Eamon Grennan referred to this "chewy" texture of Brooks's poetry.

22. Gloria Wade Gayles, ed., "Update on Part One: An Interview with Gwendolyn Brooks" (1977), Gloria Hull and Posey Gallagher, in *Conversations with Gwendolyn Brooks* (Jackson: University Press of Mississippi, 2003), 85–103.

23. *Report from Part One,* 30.

24. Imamu Amiri Baraka and Fundi (Billy Abernathy), *In Our Terribleness* (Indianapolis and New York: The Bobbs-Merrill Company, Inc., 1970), 122. In this "long image story in motion . . . papermotion," no page numbers are included. Page numbers would arrest the steady flow of images.

25. Bob Crawford began photographing "Black life in America, mainly Chicago" in 1964. Crawford defines his work in this manner in the biography accompanying the photographs shown in the "41st Annual Arts Festival—The Arts in a Changing Society," held in April 1970 at Fisk University.

26. Judith Butler, "Performative Acts and Gender Constitution: An Essay in Phenomenology and Feminist Theory," in *Performing Feminisms,* ed. Sue-Ellen Case (Baltimore: Johns Hopkins University, 1990), 272.

27. Houston A. Baker, Jr., *Modernism and the Harlem Renaissance* (Chicago and London: The University of Chicago Press, 1987), 15.

28. Baraka and Neal, *In Our Terribleness,* 100.

29. *James Baldwin: The Price of the Ticket.* Directed by Karen Thorsen. Nobody Knows Productions, 1989.

30. Eve Sedgwick, *Epistemology of the Closet* (Berkeley: University of California Press, 1990), 72.

31. James Baldwin, *Tell Me How Long the Train's Been Gone* (New York: Vintage International, 1968), 6.

32. William Faulkner, *Absalom, Absalom!* (New York: Vintage, 1986 [1936]), 285.

33. In contrast to the incestuous male rage of this scene, when the "miscegenation" between Leo and Barbara, a white actress, occurs, a "black woman moaning" becomes the background music (361). The "black woman moaning," inside the white woman's body, is a disturbing example of the overcompensation for lack that shapes fetishism. The "black woman moaning" overcompensates for the supposed lack attached to the white woman. The white woman's body covers and masks the lack attributed to the black body that produces this moan. This "black woman moaning" is heard in the moment of

orgasm Leo and Barbara experience; the black phallus literally secretes black womanhood. The "black woman moaning" becomes the background music during the sexual intimacy of the black man and white woman (361).

34. Cleaver's dilution anxiety emerges as he explains African American racial self-hatred: "Quite simply, many Negroes believe, as the principle of assimilation into white America implies, that the race problem in America cannot be settled until all traces of the black race are eliminated. Toward this end, many Negroes loathe the idea of two very dark Negroes mating. The children, they say, will come out ugly. What they mean is that the children are sure to be black, and this is not desirable." Eldridge Cleaver, *Soul on Ice* (New York: Delta, 1968), 127.

35. The crossdressing ball was held at the "Old Coliseum." It was located at 18th and Wabash in Chicago.

36. In Charles Markmann's translation of the French original (1952) of *Black Skin, White Masks,* Fanon writes, "The Negro is the genital" (180). Frantz Fanon, *Black Skin, White Masks,* trans. Charles Markmann (New York: Grove Press, 1967), 180.

37. Baraka and Neal, *In Our Terribleness,* 152.

38. Ibid., 122.

39. Baldwin, *Tell Me,* 82.

40. The "long career" of black drag stems from the "long career of blackmail," his understanding of what it means to have the "imperious bit of flesh," the black penis, in an antiblack world (6).

41. Leo muses about the possibility that if he and his family, and, by extension, all African Americans, did not bear the history of being uprooted from "home," "[they] would have known less about vanished African kingdoms and more about each other. Or, not at all impossibly, more about both" (23). In this passage, Baldwin is thinking about the self-alienation, the sense of loss, that fueled some of the psychological journeys to "Africa" during the Black Arts and Black Power movements.

42. Dudley Randall, *The Black Poets* (New York: Bantam Books, 1970), 223.

43. William Spurlin, "Culture, Rhetoric, and Queer Identity," in *James Baldwin Now,* ed. Dwight McBride (New York and London: New York University Press, 1999), 109.

44. Kimberle Williams Crenshaw, *Black Men on Race, Gender, and Sexuality* (New York and London: New York University Press, 1999), 314.

45. Madhubuti, *GroundWork,* 84–85.

46. Brooks, *Blacks,* 460.

47. Ibid., 460.

48. Baldwin, *Tell Me,* 11, 53.

49. Baraka and Abernathy, *In Our Terribleness,* 122.

50. LeRoi Jones and Larry Neal, eds., *Black Fire: An Anthology of Afro-American Writing* (New York: William Morrow, 1968), 286.

51. Ibid., 288.

52. Ibid., 327–28.

53. Baraka and Abernathy, *In Our Terribleness,* 99.

chapter four

1. The analysis of *The Bluest Eye* includes many milestones: Michael Awkward's

analysis of Morrison's revision of the work of Richard Wright and James Baldwin in *The Bluest Eye;* Trudier Harris's analysis of folk traditions in *The Bluest Eye;* Susan Willis's analysis of the critique of commodity culture in *The Bluest Eye;* and Patrice Hamilton-Cormier's "Black Naturalism and Toni Morrison: The Journey Away from Self-Love in *The Bluest Eye.*" Other foundational criticism includes Philip Weinstein's analysis of the connections between Faulkner and Morrison, Craig Werner's analysis of myth in *Tar Baby*, and Yogita Goyal's recent study of gender and diaspora in *Tar Baby* (2006). My focus on the images of the phallus, within a "race and psychoanalysis" framework, has real affinity with the work of Jean Wyatt. In *Risking Difference: Identification, Race and Community in Contemporary Fiction and Feminism* (2004), Wyatt's use of Lacan's theory of misrecognition (the images that are mistaken as the "real thing"), as she explores Morrison's multicultural feminist vision, hails the reading of *Paradise* that I set up in the next chapter.

2. In "Mama's Baby, Papa's Maybe" (1987), Spillers explains this gender confusion in the following manner: "In other words, in the historic outline of dominance, the respective subject-positions of 'female' and 'male' adhere to no symbolic integrity."

3. Wahneema Lubiano, "Black Nationalism and Black Common Sense," in *The House That Race Built* (New York: Vintage Books, 1998), 238.

4. Danille Taylor-Guthrie, *Conversations with Toni Morrison* (Jackson: University Press of Mississippi, 1994), 160.

5. Toni Morrison, *The Bluest Eye* (New York: Plume/Penguin, 1994 [1970]), 20.

6. Mari Evans, *I Look at Me!* (Chicago: Third World Press, 1969).

7. There are many scenes in which physical signs of race are experienced as metaphysical. For example, in the scene when Geraldine meets Pecola, Morrison writes, "She looked at Pecola. Saw the dirty torn dress, the plaits sticking out on her head, hair matted where the plaits had come undone, the muddy shoes with the wad of gum peeping out from between the cheap soles, the soiled socks, one of which had been walked down into the heel of the shoe. She saw the safety pin holding the hem of the dress up. Up over the hump of the cat's back she looked at her. She had seen this little girl all of her life" (91). "All of her life," Geraldine has been trying to detach her body from what she believes this little girl's body represents. Though they have both been interpellated as black, Geraldine herself is able to see a distinct difference. The specific details of Pecola's body fit a general picture in Geraldine's head. Her body is a clear and distinct picture of negativity that, in Geraldine's mind, should be matched with the negative words: "'Get out . . . You nasty little black bitch. Get out of my house'" (92). But these insulting words do not fully reflect all of her thoughts and emotions concerning Pecola. When she remembers other "little girls" like Pecola, she admits: "The end of the world lay in their eyes, and the beginning, and all the waste in between" (92). The sublimity of this passage is an abrupt jolt away from the narrow referentiality of the descriptions of Pecola immediately preceding it. Geraldine sees the "end of the world . . . and the beginning" in the eyes of a little girl whose physical image reminds her of poverty and a lower-class culture. The words "nasty little black bitch" (92) reduce this metaphysical moment to a moment of sheer physical revulsion. She overcompensates for her inability to "know" the "world" in Pecola's eyes by making a quick and easy visual interpretation of Pecola: "nasty little black bitch" (92).

8. Toni Morrison, "Memory, Creation, and Writing." *Thought: A Review of Culture and Ideas* 59:235 (December 1984): 388.

9. The hyphenated term "in-visible" was often used by Maurice Merleau-Ponty, and I've taken it from Galen Johnson, "Ontology and Painting: Eye and Mind," in *The Merleau-Ponty Aesthetics Reader: Philosophy and Painting*, ed. Galen Johnson (Evanston: Northwestern University Press, 1993), 53.

10. Francette Pacteau, *The Symptom of Beauty* (Cambridge: Harvard University Press, 1994), 135.

11. bell hooks, *Art on My Mind: Visual Politics* (New York: The New Press, 1995), 50.

12. W. J. T. Mitchell, *Picture Theory: Essays on Verbal and Visual Representation* (Chicago and London: The University of Chicago Press, 1994), 68.

13. Danille Taylor-Guthrie, *Conversations with Toni Morrison* (Jackson: University Press of Mississippi, 1994), 166. This interview was conducted by Claudia Tate in 1983.

14. In *Absalom, Absalom!* Faulkner uses the words "nigger in the woodpile, somewhere" in a figurative sense as he describes the mystery surrounding Sutpen's past and, in particular, his wealth. Morrison replaces the word "somewhere" with the words "literally, literally" as she foregrounds the material effects of racial trauma. William Faulkner, *Absalom, Absalom!* (New York: Vintage International, 1990 [1936]), 56.

15. Judith Butler, "Imitation and Gender Insubordination," in *The Second Wave: A Reader in Feminist Theory*, ed. Linda Nicholson (New York: Routledge, 1997), 306.

16. Ibid., 306.

17. Toni Morrison, *The Bluest Eye* (New York: Plume/Penguin, 1970), 211.

chapter five

1. William Loren Katz, *The Black West* (New York: Simon & Schuster, 1996 [1987]), 250.

2. Toni Morrison, *Paradise* (New York and Toronto: Alfred A. Knopf, 1998 [1997]), 3, 193.

3. Frantz Fanon, *Black Skin, White Masks*, trans. Charles Markmann (New York: Grove Press, 1967), 110. All other page references will be included in the text.

4. Phillip Novak, "'Circles and Circles of Sorrow': In the Wake of Morrison's *Sula*," *Publications of the Modern Language Association* 114:2 (March 1999): 186.

5. In 1920, the colors were used as the banner of the Universal Negro Improvement Association (UNIA).

chapter six

1. Carol Barnes, *Melanin: The Chemical Key to Black Greatness* (Chicago: Lushena Books, 1988), 21.

2. Bonnie TuSmith, ed., *Conversations with John Edgar Wideman* (Jackson: University Press of Mississippi, 1998), 130.

3. In *Faces of Nationalism: Janus Revisited* (1998), Tom Nairn playfully uses this Superman reference as he explains that Afrocentrism often makes melanin into a type of kryptonite.

4. In addition to deciphering this object, he also imagines that Lucy is an object he must interpret. As a middle-aged man, when he and Lucy remain close friends and lovers, he reminisces of how he "used to take pictures of her with his mind," in order to "trap her in those little white-framed pictures like a bee in a bottle he could study without getting stung" (103).

5. Frantz Fanon, *Peau noire, masques blancs* (Paris: Editions de Seuil, 1952), 26. Frantz Fanon, *Black Skin, White Masks,* trans. Charles Markmann (New York: Grove Press, 1967), 28.

6. Elizabeth Grosz, *Jacques Lacan: A Feminist Introduction* (London and New York: Routledge, 1990), 135.

7. Eduard Hanslick, "A Musical Theory of Sound and Motion," in *Aesthetics: A Critical Anthology,* ed. George Dickie (New York: St. Martin's Press, 1977), 602.

8. Grosz, 119.

9. John Edgar Wideman, *Reuben* (New York: Penguin Books, 1987), 15. All other page references will be in the text.

10. When Brother is "beckoned" by the tracks, as he is "beckoned . . . into [Samantha's] dance" (131), and lies on the tracks in a seemingly peaceful surrender and "no blood" is seen afterward (120), as if the train did not hit him and is a benevolent force, he feels that he is still playing and winning the "scare game." Before he lies on the train tracks and dies, he imagines himself "whispering . . . in Junebug's ear," "Watch me play" (182), and remembers when he taught Junebug "how to get ready to sleep" by praying (181). When he is on the tracks, he feels "[s]omething purring in the sleep of the tracks. Something whispering like him in Junebug's ear" (182). The prayer he remembers whispering to Junebug is "Now I lay me down to sleep. I pray the Lord my soul to keep" (182). Seemingly, when he kills himself, he feels the serenity and peace of one who is simply going to sleep and going to his final "resting place" (135).

11. Karla Holloway, "Cultural Narratives Passed On: African American Mourning Stories," *National Council of Teachers of English* 59 (January 1997): 37.

12. For example, at one point, while she and Carl attempt to tell the full story of Brother to Doot, Lucy asserts: "Brother picked the way he wanted to live. And how he wanted to die. Now how many people have you heard of like that? Jesus maybe. And one, two others like the Africans flying and walking cross water and turning sticks to snakes. Believe what you need to believe, but Brother was special like that. Not some spook or hoodoo, but a man who could be whatever he wanted to be" (199). Lucy contradicts her previous statement to Doot that "something else or somebody else killed him" (120). Her assertion that he "could be whatever he wanted to be" (199) expresses an idea exactly opposite to the descriptions of how his albinism makes others experience him as grotesque. In fact, once Lucy is commemorating Brother in this last chapter of the novel, his albinism is represented very differently from the way it is described in the first two chapters of the novel. While she is commemorating Brother, Lucy tells Carl that "Brother didn't even have skin, but he stopped people's eyes" (198). She remembers Brother seeming "solid," even though she admits that she saw him as lacking skin. At the beginning of the novel, when Doot articulates the opposite idea, he argues, "To see Brother I'd have to look away from where he was standing, focus on something safe and solid near him so that Brother would hover like the height of a mountain at the skittish edges of my vision" (15). Doot's replacement of the visuality of Brother with the visuality of other signifiers and his claim that the alternative vision actually enables him "[t]o see" Brother further reveal the process of fetishism and the masking of what

is understood to be lack and absence.

Doot's image of the hovering of Brother also illuminates the reappearance of Brother at the very end of the novel in the doorway of Lucy's home. References to doorways in the novel convey the image of suspension and transition. When Brother first meets Samantha, she sees him "in the doorway" and "knew he was a ghost" (131). When Carl decides he must seek counseling for his drug addiction, he experiences the following disorientation: "Coming through the door you'd see yourself going. Coming and going like you a ghost and you'd bump into yourself going in when you'd be coming out. Meet yourself in the vestibule and be half out your mind trying to figure whether you supposed to be leaving or just getting back" (154). At the end of the novel, when Brother "appears in the doorway" as a resurrected figure (207–8), he is seemingly the link between the world of bodies and the realm of disembodiment. As an appearance in the doorway, he is not anchored to the "earth" as he felt while alive, and the reader might wonder if his reappearance should be likened to the "dirty rubber" that he feared a young child might find and "blow . . . up again" (172).

13. This impossibility is what Samantha believes she achieves, when she experiences Brother as an embodiment of "blackness . . . [as] a way of being unseen" (135).

14. John Edgar Wideman, *Philadelphia Fire* (New York: Vintage Books, 1990), 81. All other page references will appear in the text.

15. Achille Mbembe, *On the Postcolony* (Berkeley: University of California Press, 2001), 17, 15.

16. John Edgar Wideman, *Two Cities* (Boston and New York: Houghton Mifflin, 1998), 12.

17. The arrested development images of blackness in racial primitivism are troubled by Wideman's interrogation of the meaning of "Africa" in the African American imagination as he contemplates arrested motion and the layering of time and space. In one of the final scenes in *Two Cities,* Wideman imagines John Africa telling his angst-ridden friend and photographer Martin Mallory, "Move's about not standing still" (229). The stasis attributed to the black primitive in modernist primitivism is defied when Wideman presents the black urban primitive as that which does not "stand still." As Wideman makes Martin Mallory's process of creating photography a mirror of his own writing process, he wonders how he can remember John Africa without making him "stand still." In *On Photography,* Susan Sontag wonders if photographs are "a way of imprisoning reality, understood as recalcitrant, inaccessible; of making it stand still" (163). When Wideman asserts, "Move's about not standing still," it is clear that his photographer/narrator is aiming for a type of photography that is very different from the dominant lens that Sontag laments. In contrast to the passage in which John Africa asserts that his organization represents constant movement, Wideman unveils the insidious timeline that naturalizes the idea that John Africa is an embodiment of the old. As Reverend Watt recounts his visual memories of the dreadlocked hair of the MOVE members, Martin Mallory superimposes the old body of the Reverend and the old aura tied to "Africa." When Wideman describes the old body of the Reverend, he also evokes the racial primitiveness written on the black body. The text reads: "His face a carved wooden mask, old as Africa, and Africa stamped in his mouth and nose, the mahogany of his skin scored by folds deep enough to poke a camera's eye in. And what that camera would see" (151). In *Camera Lucida,* Roland Barthes includes a photograph entitled "William Casby, Born a Slave," as he considers the "stubborn referent" of photography. As Barthes responds to this photograph taken by R. Avedon, he muses,

"The essence of slavery is here laid bare: the mask is the meaning, insofar as it is absolutely pure." When Wideman describes the mahogany skin as being "old as Africa," "Africa" emerges as a "stubborn referent" of visual images of blackness, the mask that is imagined as the "essence."

18. John Edgar Wideman, *Reuben* (New York: Penguin Books, 1987), 127.

19. Myron Schwartzman, *Romare Bearden: His Life and Art* (New York: Harry N. Abrams, Inc., 1990), 128.

20. Paul Connerton, *How Societies Remember* (Cambridge: Cambridge University Press, 1989), 95.

epilogue

1. Bonnie TuSmith, ed., *Conversations with John Edgar Wideman* (Jackson: University Press of Mississippi, 1998), 202.

2. In *Our America: Nativism, Modernism, and Pluralism* (1995), Walter Benn Michaels explores the ways in which cultural identities, like racial identities, continue to be understood as what people "are" as opposed to what they do or believe. He argues, at one crucial point, that "[t]he modern concept of culture is not, in other words, a critique of racism; it is a form of racism" (129).

3. In *The Location of Culture* (1994), Homi Bhabha argues, "First, the fetish of colonial discourse—what Fanon calls the epidermal schema—is not, like the sexual fetish, a secret. Skin, as the key signifier of cultural and racial difference in the stereotype, is the most visible of fetishes, recognized as 'common knowledge' in a range of cultural, political, and historical discourses, and plays a public part in the racial drama that is enacted every day in colonial societies" (78).

4. Quoted in: Richard Meyer, "Light it Up, or How Glenn Ligon Got Over," *Art Forum* (May 2006): 247.

5. Angelyn Mitchell, ed., *Within the Circle: An Anthology of African American Literary Criticism from the Harlem Renaissance to the Present* (Durham and London: Duke University Press, 1994), 59.

6. John Edgar Wideman, *Sent for You Yesterday* (New York: Vintage Books, 1983), 135.

7. Colson Whitehead, *Apex Hides the Hurt* (New York: Doubleday, 2006), 177.

8. Baraka and Abernathy, *In Our Terribleness*, 99.

works cited

Alhamisi, Ahmed and Harun Kofi Wangara, eds. *Black Arts: An Anthology of Black Creations.* Detroit: Black Arts Publications, 1969.

Baker, Houston A., Jr. *Modernism and the Harlem Renaissance.* Chicago and London: The University of Chicago Press, 1987.

Bakhtin, M. M. *The Dialogic Imagination,* ed. Michael Holquist. Austin: University of Texas Press, 1981.

Baldwin, James. *Nobody Knows My Name.* New York: Vintage Books, 1954.

———. *Tell Me How Long the Train's Been Gone.* New York: Vintage International, 1968.

———. *Just above My Head.* New York: The Dial Press, 1978.

Bambara, Toni Cade, ed. *The Black Woman: An Anthology.* New York: Penguin, 1970.

Baraka, Imamu Amiri and Fundi (Billy Abernathy). *In Our Terribleness.* Indianapolis and New York: The Bobbs-Merrill Company, 1970.

Barnes, Carol. *Melanin: The Chemical Key to Black Greatness.* Chicago: Lushena Books, 1988.

Bey, Mia. *The White Image in the Black Mind.* New York and Oxford: Oxford University Press, 2000.

Bhabha, Homi. "The Other Question: Stereotype, Discrimination, and the Discourse of Colonialism," in *The Location of Culture.* London and New York: Routledge, 1994.

Blotner, Joseph, ed. *Selected Letters of William Faulkner.* New York: Random House, 1977.

Bordo, Susan. *The Male Body.* New York: Farrar, Straus and Giroux, 1999.

Brooks, Gwendolyn. *Blacks.* Chicago: Third World Press, 1987.

———. *Report from Part One.* Detroit: Broadside Press, 1972.

———. *Primer for Blacks.* Chicago: Third World Press, 1980.

Brown, H. Rap. *Die Nigger Die!* Chicago: Lawrence Hill Books, 1969.

Butler, Judith. "Performative Acts and Gender Constitution: An Essay in Phenomenology and Feminist Theory." In *Performing Feminisms,* ed. Sue-Ellen Case. Baltimore: Johns Hopkins University Press, 1990.

———. *The Judith Butler Reader*, ed. Sara Salih with Judith Butler. Oxford: Blackwell Publishing, 2004.

———. "Imitation and Gender Insubordination." In *The Second Wave: A Reader in Feminist Theory*, ed. Linda Nicholson. New York: Routledge, 1997.

Cameron, Dan, Richard Powell, and Michelle Wallace, eds. *Dancing at the Louvre: Faith Ringgold's French Collection and Other Story Quilts.* Berkeley: University of California Press, 1998.

Cleaver, Eldridge. *Soul on Ice.* New York: Delta, 1991. Originally published in 1968.

Connerton, Paul. *How Societies Remember.* Cambridge: Cambridge University Press, 1989.

Crenshaw, Kimberle Williams. *Black Men on Race, Gender, and Sexuality.* New York and London: New York University Press, 1999.

Cress Welsing, Frances. *The Isis Papers: The Keys to the Colors.* Chicago: Third World Press, 1991.

Cruse, Harold. *The Crisis of the Negro Intellectual.* New York: Quill, 1984. Originally published 1967.

Davis, F. James. *Who Is Black? One Nation's Definition.* University Park: The Pennsylvania State University Press, 1991.

Du Bois, W. E. B. *The Souls of Black Folk.* New York: Signet Classic, 1995. Originally published in 1903.

Eagleton, Terry. "Ideology and Its Vicissitudes in Western Marxism." In *Mapping Ideology*, ed. Slavoj Žižek. London and New York: Verso, 1994.

Eng, David. *Racial Castration: Managing Masculinity in Asian America.* Durham and London: Duke University Press, 2001.

Erikson, Kai. "Notes on Trauma and Community." In *Trauma: Explorations in Memory*, ed. Cathy Caruth. Baltimore and London: Johns Hopkins University Press, 1995.

Evans, Mari. *I Look at Me!* Chicago: Third World Press, 1969.

Fanon, Frantz. *Peau noire, masques blancs.* Paris: Editions de Seuil, 1952.

———. *Black Skin, White Masks*, trans. Charles Markmann. New York: Grove Press, 1967.

Faulkner, William. *Absalom, Absalom!* New York: Vintage Books, 1990. Originally published in 1936.

———. *The Mansion.* New York: Vintage Books, 1959.

Flam, Jack and Miriam Deutch. *Primitivism and Twentieth Century Art.* Berkeley: University of California Press, 2003.

Freud, Sigmund. *Civilization and Its Discontents*, trans. James Strachey. New York and London: W. W. Norton, 1961.

Gilman, Sander L. *Freud, Race, and Gender.* Princeton: Princeton University Press, 1993.

Goodwyn Jones, Anne. "Desire and Dismemberment: Faulkner and the Ideology of Penetration." In *Faulkner & Ideology*, ed. Donald Kartiganer and Ann Abadie. Jackson: University Press of Mississippi, 1995.

Grier, William H. and Price M. Cobbs. *Black Rage.* New York: Basic Books, 1968.

Grosz, Elizabeth. *Jacques Lacan: A Feminist Introduction.* London and New York: Routledge, 1990.

Haney, Lynn. *Naked at the Feast: A Biography of Josephine Baker.* New York: Dobb Mead, 1981.

Hanslick, Eduard. "A Musical Theory of Sound and Motion." In *Aesthetics: A Critical Anthology,* ed. George Dickie. New York: St. Martin's Press, 1977.
Harris, William J., ed. *The LeRoi Jones/Amiri Baraka Reader.* New York: Thunder's Mouth Press, 1991.
Holloway, Karla. "Cultural Narratives Passed On: African American Mourning Stories." *National Council of Teachers of English* 59 (January 1997).
hooks, bell. *Art on My Mind: Visual Politics.* New York: The New Press, 1995.
Hull, Gloria and Posey Gallagher. "Update on Part One: An Interview with Gwendolyn Brooks" (1977). In *Conversations with Gwendolyn Brooks.* Jackson: University Press of Mississippi, 2003.
Hunter, Margaret. *Race, Gender, and the Politics of Skin Tone.* New York: Routledge, 2005.
Johnson, Galen. "Ontology and Painting: Eye and Mind." In *The Merleau-Ponty Aesthetics Reader: Philosophy and Painting,* ed. Galen Johnson. Evanston: Northwestern University Press, 1993.
Jones, Charisse and Kumea Shorter-Gooden. *Shifting: The Double Lives of Black Women in America.* New York: Harper Perennial, 2003.
Jones, LeRoi. *Black Art.* Newark, NJ: Jihad Productions, 1966.
——— and Larry Neal, eds. *Black Fire: An Anthology of Afro-American Writing.* New York: William Morrow, 1968.
Karenga, Maulana Ron. *The Quotable Karenga.* Los Angeles: US Organization, 1967.
Katz, William Loren. *The Black West.* New York: Simon & Schuster, 1996.
Kaufman, Jonathan. "Obama's Bid Turns Focus on Class Split among Blacks." *Wall Street Journal* (January 22, 2008).
Kerr, Audrey Elisa. "The Paper Bag Principle: Of the Myth and the Motion of Colorism." *Journal of American Folklore* 118.469 (2005): 271–89.
Lemke, Sieglinde. *Primitivist Modernism: Black Culture and the Origins of Transatlantic Modernism.* Oxford: Oxford University Press, 1998.
Llorens, David. "Natural Hair—New Symbol of Race Pride." *Ebony* 23:2 (December 1967): 139–44.
Lorde, Audre. "Uses of the Erotic: The Erotic as Power." In *Sister Outsider: Essays and Speeches.* Freedom, CA: Crossing Press, 1984.
Lott, Tommy. "Du Bois's Anthropological Notion of Race." In *Race,* ed. Robert Bernasconi. Oxford: Blackwell, 2000.
Lubiano, Wahneema. "Black Nationalism and Black Common Sense." In *The House That Race Built.* New York: Vintage Books, 1998.
Madhubuti, Haki R. *GroundWork: New and Selected Poems of Don L. Lee/Haki R. Madhubuti.* Chicago: Third World Press, 1996.
Mbembe, Achille. *On the Postcolony.* Berkeley: University of California Press, 2001.
McClintock, Anne. *Imperial Leather.* New York and London: Routledge, 1995.
McLendon, Jacquelyn. *The Politics of Color in the Fiction of Jessie Fauset and Nella Larsen.* Charlottesville and London: University Press of Virginia, 1995.
Meyer, Richard. "Light It Up, or How Glenn Ligon Got Over." *Art Forum* (May 2006).
Mitchell, Angelyn, ed. *Within the Circle: An Anthology of African American Literary Criticism from the Harlem Renaissance to the Present.* Durham and London: Duke University Press, 1994.
Mitchell, W. J. T. *Picture Theory: Essays on Verbal and Visual Representation.* Chicago

and London: The University of Chicago Press, 1994.

Mix, Deborah. "Tender Revisions: Harryette Mullen's *Trimmings* and *S*PeRM**K*T*." *American Literature* 77, no. 1 (March 2005): 65–92.

Morrison, Toni. *The Bluest Eye*. New York: Plume/Penguin, 1994. Originally published in 1970.

———. "Memory, Creation, and Writing." *Thought: A Review of Culture and Idea* 59, no. 235 (December 1984).

———. *Tar Baby*. New York: Plume/Penguin, 1981.

———. *Paradise*. New York and Toronto: Alfred A. Knopf, 1998. Originally published in 1997.

Mulvey, Laura. *Fetishism and Curiosity*. Bloomington and Indianapolis: Indiana University Press, 1996.

Neal, Larry. "Any Day Now: Black Art and Black Liberation." *Ebony* 24:10 (August 1969): 58.

Novak, Phillip. "'Circles and Circles of Sorrow': In the Wake of Morrison's *Sula*." *Publications of the Modern Language Association* 114.2 (March 1999).

Nora, Pierre. "Between Memory and History: Les Lieux de Memoire," trans. Marc Roudebush. In *History & Memory in African American Culture*, ed. Genevieve Fabre and Robert O'Meally. New York and Oxford: Oxford University Press, 1994.

Pacteau, Francette. *The Symptom of Beauty*. Cambridge: Harvard University Press, 1994.

Peavy, Charles. *Go Slow Now: Faulkner and the Race Question*. Eugene: University of Oregon Books, 1971.

Randall, Dudley, ed. *The Black Poets*. New York: Bantam Books, 1970.

———. *After the* Killing. Chicago: Third World Press, 1973.

Russell, Kathy, Midge Wilson, and Ronald Hall. *The Color Complex: The Politics of Skin Color among African Americans*. New York: Doubleday, 1993.

Schwartzman, Myron. *Romare Bearden: His Life and Art*. New York: Harry N. Abrams, 1990.

Sedgwick, Eve. *Epistemology of the Closet*. Berkeley: University of California Press, 1990.

Seshadri-Crooks, Kalpana. *Desiring Whiteness: A Lacanian Analysis of Race*. London and New York: Routledge, 2000.

Somerville, Siobhan. *Queering the Color Line*. Durham and London: Duke University Press, 2000.

Spellman, A. B. "Big Bushy Afros." *International Review of African American Art* 15.1 (1998): 53.

Spillers, Hortense. *Black, White, and in Color: Essays on American Literature and Culture*. Chicago and London: University of Chicago Press, 2003.

Spurlin, William. "Culture, Rhetoric, and Queer Identity." In *James Baldwin Now*, ed. Dwight McBride. New York and London: New York University Press, 1999.

Stein, Gertrude. *Three Lives*. New York: Vintage, 1909.

Taylor-Guthrie, Danille. *Conversations with Toni Morrison*. Jackson: University Press of Mississippi, 1994.

Toomer, Jean. *The Wayward and the Seeking: A Collection of Writings by Jean Toomer*, ed. Darwin Turner. Washington, DC: Howard University Press, 1980.

———. *Cane*, ed. Darwin Turner. New York: W. W. Norton, 1988. Originally published in 1923.

Thorsen, Karen, director. *James Baldwin: The Price of the Ticket.* Nobody Knows Productions, 1989.

Thurman, Wallace. *The Blacker the Berry.* London: The X Press, 1997. Originally published in 1929.

Torgovnick, Marianna. *Gone Primitive: Savage Intellects, Modern Lives.* Chicago and London: The University of Chicago Press, 1990.

TuSmith, Bonnie, ed. *Conversations with John Edgar Wideman.* Jackson: University Press of Mississippi, 1998.

Walker, Alice. *The Temple of My Familiar.* New York: Washington Square Press, 1989.

Watson Sherman, Charlotte. *One Dark Body.* New York: Harper Perennial, 1993.

Weiss, Lynn. *Gertrude Stein and Richard Wright: The Poetics and Politics of Modernism.* Jackson: University Press of Mississippi, 1998.

Whitehead, Colson. *Apex Hides the Hurt.* New York: Doubleday, 2006.

Wideman, John Edgar. *Sent for You Yesterday.* London: Flamingo, 1981.

———. *Reuben.* New York: Penguin Books, 1987.

———. *Philadelphia Fire.* New York: Vintage Books, 1990.

———. *Two Cities.* Boston and New York: Houghton Mifflin Company, 1998.

Wonham, Henry B., ed. *Criticism and the Color Line: Desegregating American Literary Studies.* New Brunswick: Rutgers University Press, 1996.

Worringer, Wilhelm. "Im Kampf um die moderne Kunst: Die Antwort auf den Protest Deutscher Kunstler." In *German Expressionism: Primitivism and Modernity,* trans. Jill Lloyd. New Haven: Yale University Press, 1991.

index